Eduqas GCSE Religious Studies (9–1)

Christianity, Islam and themes

Route A

Clare Lloyd

OXFORD
UNIVERSITY PRESS

OXFORD
UNIVERSITY PRESS

Great Clarendon Street, Oxford, OX2 6DP, United Kingdom

Oxford University Press is a department of the University of Oxford.

It furthers the University's objective of excellence in research, scholarship, and education by publishing worldwide. Oxford is a registered trade mark of Oxford University Press in the UK and in certain other countries

British Library Cataloguing in Publication Data
Data available

978-1-38-200952-2

10 9 8 7 6 5 4 3

Paper used in the production of this book is a natural, recyclable product made from wood grown in sustainable forests.
The manufacturing process conforms to the environmental regulations of the country of origin.

Printed in Great Britain by Ashford Colour Press Ltd.

Acknowledgements

We are grateful to the authors and publishers for use of extracts from their titles and in particular for the following:

Scripture quotations taken from **The Holy Bible, New International Version®** NIV® Copyright © 1973 1978 1984 2011 by Biblica, Inc.TM Used by permission. All rights reserved worldwide.

Excerpts from **The Qur'an OWC**, translated by M. A. S. Abdel Haleem (Oxford University Press, 2008). Reproduced with permission from Oxford University Press.

Excerpts from **Catechism of the Catholic Church**, http://www.vatican.va/archive/ccc_css/archive/catechism/ccc_toc.htm (Strathfield, NSW: St Pauls, 2000). © Libreria Editrice Vaticana. Reproduced with permission from The Vatican.

Excerpts from the **Nicene-Constantinopolitan Creed**, http://www.vatican.va/roman_curia/congregations/cfaith/documents/rc_con_cfaith_doc_1998_professio-fidei_en.html © Libreria Editrice Vaticana. Reproduced with permission from The Vatican.

United Nations: *The Universal Declaration of Human Rights*, http://www.un.org/en/universal-declaration-human-rights/ (United Nations, 1948). Reproduced with permission from United Nations.

World Council of Churches: *The Basis of the WCC*, https://www.oikoumene.org/node/6243 (World Council of Churches, 2020). Reproduced with permission from the World Council of Churches.

Cover illustrations: Eleanor Grosch

Photos: p11 Maryna Pleshkun/Shutterstock; p13(T) Mladen Mitrinovic/Alamy Stock Photo; p13(B) Rido/Shutterstock; p14 Rawpixelimages/Dreamstime.com; p15 Panther Media GmbH/Alamy Stock Photo; p17 Dominic Lipinski - WPA Pool/Getty Images; p18 Alex Liew/E+/Getty Images; p20 Panther Media GmbH/Alamy Stock Photo; p22 ZouZou/Shutterstock; p24 Adam Ján Figel/Alamy Stock Photo; p25 Dale Cherry/Shutterstock; p26 robertharding/Alamy Stock Photo; p33 Grejak/Shutterstock; p34 NASA images/Shutterstock; p35 VanderWolf Images/Shutterstock; p36 Godong/Getty Images; p37 Neneo/Shutterstock; p38 Mansoreh Motamedi/Getty Images; p39 Odua Images/Shutterstock; p40 Ryan M. Bolton/Shutterstock; p41 Henrik5000/Getty Images; p42 Hemant Mehta/Getty Images; p43 Jack Cunliffe/Alamy Stock Photo; p44 HQuality/Shutterstock; p45 Sturti/E+/Getty Images; p47 ESB Professional/Shutterstock; p48 Lightspring/Shutterstock; p49 Julian Kumar /GODONG/The Image Bank/Getty Images; p50 Mustafagull/E+/Getty Images; p51 Godong/Alamy Stock Photo; p57 Gts/Shutterstock; p58 Piosi/Shutterstock; p59 VictorHuang/Getty Images; p61 ildintorlak/Shutterstock; p63 Peppinuzzo/Shutterstock; p64 Jasmin Merdan/Moment/Getty Images; p65 In Pictures Ltd./Corbis via Getty Images; p67 Joe Raedle/Getty Images News/Getty Images; p68 Anadolu Agency/Getty Images; p69 PA Images/Alamy Stock Photo; p71 Chronicle/Alamy Stock Photo; p73 Kavram/Shutterstock; p79 Francis Miller/The LIFE Picture Collection/Getty Images; p81 John Gomez/Shutterstock; p83 BRENDAN ESPOSITO/EPA-EFE/Shutterstock; p84 Christian Climate Action; p85 Matt Rourke/AP/Shutterstock; p86 Reuters; p87 Hagen Hopkins/Stringer/Getty Images; p89 Alpha Historica/Alamy Stock Photo; p91 Tom Corban/Alamy Stock Photo; p93 imageBROKER/Alamy Stock Photo; p94 Boston Globe/Getty Images; p95 esp_imaging/iStockphoto; p101 Hfng/Shutterstock; p102 Photo 12/Alamy Stock Photo; p107 Bruce Rolff/Shutterstock; p108 FotograFFF/Shutterstock; p109 Vladimir Wrangel/Shutterstock; p110 Panther Media GmbH/Alamy Stock Photo; p113 Aldeca Productions/Shutterstock; p114 Sturti/E+/Getty Images; p115 Sedmak/iStock/Getty Images; p117 DEA/G. DAGLI ORTI/Getty Images; p123 Bobby Stevens Photo/Shutterstock; p124 Amer ghazzal/Alamy Stock Photo; p125 BRIAN HARRIS/Alamy Stock Photo; p126 AB Forces News Collection/Alamy Stock Photo; p127 Sweet marshmallow/Shutterstock; p128 Renata Sedmakova/Shutterstock; p129 Godong/Universal Images Group/Getty Images; p130 Homer Sykes/Alamy Stock Photo; p131 Godong/The Image Bank/Getty Images; p132 AFP/Getty Images; p133 ALBERTO PIZZOLI/AFP/Getty Images; p134 Matt Cardy/Stringer/Getty Images; p135 Al Seib/Los Angeles Times/Getty Images; p136 Jake Lyell/Alamy Stock Photo; p137 Andrew Philip/Tearfund; p139 DENIS BALIBOUSE/AFP/Getty Images; p145 André Dias Duarte/Alamy Stock Photo; p146 imageBROKER/Alamy Stock Photo; p149 Sufi/Shutterstock; p150 Anadolu Agency/Getty Images; p151 Hikrcn/Shutterstock; p152 Fouad A. Saad/Shutterstock; p153 Dark Moon Pictures/Shutterstock; p154 CiydemImages/E+/Getty Images; p155 Omar Chatriwala/Moment/Getty Images; p156 Soltan Frédéric/The Image Bank/Getty Images; p157 Jim West/Alamy Stock Photo; p158 Marvin del Cid/Moment/Getty Images; p159 Pacific Press/LightRocket/Getty Images; p160 istanbulimage/E+/Getty Images; p167 Dan Kitwood/Getty Images News/Getty Images; p168 Yulia_B/Shutterstock; p169 Arterra/Universal Images Group/Getty Images; p171(T) Jasminko Ibrakovic/Shutterstock; p171(B) Rawpixel.com/Shutterstock; p172 SOPA Images/LightRocket/Getty Images; p173 Kertu/Shutterstock; p175 Sony Herdiana/Shutterstock; p177 Zurijeta/Shutterstock; p176 FS Stock/Shutterstock; p178 Mr.Whiskey/Shutterstock; p179 PA Images/Alamy Stock Photo; p180 Mamunur Rashid/Shutterstock; p181 UPI/Alamy Stock Photo; p182 yunlutas/iStockphoto; and p183 JEP News/Alamy Stock Photo.

All other **illustrations** by Integra Software Services.

Although we have made every effort to trace and contact all copyright holders before publication this has not been possible in all cases. If notified, the publisher will rectify any errors or omissions at the earliest opportunity.

Thank you

The publishers would like to thank Dr Greg Barker who originated the ABCD paradigm quoted on pages 32, 56, 122, 144 and 166. The publishers would also like to thank Mohammed Al-Hilli, Mary Cunniffe, Mark Griffiths, Julie Haigh, Ibrahim Mogra and Christopher Owens for their help in reviewing this book. We would also like to thank Emma Raven, Caroline McVicker and Nicola McGee for their help in reviewing the early stages of this book. The publishers would like to thank James Helling for compiling the index for this book.

The teaching content of this resource is endorsed by WJEC Eduqas to support WJEC Eduqas GCSE in Religious Studies Route A. This resource has been reviewed against WJEC Eduqas' endorsement criteria. As this resource belongs to a third party, there may be occasions where a specification may be updated and that update will not be reflected in the third party resource. Users should always refer to WJEC Eduqas' specification and Sample Assessment Materials to ensure that learners are studying the most up to date course. It is recommended that teachers use a range of resources to fully prepare their learners for the exam and not rely solely on one textbook or digital resource. WJEC, nor anyone employed by WJEC has been paid for the endorsement of this resource, nor does WJEC receive any royalties from its sale. All exam questions in Skills Practice are used under licence from WJEC CBAC Ltd. WJEC bears no responsibility for the example answers to questions taken from its past question papers which are contained in this publication.

Contents

For the Short Course, Chapters 1, 2, 5 and 7 should be studied.
For the Full Course, all chapters should be studied.

Contents

Eduqas GCSE in Religious Studies

This book covers all you will need to study for a GCSE examination in Religious Studies with Eduqas if you are combining the study of Christianity and Islam. It includes the knowledge that you need for all your examinations, plus help in developing those crucial examination skills.

How is the specification covered?

The content that you will need is divided into three examination papers or 'components'. This book covers all three of those papers.

Component 1 – Religious, philosophical and ethical studies in the modern world

This paper is worth 50% of your overall marks. It is sometimes referred to as the 'Themes' paper. It is a compulsory paper and you are expected to answer every question. You can answer the questions from the perspective of any world faith. In this book we cover the themes through the perspectives of Christianity and Islam.

The examination paper for this component is split into four themes:

- **Theme 1** – Issues of relationships
- **Theme 2** – Issues of life and death
- **Theme 3** – Issues of good and evil
- **Theme 4** – Issues of human rights

Component 2 – Study of Christianity

This paper is worth 25% of your overall marks. It is also a compulsory paper and you are expected to answer every question.

The examination for this component is split into two sections:

- Beliefs and teachings
- Practices

Component 3 – Study of a World Faith

This paper is worth 25% of your overall marks. This book will cover **Option 3: Islam** as a world faith. Some schools and colleges may have selected a different world faith to study. You are expected to answer every question on this paper.

The examination for this component is split into two sections:

- Beliefs and teachings
- Practices

It is vital that you study the whole course and do not miss any bits out because there will be questions on all three of these components. This book contains everything you will need to be able to do this.

Tip

Your study of Christianity and Islam should underpin and support your learning in the Themes paper.

Short course GCSE

If you are studying the short course, then you will cover half of the content that has been outlined on the previous page. This means that you will study:

Component 1 – Religious, philosophical and ethical studies in the modern world

This paper is worth 50% of your overall marks and is 1 hour long. It is split into two themes:

- **Theme 1** – Issues of relationships
- **Theme 2** – Issues of life and death

In this paper, there are two questions with four parts each. Each question covers one theme.

Component 2 – Study of Christianity

The paper is worth 25% of your overall marks and it is 35 minutes long. There will be one question with four parts on **beliefs and teachings**.

Component 3 – Study of a World Faith

For Component 3, this book will cover the beliefs and teachings of **Option 3: Islam**. Component 2 and 3 is worth 25% of your overall marks and is 35 minutes long.

How do I use this book?

As you work through this book, you will find features to help you develop your knowledge and your examination skills so that you can feel confident on the day of your examination.

There is an Introduction to every new chapter.

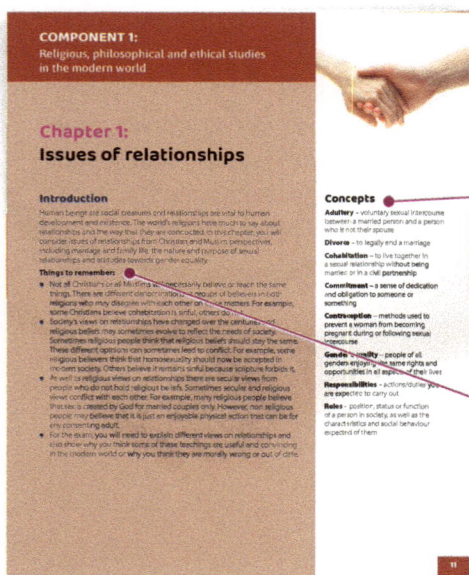

Concepts – At the start of every chapter is a list of the concepts you are expected to know and the definitions that Eduqas have provided. These terms are then highlighted in the main text, so you can see how and when they are used.

Things to remember – These are points that are important to bear in mind as you study the religions or themes. They will help you to understand the material in each chapter.

The content that you will need to study is covered in a number of double page spreads.

Specification focus – This shows you which detail from the specification is being covered on these pages, so you can be confident you are covering all the required content.

Quotes – Quotes from religious texts are shown in yellow boxes. We have included all the essential quotations named in the specification - these appear with a blue outline.

Useful terms – These boxes give definitions of some specialist language used on the pages that has not been included in the list of concepts but is still helpful to know. These terms are in bold and blue on the main page.

Knowledge recall – There are three questions at the end of each double page that ask you to recall knowledge and understanding from the pages you have just covered. These help you to repeat key information so that it sticks in your mind.

Evaluation practice – There are two questions at the end of each double page that ask you to provide arguments and weigh up how effective they are. These questions help you to practise thinking of ideas and reasoning, just as you will in an exam.

There are skills practice pages at the end of each chapter that will help you to become familiar with the different question types that you will encounter in the exam.

Exemplar questions – Each skills section contains examples of questions from real examination papers, and some exemplar answers. In each case, there is an answer with some problems and an improved response.

What went well – An explanation of the successful features of a student's answer.

How to improve – These boxes suggest things you must, should and could do to improve an examination response.

Helpful hints and Tips – Support and guidance in writing your own answers.

Over to You – Opportunities to try your hand at real examination questions.

Commentaries – These show how and why an improved answer is successful.

What will the exams be like?

To match the three components that you will study, there are three examination papers that you will have to answer.

Examination 1:
Component 1 –
(Themes) 2 hours

In this examination paper, there are four questions with four parts each. Each question covers one theme from the specification.

Examination 2:
Component 2 –
(Christianity) 1 hour

In this examination paper, there are two questions with four parts each. Question 1 will always be about beliefs and teachings and question 2 will always be about practices.

Examination 3:
Component 3 – (Option 3: Islam) 1 hour

In this examination paper, there are two questions with four parts each. Question 1 will always be about beliefs and teachings and question 2 will always be about practices.

Tip

You need to answer every question on each examination paper. If you have enough time, always try to write something, even if you are not sure of the answer. You won't lose marks for writing the wrong thing!

What kinds of questions will be asked?

Each question is always divided into four parts: *(a)*, *(b)*, *(c)* and *(d)*.

(a) question

(a) will always begin with the words:

What is meant by…

Or *What do Christians mean by…*

Or *What do Muslims mean by…*

Question *(a)* is worth two marks and it always requires you to define one of the concepts listed on the specification. These are listed for you at the start of each chapter. You should aim to spend no longer than two minutes on an *(a)* question before you move on.

A partially correct answer will get 1 mark. You will need an accurate and appropriate definition for the full 2 marks.

Tip

Learn the definitions for the concepts provided by Eduqas and listed at the start of each chapter. These definitions will get you two marks with no need for extra information to be added.

(b) question

(b) will always begin with the word:

Describe…

Question *(b)* is worth five marks and always requires you to show your knowledge and understanding of a specific area of religion or the themes. You will find the content needed for these questions in the main body of each chapter. The skills pages will help you learn to answer these kinds of questions. You should aim to spend no longer than five minutes on a *(b)* question before you move on.

Here is what Eduqas want to see in your answer for a *(b)* question:

- Knowledge – of a religious idea, belief, practice, teaching or concept.
- Understanding – of how belief influences individuals, communities and societies.
- Specialist language – used correctly and in context.
- Sources of authority – quoted or referred to accurately and in context.

(c) question

(c) will always begin with the word:

Explain…

In Component 1 only (Themes), you will be asked to show an understanding of diversity. This means that the question will always go on to say:

*… from **two** religions **or two** religious traditions…*

Responses to a *(c)* question in the Themes paper only should always clearly show two different religious responses. These can be from two different religions (e.g. Christianity and Islam), or you can give two different responses from within one religion (e.g. Catholic and Church of England, or Sunni and Shi'a). This book shows you both options. This is not required in either of the religion papers.

Question *(c)* on all the papers is worth 8 marks and requires more detail than a *(b)* question. You still need to show knowledge and understanding, but you also need to include supporting evidence or reasoning. You can find help with this on the skills pages. You should aim to spend roughly eight minutes on a *(c)* question.

As with the *(b)* question, Eduqas will credit you for showing knowledge and understanding, for using specialist language and sources of authority, but the *(c)* question is worth 8 marks and requires more detail.

In a *(c)* question, Eduqas want you to show **how** or **why** a belief or practice is **important** OR to give details on the **main features** of beliefs, teachings or attitudes about a topic.

- Include supporting evidence or reasoning to 'explain' your answer.
- Give a detailed response – spend up to 8 minutes answering this question.
- For the Themes paper only, show an understanding of ideas, beliefs, practices, teachings and concepts from two different religions or religious traditions.

Tip

Avoid writing a list of bullet points in answer to a *(b)* question, but remember you are not expected to include large amounts of detail. It is more important to answer the question clearly and accurately than to give lots of detailed information.

Tip

Question *(c)* requires you to write about *religious* beliefs and attitudes. You will not gain any marks for writing about Atheists or Humanists in your response.

(d) question

(d) will always begin with a controversial statement and then tell you to:

Discuss this statement showing that you have considered more than one point of view (you must refer to religion and belief in your answer).

Question (d) is worth 15 marks and you should aim to spend 15 minutes on it. This question is different from the others because instead of testing your knowledge and understanding, it tests your evaluation skills. You will need to look at the statement and show how some religious people might argue one response, but other religious people may argue differently. You then need to weigh up which response is better and give reasons why. You can see lots of hints and ideas for how to do this on the skills pages of this book.

Here is what Eduqas wants to see in your answer for a (d) question:

- Analysis and evaluation – of the issue raised in the question statement.
- Judgement – backed up by knowledge of religion, teaching or moral reasoning.
- Understanding – of how belief influences individuals, communities and societies.
- Specialist language – used correctly and in context.
- Sources of authority – quoted or referred to accurately and in context.

On Question 1 in the Themes paper (Issues of relationships) and the Christianity paper (Beliefs and teachings) you will be marked on **SPaG** (spelling, punctuation and grammar). So always try to use your best written English as it is a chance to pick up extra marks. There are 6 SPaG marks for the Full Course and 3 for the Short Course.

Tip

The (d) question asks you to demonstrate your evaluative skills. The examiner wants to see you analyse and evaluate the issues so that you can make a reasoned judgement.

Tip

On Question 2 in the Themes paper only (Issues of life and death), you will be asked to include beliefs of non-religious people such as Humanists or Atheists in your answer.

COMPONENT 1:
Religious, philosophical and ethical studies
in the modern world

Chapter 1:
Issues of relationships

Introduction

Human beings are social creatures and relationships are vital to human development and existence. The world's religions have much to say about relationships and the way that they are conducted. In this chapter, you will consider issues of relationships from Christian and Muslim perspectives, including marriage and family life, the nature and purpose of sexual relationships and attitudes towards gender equality.

Things to remember:

- Not all Christians or all Muslims will necessarily believe or teach the same things. There are different denominations or groups of believers in both religions who may disagree with each other on these matters. For example, some Christians believe cohabitation is sinful, others do not.
- Society's views on relationships have changed over the centuries and religious beliefs may sometimes evolve to reflect the needs of society. Sometimes religious people think that religious beliefs should stay the same. These different opinions can sometimes lead to conflict. For example, some religious believers think that homosexuality should now be accepted in modern society. Others believe it remains sinful because scripture forbids it.
- As well as religious views on relationships there are secular views from people who do not hold religious beliefs. Sometimes secular and religious views conflict with each other. For example, many religious people believe that sex is created by God for married couples only. However, non-religious people may believe that it is just an enjoyable physical action that can be for any consenting adult.
- For the exam, you will need to explain different views on relationships and also show why you think some of these teachings are useful and convincing in the modern world or why you think they are morally wrong or out of date.

Concepts

Adultery – voluntary sexual intercourse between a married person and a person who is not their spouse

Divorce – to legally end a marriage

Cohabitation – to live together in a sexual relationship without being married or in a civil partnership

Commitment – a sense of dedication and obligation to someone or something

Contraception – methods used to prevent a woman from becoming pregnant during or following sexual intercourse

Gender equality – people of all genders enjoying the same rights and opportunities in all aspects of their lives

Responsibilities – actions/duties you are expected to carry out

Roles – position, status or function of a person in society, as well as the characteristics and social behaviour expected of them

Christianity and relationships in the twenty first century

Specification focus

Relationships: Christian beliefs, attitudes and teachings about the nature and purpose of relationships in the twenty first century: families, roles of women and men, marriage outside the religious tradition and cohabitation.

Families

Modern families do not all look the same, but they all consist of some combination of adults and children who live together and operate as a unit. Christian **scripture** teaches that the purpose of a family was set at the time of creation. For Christianity, the family is:

- the building block of society – enabling it to be well-organised and stable
- where children are produced, protected and educated in the Christian faith.

Scripture depicts **nuclear families** as the ideal family unit. However, Christians have had to respond to the fact that in modern society there are **single parent families**, **blended families**, families without children and families with adults of the same sex.

Different Christian **denominations** have slightly different beliefs and teachings about the nature, purpose and **role** of the family. For example:

- the Catholic Church teaches that the ideal family is a nuclear family. The role of parents is to provide a safe and stable home where children are protected and educated in their faith. The children's role is to respect and obey their parents.
- Quakers welcome any family where children are taught religious and moral values. Children are taught by following the example of any loving parent who demonstrates those values.

> ❛Children obey your parents in everything, for this pleases the Lord. Fathers do not embitter your children, or they will become discouraged.❜
> *Colossians 3:20-21*

Roles of women and men

Christianity teaches that women and men were both created by God, in his image and that they are of equal value. They are made to be partners and to help and support each other.

In the Bible, St. Paul does not clearly state gender roles for a family, but his teaching generally supports the historical context in which he wrote which was **patriarchal**. Husbands work and earn a wage, whilst wives remain at home, raising children and keeping the house.

> ❛Wives, submit yourselves to your husbands as you do to the Lord.❜
> *Ephesians 5:22*

However, he also teaches that men and women are equal, so many modern Christian families reject **gender stereotypes**. Parents help each other with wage earning, housework and child rearing, or sometimes fathers stay at home whilst mothers earn a wage.

> ❛There is no longer Jew nor Gentile, neither slave nor free, nor is there male and female, for you are all one in Christ Jesus.❜
> *Galatians 3:28*

Useful terms

scripture – a sacred writing or book (for Christians this is the Bible)

nuclear family – two parents – one male, one female – and their children

single parent family – one parent raising a child or children alone

blended family – when a divorced person forms a new relationship, the family may contain a mixture of step-parents and step-children

denominations – organised groups of Christians with their own leaders and traditions

patriarchal – a system controlled by men

gender stereotypes – generalisations made about male and female behaviour based on their biological sex

Whilst most Christian denominations emphasise equality between men and women, different denominations may state slightly different things in their teachings. For example:

- the Catholic Church teaches that men and women have equal worth in the eyes of God, but different, complementary roles and **responsibilities**. Therefore, some choose to take on traditional family roles.
- Quakers actively use inclusive language and reject gender stereotyping in all its teaching. They say that women can be included in all the same kinds of roles as men.

Marriage outside the religious tradition

An interfaith marriage is where two people of different faiths marry, such as a Muslim and a Christian or a religious person and an Atheist. Not all Christians encourage interfaith marriages, because they risk arguments over how to raise any children. Many Christians don't want to marry someone who might teach their children the faith or behaviour that they believe is wrong.

- The Orthodox Church does not allow an interfaith marriage to take place in an Orthodox church and the Orthodox partner cannot join in Holy Communion if they have married a non-Christian.
- The Church of England recognises and supports couples in interfaith marriages. They offer other options if one partner cannot agree to saying Christian marriage vows. For example, a couple could have a non-religious service followed by religious blessings.

Cohabitation

In modern society it is popular for couples to live together in a romantic and sexual relationship before marriage, or with no intention of marrying. The Office for National Statistics estimates that between 2002 and 2019, the numbers of cohabiting couples had risen by over 2 million. Christian teaching traditionally forbids this.

- The Catholic Church considers sex before and outside marriage a sin, called 'fornication', and only allows sex to take place within marriage. **Cohabitation** is not consistent with God's plan for marriage.

But, increasing numbers of Christians today do cohabit before getting married.

- Quakers accept couples that are faithful to each other in a loving relationship outside of marriage. They teach that marriage is special and is God's work but that people should be included and valued in the church whatever their living situation.

Many modern Christian families do not reflect traditional gender roles

'Do not be yoked together with unbelievers. For what do righteousness and wickedness have in common?'
2 Corinthians 6:14

Cohabitation before or instead of marriage is increasingly popular in modern society

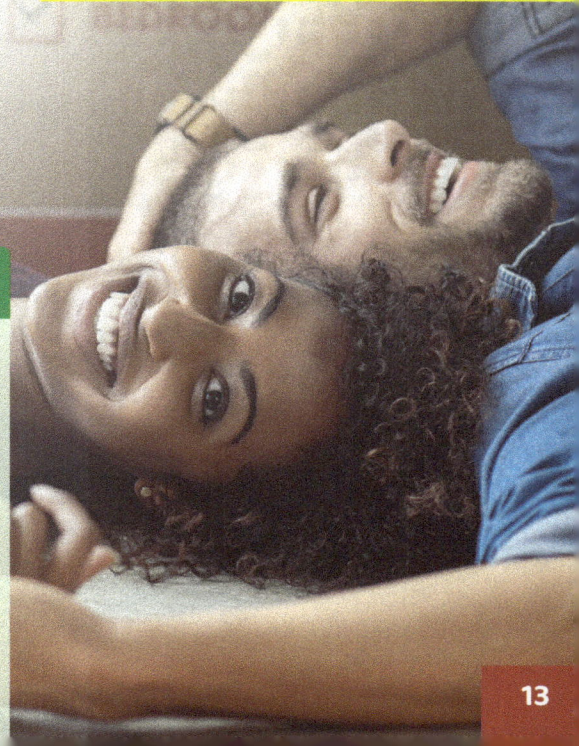

Knowledge recall

1 Define the following concepts: cohabitation, responsibilities, roles. (You can find these definitions on page 11.)
2 List three roles that parents may perform in a family.
3 State one example of a religious teaching regarding interfaith marriages.

Evaluation practice

4 Give one reason why some Christians might reject cohabiting and one reason why some Christians might agree with it.
5 Which of these views do you find most persuasive? Give two reasons for your view.

Islam and relationships in the twenty first century

Specification focus

Relationships: Islamic beliefs, attitudes and teachings about the nature and purpose of relationships in the twenty first century: families, roles of women and men, marriage outside the religious tradition and cohabitation: *Hadith Sahih al-Bukhari 9:89:252.*

Families

In Islam, the family is the most important institution and considered a gift from Allah. Muslims are encouraged to follow the example of the Prophet Muhammad who married and had children. The purpose of the family in Islam is:

- to provide a stable foundation for society
- to raise and nurture children – bringing them up as faithful Muslims, loved and educated in Islam and its tradition.

Children are a blessing from Allah. Parents have a duty to provide a stable, loving home for their children and to raise them to be faithful Muslims. Muslim children may go to a religious school or **madrasah**, to help them grow in the Muslim faith.

In Islam, the family consists of a heterosexual couple (a man and woman), their children and often, **extended family**. Muslims have a duty to care for their parents with kindness and respect when they are elderly, just as their parents cared for them when they were children. Grandparents in extended families can offer additional support in caring for and educating children.

Roles of women and men

Women are not inferior in Islamic teaching; men and women are made from the same soul and so they are equal. However, men and women have different rights and responsibilities according to their biological differences.

- Men are the head of the family. They are protectors or guardians of women and must provide financially for them, even if they have their own wealth, as men are often physically stronger and do not suffer the physical burdens of menstruation, pregnancy, childbirth and nursing.
- Women are the heart of the family. They see to the wellbeing of everyone and set the standard of morality, manners and religious education.

> 'And lower your wing in humility towards them in kindness and say, "Lord, have mercy on them, just as they cared for me when I was little."'
> *Qur'an 17:24*

Extended families can offer additional support in raising children

Useful terms

madrasah – an Islamic school, often attached to the mosque, for learning about the faith
extended family – a family that includes near relatives such as grandparents, aunts and uncles in the same household as parents and children
hadiths – Islamic scriptures, a record of the words of Muhammad
Shi'a – a branch of Islam that regards Ali as the successor of Muhammad
Sunni – a branch of Islam that accepts the first four caliphs as successors of Muhammad
zina – unlawful sexual intercourse, e.g. sex before marriage or adultery
Qur'an – Islamic scripture, a record of the words of Allah to Muhammad

> 'Allah's Apostle said "Surely! Everyone of you is a guardian and is responsible for his charges; The Imam (ruler) of the people is the guardian and is responsible for his subjects; **a man is the guardian of his family (household) and is responsible for his subjects; a woman is the guardian of her husband's home and of his children and is responsible for them;** and the slave of a man is a guardian of his master's property and is responsible for it. Surely, everyone of you is a guardian and responsible for his charges."'
> *Hadith Sahih al-Bukhari 9:89:252*

The family is patriarchal but there is no Islamic law against women working if it is compatible with Islamic principles and doesn't threaten the wellbeing of the home. Khadijah, the first wife of Muhammad, was originally his employer and a highly successful businesswoman according to the **hadiths**.

A woman's duty is to be the guardian of the children in the family

Marriage outside the religious tradition

Marriage outside of Islam is strongly discouraged.

- Some Muslims agree that a Muslim man can marry a Christian or Jewish woman, but a Muslim woman should only marry a Muslim man. It is thought that this stems from patriarchal tradition: Muslim men have a duty to respect any religious requirements that their wives have, but a non-Muslim man might not allow his Muslim wife to keep her religion. However, many **Shi'a** scholars argue that no Muslim should marry outside the faith.
- A Muslim may not marry a Hindu or a Buddhist unless that person converts to Islam. It is thought that the challenges to faith would be too great for a family to bear.
- In non-Muslim countries, marriages between **Sunni** and Shi'a Muslims are uncommon, but they do take place. In Shi'a majority countries, Shi'a men may marry Sunni women. In areas where Sunni Muslims are in the majority, then Sunni men may marry Shi'a women.

Cohabitation

Cohabitation is forbidden in Islam without being married first. This is because **zina** or sexual immorality is a sin. It is not acceptable for an unmarried couple to live together, even if they do not have sexual intercourse. The **Qur'an** advises that Muslims should not even come close to committing zina so a male and female who are not related, should not even be in the same room alone together.

Although in practice some Muslims might choose to cohabit, it is not considered acceptable. However, most Shi'a traditions allow temporary marriage as a morally better solution to having sexual relationships outside of marriage.

> 'And do not go anywhere near adultery: it is an outrage, and an evil path.'
> *Qur'an 17:32*

Read about temporary marriage on page 18.

Knowledge recall

1 Define the following concepts: roles, responsibilities, cohabitation. (You can find these definitions on page 11.)
2 List two reasons for living in an extended family.
3 State why the traditional duties of Muslim husbands and wives may differ from each other.

Evaluation practice

4 Give one reason why some Muslims might believe that women should remain in the home and one reason why other Muslims may think that women can go out to work.
5 Which of these views do you think is more convincing? Give two reasons for your view.

Christian attitudes to marriage and divorce

Specification focus

Relationships: The nature and purpose of marriage as expressed through Christian marriage ceremonies in Britain and teachings: Mark 10:6-8 and the Church of England Synod; Varying Christian attitudes towards adultery, divorce and annulment and separation and remarriage. Interpretations of Matthew 19:8-9, Mark 10:9.

The nature and purpose of marriage

For many Christians, marriage is a **sacrament**. It is a lifelong, **monogamous** union between one man and one woman that is blessed by God. For other Christians it is still a gift from God that is holy and to be respected.

In 2002 the General Synod of the Church of England affirmed the Christian teaching that marriage is a permanent lifelong union between one man and one woman for:

- **P**rocreation – it is a stable environment to produce and raise children in the Christian faith
- **P**artnership – it is a lifelong **commitment** to unite and support each other physically, emotionally and spiritually, even in difficult times
- **P**urity – marriage is the right place for a sexual relationship. It prevents sexual immorality
- **P**rotection – marriage is fundamental to an organised, stable society.

Jesus said that marriage was God's intention for humans since creation. God joins the couple physically and spiritually as one flesh through marriage that is **consummated** by sex.

'But at the beginning of creation God "made them male and female." For this reason a man will leave his father and mother and be united to his wife, and **the two will become one flesh**.'
Mark 10:6-8

Christian marriage ceremonies in Britain

Different denominations mark this **rite** in different ways. The rituals involved show that marriage is a **covenant**, a promise between a husband, a wife and God:

The Orthodox Church	The Church of England
Called a Betrothal Service, followed by a Crowning Service.	Called a Marriage Service.
A sacrament performed by the Presbyter (Orthodox Priest).	Not a gospel sacrament, but a sacred ceremony performed by God through the Vicar.
Two lit candles are presented to the couple representing Christ's light to the world.	The couple make declarations to love, honour, comfort and protect their partner.
No vows are recited. Wedding crowns are placed on the couple's heads as they participate in Christ's kingship and give themselves up to each other and to God.	The couple vow: 'To have and to hold, from this day forward, for better, for worse, for richer, for poorer, in sickness and in health, to love and to cherish until death parts us according to God's holy law.'
There are readings, wine is drunk by the couple from a shared cup and there is a procession around the central altar whilst hymns are sung.	The couple exchange rings and say: 'With my body I honour you, all that I am I give to you and all that I have I share with you, within the love of God, Father, Son and Holy Spirit.'

Christian attitudes towards adultery and divorce

Christianity generally does not support **divorce**, although some denominations accept that it is sometimes necessary. In the Gospel of Mark, Jesus emphasises that the act of marriage is performed by God so cannot be ended by humans:

Useful terms

sacrament – an outward sign of an invisible and inward blessing by God. For example, Baptism, the Eucharist
monogamous – having only one sexual partner
consummate – to complete a marriage by having sex after the ceremony has taken place
rite – religious ceremony or practice
covenant – an agreement or promise between human beings and God
Matthean exemption – the exception to Jesus' rule forbidding divorce, allowing it if one partner has been unfaithful
sacred – holy, devoted to God for a religious purpose
General Synod of the Church of England – the national assembly of the Church of England that considers, debates and approves laws affecting the whole of the Church
annulment – a legal process in which a marriage is declared invalid or void

> ❝Therefore what God has joined together, let no one separate.❞
> Mark 10:9

Under Jewish law divorce was permitted, but Jesus makes the law stricter by forbidding divorce unless a partner has been unfaithful. **Adultery** is considered a sin because it is a violation of vows made before God. It damages trust within a marriage and can cause the breakdown of the family.

This rule is called the '**Matthean exemption**' because it is described in these verses from the Gospel of Matthew:

> ❝Moses permitted you to divorce your wives because your hearts were hard. But it was not this way from the beginning. I tell you that **anyone who divorces his wife, except for sexual immorality, and marries another woman commits adultery.**❞
> Matthew 19:8-9

Christian attitudes towards annulment, separation and remarriage

The verses from Matthew state that since marriage is a **sacred** bond between two people, to divorce and remarry is to commit adultery. However, not all Christians agree that this is the case.

- The Catholic Church forbids remarriage because Matthew 19 has declared it sinful. Whilst people may remarry after an annulment, those who remarry after divorce are barred from receiving Holy Communion.
- The Church of England has previously forbidden remarriage. However, in 2002 the **General Synod of the Church of England** changed Church teaching to allow remarriage in church in exceptional circumstances. Church of England vicars may offer a blessing instead.

The Catholic Church forbids divorce but allows **annulment** as the only way to dissolve a marriage. For a marriage to be annulled, it must be proven to have not been a legitimate marriage in the first place. For example:

- the couple did not consummate their marriage
- one partner was already married to someone else
- one partner was forced into the marriage.

Alternatively, Catholics may see separation as acceptable if a marriage breaks down. Separation is where the partners no longer live together but are not divorced.

Harry and Meghan were married by the Archbishop of Canterbury in St. George's Chapel, Windsor. This is Meghan Markle's second marriage

Knowledge recall

1 Define the following concepts: adultery, divorce, commitment. (You can find these definitions on page 11.)
2 List three purposes of Christian marriage.
3 State two examples of how Christians might show the importance of marriage in their wedding ceremonies.

Evaluation practice

4 Give two reasons why some Churches might refuse to perform second marriages and two reasons why other Churches might tolerate, bless or perform remarriages.
5 Which of these views do you think is the most persuasive for Christians? Give a reason why.

Islamic attitudes to marriage and divorce

Specification focus

Relationships: The nature and purpose of marriage as expressed through Muslim marriage ceremonies and teachings: Qur'an 30:21; Diversity of belief between Shi'a and Sunni Muslims regarding temporary and unannounced marriage; Islamic attitudes towards adultery, divorce and annulment and separation and remarriage. Qur'an 4:35, 4:128-130, 2:229; Arranged marriage in Britain.

The nature and purpose of marriage

In Islam marriage is a contract or commitment, not a sacrament, between a consenting man and woman. It is a vital part of religious life. According to the Qur'an, men and women are gifts from Allah for each other. Marriage is for:

- mutual support and care
- a flourishing society
- safeguarding against sin by allowing sexual needs to be met
- meeting religious obligation.

> ❛Another of His signs is that **He created spouses from among yourselves** for you to live with in tranquillity: He ordained love and kindness between you.❜
> *Qur'an 30:21*

Muslim marriage ceremonies

A Muslim wedding is performed before Allah as a religious duty. The ceremony is called a **nikah**. It is performed by an **Imam**, but any Muslim can also perform it. It can take place at the home of the bride, at a banqueting hall or in a mosque.

Muslim weddings require a **mahr**: a dowry of money, jewellery or other high value gifts, given to the bride by the groom. This is kept by the bride, even in the event of a divorce. Traditionally, the couple must have permission to marry from a **wali** (a guardian – often a father) and the bride must agree to the marriage. For Shi'a Muslims the woman must say in Arabic, 'I have made myself your wife on the agreed dowry.' The husband replies, 'I accept the marriage.'

There are many customs that may be observed at a Muslim wedding, for example, the couple may sit on thrones or recite vows, but most of these are cultural and are not obliged by Islam. The most important part of the nikah is the signing of the marriage contract in front of at least two witnesses. There may be verses from the Qur'an, prayers, blessings and a short talk if there is an Imam. The nikah must be public and never secret. A separate civil ceremony must also take place to make the marriage legal under UK law. For Muslims, the religious ceremony is the most important.

Temporary and unannounced marriage

The Qur'an allows men to make temporary marriages. This practice arose to prevent zina in the early history of Islam, when Muslim armies travelled long distances away from their families.

All Muslims accept the Qur'an and broadly have the same beliefs. However, Sunni and Shi'a Muslims accept some different hadiths. Sunni Muslims accept a hadith that suggests that Muhammad later forbade temporary marriages. Most Shi'a Muslims reject this hadith and allow temporary and unannounced marriages.

Useful terms

nikah – Muslim wedding ceremony
Imam – for Sunni Muslims: a Muslim prayer leader. For Shi'a Muslims: one of the twelve infallible successors to Muhammad chosen by Allah to guide humans towards Him
mahr – (dowry) the money or goods given to the wife to fall back on in the instance of divorce
wali – guardian or father
haram – any actions or things which are forbidden within Islam, such as eating forbidden foods
ummah – means 'community' and refers to the worldwide community of Muslims who share a common religious identity
Shariah Council – an organisation that rules on Islamic laws derived from the Qur'an and hadiths
tallaqtuki – in Arabic: 'I divorce you'

A nikah is a religious duty before Allah

Temporary marriages usually require permission from a wali. They should be agreed with a contract that specifies the length of the marriage and a mahr, but do not require a divorce as the marriage ends as soon as the agreed time expires.

Muslim attitudes towards adultery, divorce, separation and remarriage

In Islam, adultery, like any sex outside of marriage, is **haram** and harmful to the **ummah**.

If a couple experience marriage difficulties, there are Muslim counselling services in the UK, and mosques or extended families often try to help with mediation in the hope that divorce can be avoided.

Divorce is a last resort after all attempts at reconciliation have failed. It is not permissible during menstruation, pregnancy or just after childbirth. Religious divorces are granted by a **Shariah Council** that gives legal rulings to Muslims based on Shariah Law. For a religious divorce to happen, a man must say **'tallaqtuki'** – 'I divorce you' in Arabic – either verbally or in writing. For Shi'a Muslims there must be two witnesses to this. There is a three month waiting period before the divorce is granted. This gives the couple a chance to ensure that the wife is not pregnant and during this time the man can take the woman back as his wife. The wife may keep the mahr and the husband must support any children. If the couple have had a civil marriage, they must legally dissolve this too.

Remarriage after divorce is encouraged since there is no tradition of celibacy in the Islamic faith. Muhammad led by example and several of his wives, were widows or divorcees.

> ❝Divorce can happen twice, and each time **wives either be kept on in an acceptable manner or released in a good way.** It is not lawful for you to take anything back that you have given your wives, except where both fear that they cannot maintain the bounds set by God.❞
> *Qur'an 2:229*

> ❝If a wife fears high-handedness or alienation from her husband, neither of them will be blamed if they come to a peaceful settlement, for peace is best. Although human souls are prone to selfishness, if you do good and are mindful of God, He is well aware of all that you do. If you make amends and remain conscious of God, He is most forgiving and merciful, but **if husband and wife do separate, God will provide for each out of His plenty.**❞
> *Qur'an 4:128-130*

Arranged marriage in Britain

Muslim marriages are traditionally arranged since Islam does not allow men and women to socialise freely and form romantic relationships. The wali arranges the marriage on behalf of the couple to ensure they are compatible. Islam forbids forced marriages so both the man and woman have the right to refuse. However, arranged marriage is a cultural practice, not an Islamic requirement. In Britain, love marriages are becoming more popular amongst young Muslims.

> ❝If you fear that a couple may break up, **appoint one arbiter from his family and one from hers.** Then, if the couple want to put things right, God will bring about a reconciliation between them.❞
> *Qur'an 4:35*

Knowledge recall

1 Define the following concepts: commitment, adultery, divorce. (You can find these definitions on page 11.)
2 List three purposes of Muslim marriage.
3 State one reason why temporary marriage may be accepted by some Muslims and one reason why it might be rejected by others.

Evaluation practice

4 Give two reasons why some Muslim families might arrange marriages for their children and two reasons why other Muslims might not do this.
5 Which of these views do you find most convincing? Give a reason why.

Christian attitudes to sexual relationships

Christian teachings about the nature and purpose of sex

Christianity teaches that sex is a gift, given by God at creation, for one man and one woman within marriage. Following the guidance of St. Thomas Aquinas in the thirteenth century, the Church has taught that sex has several purposes:

- **P**rocreation – the primary purpose of sex is to reproduce
- **P**artnership – sex unites the husband and wife physically and spiritually within a marriage
- **P**leasure – sex is for enjoyment, between a husband and wife.

Most Christian Churches teach that sex is only for a husband and wife, so **promiscuity** is considered sinful. Couples are taught to avoid sex before marriage and adultery. Unmarried people are encouraged to be **chaste**. Some more Liberal Christians consider it possible for sex to fulfil its God-given purpose outside marriage, but in a committed, loving relationship.

The use of contraception

Contraception is the use of methods during or following sex to prevent pregnancy. There are two types:

1 Artificial contraception – preventing pregnancy or conception during sex by use of a device, drugs or surgery, e.g. implants, condoms, the morning after pill.
2 Natural contraception – preventing pregnancy by natural means, e.g. avoiding sex during the fertile days of a woman's menstrual cycle.

Most Protestant Churches welcome natural and artificial contraceptive methods for the use of family planning and so that partnership and pleasure can be enjoyed by a married couple, but still reject promiscuity.

The Catholic and Orthodox Churches teach that any method of birth control that destroys a fertilised egg, such as the morning after pill, is sinful because it is destroying a human life. Catholics also reject artificial contraception in any form because it interferes with the God-given purpose of sexual intercourse – procreation. They accept natural contraceptive methods because these do not make it impossible for God to create new life but do allow couples to plan their families effectively.

Natural Law

The Catholic approach to contraception comes from scripture and the teachings of Aquinas in his Natural Law. Aquinas taught that there are **Five Primary Precepts**. These are commands or rules that we can use reason to understand. They are absolute and must never be broken:

1 **P**reserve innocent life/ self-preservation
2 **R**eproduce
3 **E**ducate children
4 **O**rder society
5 **W**orship God

The primary precept of 'reproduce' means that any behaviour that prevents reproduction is unacceptable. Therefore, artificial contraception, same sex relationships and abortion are forbidden by the Catholic Church.

Specification focus

Sexual relationships: Christian teachings about the nature and purpose of sex and the use of contraception including varied interpretations of the Natural Law / Absolutist approach of Thomas Aquinas' Five Primary Precepts with reference to the second Primary Precept; Diverse attitudes within and across Christian traditions towards same sex relationships, including varied interpretations of: Leviticus 20:13 and 1 Timothy 1:8-10.

Some churches are working to find ways to make gay and bi people feel welcome in their congregations

Useful terms

promiscuity – having several sexual partners on a casual basis
chaste – refraining from sexual intercourse
Five Primary Precepts – five absolute rules that guide moral action
celibate – remaining unmarried and not having sexual intercourse. Monks and nuns take a vow to be celibate

Christian attitudes towards same sex relationships

Traditionally, Christianity has taught that same sex relationships are sinful because:

- they violate the primary precept to reproduce
- they go against the purpose of marriage as set out by God at creation
- they are directly forbidden in scripture.

Some Christians use Bible passages such as the ones below from Leviticus and Timothy to argue that Christians should reject same sex relationships.

> ❝We know that the law is good if one uses it properly. **We also know that the law is made not for the righteous but for lawbreakers and rebels, the ungodly and sinful, the unholy and irreligious; for those who kill their fathers or mothers, for murderers, for the sexually immoral, for those practising homosexuality,** for slave traders and liars and perjurers – and whatever else is contrary to the sound doctrine.❞
> *1 Timothy 1:8-10*

- This is a New Testament letter from St. Paul.
- The letter lists people who exhibit 'immoral' behaviour.
- Some Christians argue that the original text did not refer to homosexuality in ancient Greek and therefore it is not directly forbidden.
- Other Christians believe the law is very clear and forbids same sex relationships.

> ❝If a man has sexual relations with a man as one does with a woman, both of them have done what is detestable. They are to be put to death; their blood will be on their own heads.❞
> *Leviticus 20:13*

- This is Old Testament law given by God to Moses.
- Christianity no longer advocates capital punishment for sexual acts between people of the same sex because society has changed. Therefore, it is also possible for the rules against same sex relationships to be changed.
- Conservative Christians argue that scripture cannot be wrong since it is the word of God.

Other Christians argue that these biblical laws were for a particular time in history and are no longer needed or that they have been misunderstood. Jesus never refers to or forbids same sex relationships. Today, there are many gay or bi people who are also Christian. In UK law, homosexuality was decriminalised in 1967, **civil partnerships** were introduced for same sex couples in 2004 and same sex marriages were legalised in 2013.

The Catholic Church believes that gay and bi people are not sinful for their feelings, but only if they engage in sexual activity, so they should remain **celibate**. Sex with someone of the same gender is 'intrinsically disordered' - it is against the primary precepts and therefore always wrong.

In 2017, the Church of England General Synod rejected a report opposing same sex marriage because they wanted to become more welcoming for homosexual couples. Some vicars are openly gay, but they are instructed to remain celibate. Same sex couples cannot get married in the Church of England.

Quakers welcome same sex couples and perform or bless same sex unions. They accept that people may show their love for each other in diverse ways.

Knowledge recall

1 Define the following concepts: contraception, commitment, cohabitation. (You can find these definitions on page 11.)
2 List three Christian ideas about the purpose of sex.
3 State two examples of Christian teachings about same sex relationships.

Evaluation practice

4 Give one reason why some Christians might object to the use of contraception and one reason why others may welcome it.
5 What problems can you see with this teaching?

Islamic attitudes to sexual relationships

Specification focus

Sexual relationships: Islamic teachings about the nature and purpose of sex and the use of contraception. Qur'an 17:32; Islamic attitudes towards same sex relationships. Qur'an 7:80-81.

Muslim teachings on the nature and purpose of sex

The greatest purpose of sex in Islam is procreation. Bringing new life into the world is highly valued in Islam. Sex is also a gift from Allah for the enjoyment of the couple and an act of worship. Sex is encouraged for married couples only, for each to be faithful and respectfully meet each other's needs.

Islam has very strict rules about sex. Unlawful sexual intercourse is called **zina**, and it is considered an abuse of Allah's intention for human beings. Zina includes sex before marriage, casual sex and adultery. Muslims are expected to remain chaste until they are married. Therefore, having boyfriends or girlfriends is prohibited, there is to be no touching, intimate talking or even looking with desire that could be considered zina or that might lead to zina. Men and women who are unrelated should not be alone together. This is believed to protect the individual and society from sin. Muslim societies therefore often encourage or arrange marriages quite early, after the onset of puberty, to avoid the risk of zina.

There is no tradition of celibacy or **monasticism** in Islam. It is seen as ungrateful to Allah to live in celibacy as a life choice and should never be forced upon a husband or wife by a spouse who refuses to have sex. Muhammad was not celibate and did not encourage or recommend celibacy to his followers.

> ❝And do not approach unlawful sexual intercourse. Indeed, it is ever an immorality and is evil as a way.❞
> *Qur'an 17:32*

- This is a command to the individual but also the whole society.
- This text warns the believer not to even come close to sexual immorality.
- This means that Muslims should not perform acts that may lead to sexual immorality, e.g. being alone together, touching, speaking or looking at each other in a sexual way.

The use of contraception

Family planning and birth control is permitted by most Islamic schools of law within a marriage. It is not allowed for unmarried people as sex outside marriage is **haram**.

A couple may wish to use **contraception** to:

- protect a woman's health
- space out their children to help them cope
- limit the size of their families.

Some hadiths suggest that Muhammad used some methods of birth control. Those who agree with the use of contraception would say that it is only allowed if:

- the method is temporary and reversible, such as condoms or any device that prevents the fertilisation of the egg. (Sterilisation or abortion are not acceptable.)
- both the husband and wife agree to use it.

The purpose of sex is to bring new life into the world. Contraception should only ever be temporary

Some Muslims object to contraception because of the following verse:

> ‘Do not kill your children for fear of poverty – We shall provide for them and for you – killing them is a great sin.’
> *Qur'an 17:31*

Some think that this verse applies to contraception as well as abortion and the murder of children. Allah and the **ummah**, the Muslim community, will provide for any children that are born.

Muslim attitudes towards same sex relationships

Same sex relationships are haram in the Qur'an where Allah tells Muslims that all sexual relations should be within marriage only. Islam does not accept same sex marriage, since Allah created humans in male and female pairs to complement each other and procreate. Only relationships between a man and a woman are permissible.

Any public displays of sexual behaviour are forbidden to everyone, regardless of sexuality. It is also a sin to publicise wrong behaviour, so if someone has had sex with a person of the same gender, they are to keep it private between themselves and Allah, to whom they should repent and then alter their ways.

Islam also teaches that there should be no discrimination against gay or bi people. Everyone should be allowed to attend prayers at the mosque and receive the same treatment. Harming someone because of their sexual orientation is haram. However, in many Muslim countries, homosexual behaviour is a criminal offence and punishable in the same way as adultery.

Islam teaches that same sex relationships are haram because Allah says so in the Qur'an. According to the Qur'an, God destroyed the people of Sodom because they did not refrain from engaging in sex with people of the same gender despite being warned by Lut.

> ‘We sent Lot and he said to his people, “How can you practise this outrage? No other people has done so before. You lust after men instead of women! You transgress all bounds!”’
> *Qur'an 7:80-81*

Some Muslim people who identify as gay or bi struggle to make their faith compatible with their sexuality. There are support groups such as IMAAN who offer support to LGBTQ Muslims and campaign on their behalf.

Useful terms

zina – unlawful sexual intercourse, e.g. sex before marriage or adultery

monastic – monks or nuns who live simply under a vow of chastity with few possessions so they can dedicate themselves to worship

haram – any actions or things which are forbidden within Islam, such as eating forbidden foods

contraception – methods used to prevent a woman from becoming pregnant during or following sexual intercourse

ummah – means 'community' and refers to the worldwide community of Muslims who share a common religious identity

- This story can be also found in the Old Testament of the Bible.
- The city of Sodom was inhabited by corrupt, sinful people.
- The people of Sodom were the first to practise sex between two people of the same gender.
- Lut, Ibrahim's nephew, repeatedly appealed to them to practise sex in a lawful way.
- God's punishment was to destroy the inhabitants of the city, except for Lut and his family.
- Some Muslims argue the original passage was a rejection of non-consensual sex, not same sex relationships.

Knowledge recall

1 Define the following concepts: contraception, adultery, gender equality. (You can find these definitions on page 11.)
2 Explain two rules from within Islam that control the use of contraception.
3 State one example of Qur'anic teachings about same sex relationships.

Evaluation practice

4 Give two reasons why some Muslims may wish to restrict contact between unmarried men and women.
5 Explain one strength and one weakness to limiting contact between unmarried people.

Christian attitudes towards the roles of women and men in religion

Specification focus

Issues of equality: Gender prejudice and discrimination: Diverse attitudes within Christianity towards the roles of women and men in worship and authority with reference to Catholic, Orthodox and Anglican views on this issue; Interpretations of teachings: 1 Timothy 2:11-12, Galatians 3:27-29.

Diverse Christian attitudes towards the roles of women and men in worship

The subject of the **roles** of women and men in worship is a controversial topic within Christianity. Traditionally, women and men have had different roles, based on interpretations of Christian scripture. The Bible is thought to have been written by about 70 CE. Since then, our society has changed and Christians are faced with the challenge of understanding scripture in the light of **gender equality**.

During Jesus' life, his actions showed that he had great respect for women and women were among his closest followers. He demonstrated value for women by speaking to them publicly, respectfully and compassionately, teaching them and ministering to them as he would to men. Although all of Jesus' disciples were male, he first appeared to women after his resurrection.

Not all Christians agree about the roles that men and women should play in worship. All Christian denominations teach opposition to prejudice and discrimination against women, but they differ regarding what this means.

Catholic views

The Catholic Church teaches that men and women are equal in terms of value, but that they have different roles and **responsibilities**. In church, the priest represents Christ in the celebration of the **Eucharist**. Christ was male and he only appointed male apostles, so it is argued that his representatives today must be male too. Catholic priests are always men.

- In 2016, Pope Francis made a statement ruling out women ever becoming priests.
- Women are allowed other roles in the Church such as nuns, **religious sisters**, **abbesses** or **prioresses**.
- Currently, women are campaigning to be allowed to be ordained as **deacons** and perform some of the duties of priests but not take Mass or hear confession.
- Pope Francis recently appointed a woman, Francesca Di Giovani, to a senior Vatican diplomatic post.

Orthodox views

The Orthodox Church sees men and women as equal in terms of their value as human beings. Women are not inferior beings and must be given the same rights as men. However, women and men have significant and important roles that are unique to their gender. Women have the God-given role of motherhood and no other role is more valuable for them. In the Orthodox Church women are only able to be lay people; they cannot be **ordained**. This means that they can become a nun or, in some Orthodox traditions, a **deaconess** but never a priest. Women continue to work and campaign for their right to be accepted into ordination.

Jesus only appointed male disciples during his ministry

Useful terms

Eucharist – the celebration of the Lord's Supper with bread and wine during a church service
religious sister – a woman who takes some vows as a nun would but helps in the world instead of living separately in a convent
abbess and prioress – superior roles governing nuns in an Abbey or Priory
deacon – an ordained role, often reserved for men, who take some responsibilities assisting a priest
ordained – to be given priestly authority in a holy ceremony
deaconess – a non-ordained role, mainly concerned with helping the priest to minister to women and girls

Anglican views

The Anglican Church teaches that men and women were both created in God's image and equally reflect something of his nature. In the early Church it is thought that there were some women who took leadership roles. Whilst women have not always been allowed into the priesthood in the Anglican Church, in relatively recent years this has changed. Many feel that women can have many qualities that are useful for a calling to the priesthood and should have the same opportunities as men.

- The first women were ordained as priests or vicars in the UK in 1994.
- In 2015 the first woman bishop was ordained, the Rt Reverend Libby Lane.
- Some in the Church of England objected to these developments and left to join the Catholic Church, including some vicars.
- Female priests now have the same roles and responsibilities as male priests. For example, they can administer the sacraments of Baptism and the Eucharist.

Interpretations of teachings

The Bible contains teachings that seem to tell us about the expected roles of women in the Church.

These different interpretations mean that Christians do not all agree about whether women should take an active or authoritative role in the life and running of the Church.

Angela Berners-Wilson was the first woman to be ordained into the Church of England as a priest in 1994

> ❝A woman should learn in quietness and full submission. I do not permit a woman to teach or to assume authority over a man; she must be quiet.❞
> *1 Timothy 2:11-12*

- This is a New Testament letter from St. Paul to Timothy.
- This instruction was not surprising to Jews or Greeks at the time, because neither of them allowed women to teach.
- Some think that it is not clear whether this is a command or a suggestion to Timothy about how he could organise the church.
- Some argue that it does not rule out the ministry of women at some future stage.

> ❝For all of you who were baptised into Christ have clothed yourselves with Christ. There is neither Jew nor Gentile, neither slave nor free, **nor is there male and female; for you are all one in Christ Jesus**. If you belong to Christ, then you are Abraham's seed, and heirs according to the promise.❞
> *Galatians 3:27-29*

- This is a New Testament letter from St. Paul to the churches in Galatia.
- Under the law at the time, men had greater privileges than women.
- This teaching makes a change in the order of society.
- Paul removes all the barriers that have divided people in the past.
- Some Christians argue that this means that anyone who has faith in Christ could potentially serve in the priesthood.

Knowledge recall

1 Define the following concepts: roles, gender equality, responsibility. (You can find these definitions on page 11.)
2 List three examples of roles that women can perform within the Catholic Church.
3 Suggest one biblical teaching that could be used in a debate about women's ordination.

Evaluation practice

4 Give an argument for and an argument against the ordination of women into the priesthood.
5 Which argument do you think is the strongest and why?

Islamic attitudes towards the roles of women and men in religion

Specification focus

Issues of equality: gender prejudice and discrimination: Diverse attitudes within Islam toward the roles of women and men in worship and authority; Teachings: Qur'an 2:228, 40:40, 4:1.

The roles of women and men in Islam

Islam teaches that women and men were created as equals by Allah to complement each other. The Qur'an praises women and men equally. Allah has given each gender their own different responsibilities that reflect the roles that they were created to take on.

> ‘People, **be mindful of your Lord, who created you from a single soul and from it created its mate,** and from the pair of them spread countless men and women far and wide; be mindful of God, in whose name you make requests of one another. Beware of severing the ties of kinship: God is always watching over you. ’
> *Qur'an 4:1*

- This shows the equality of men and women as they originate from the same single soul.
- Some argue that this means they should equally be allowed to serve Allah through leading prayers in the mosque and giving sermons.

Since only women can bear children, men must work outside the home to support their wives who concentrate on the family. However, there is nothing in Islam that forbids women from working, provided they do not neglect their family. Both men and women have a duty to be educated. Educated Muslim women are vital, because of the rules regarding non-**mahrams**, female doctors, midwives, dentists, teachers and lawyers are essential to support other women.

Women in worship

Muhammad encouraged men to allow their wives to attend the mosque and join in with prayers. However, the rules regarding contact with non-mahrams require men and women to worship separately. Arrangements to enable women to worship at the mosque where there are men could be:

- Women pray beside men, with a screen to separate them.
- Women pray in a separate room or up on a balcony.
- Women pray at the back of the room behind the men.

Prayers are led by an Imam who must be male. The exception to this is if the worshippers are female only. Then a woman may lead, but she stands in the centre of the front row, not alone at the front as a man would do. In China, there has been a move to establish women-only mosques that are led by female Imams.

Aisha and Umm Salamah (two of Muhammad's wives) led congregations of women. Umm Waraqah was a contemporary of Muhammad who knew the entire Qur'an. One hadith suggests that Muhammad made her an Imam and that she led both men and women in prayers. This has led to several possible responses:

- Some scholars argue this was a privilege for Umm Waraqah and not intended for others.
- Some scholars say that she only led women.
- Some scholars reject the hadith as coming from an unreliable source.

Women are encouraged to pray separately from men and do not usually lead mixed prayers

Useful term

mahram – a member of one's family with whom marriage or sexual intercourse would be considered haram. Women may not be alone with men who are not their mahram

Many scholars argue that if women attempt to lead the prayers of men, this invalidates men's prayers. In Britain, Raheel Raza was the first Muslim woman to lead a mixed gender prayer session. She received death threats for leading a similar group in Canada, but she argues that nowhere in the Qur'an does it forbid female Imams.

Women in authority

Other leadership roles in the mosque can be found in the mosque committee, which manages the building, finances and any workers. The members are almost exclusively male. A few scholars argue that women should be included on these committees since they make up half of all Muslim communities. The Muslim Council of Britain has called for more Muslim women to be in leadership and the Al-Manaar Muslim Cultural Heritage Centre in Kensington has appointed a female director.

Many traditional Muslim societies struggle with the idea of women in leadership because the Qur'an implies that men have authority over women. However, elsewhere in the Qur'an there is reference to the ruler the Queen of Sheba, and the hadiths refer to Khadija and Aisha (two of Muhammad's wives) being political leaders. There are Muslim women around the world who have taken leadership roles. Benazir Bhautto was elected as the first female prime minister of a Muslim country (Pakistan) in 1988 and other female leaders have been elected since.

Muslim teachings on the roles of men and women

The Qur'an contains teachings that tell us about the expected roles of women in worship.

‘Whoever does evil will be repaid with its like; **whoever does good and believes, be it a man or woman, will enter Paradise** and be provided for without measure.’
Qur'an 40:40

‘Divorced women must wait for three monthly periods before remarrying, and, if they really believe in God and the Last Day, it is not lawful for them to conceal what Allah has created in their wombs: their husbands would do better to take them back during this period, provided they wish to put things right. Divorced women have rights similar to their obligations, according to what is fair, and **[ex-]husbands have a degree of right over them**: [both should remember that] God has the power to decide.’
Qur'an 2:228

- An Imam must be a good Muslim to be allowed to lead others in prayer.
- Many Muslims argue that both men and women can be good Muslims and can be judged in the afterlife.
- A small minority argue this passage means that women should be allowed to lead mosques because they are morally accountable to Allah.

- Men are given authority over women and responsibility for them.
- This means that women have the right to be provided for by their husbands and that men have the responsibility to care for women who are seen as vulnerable.
- This passage refers to marriage and divorce. However some may argue it shows that women are never suitable to be in a position of authority over men.

Knowledge recall

1 Define the following concepts: gender equality, contraception, divorce. (You can find these definitions on page 11.)
2 List three possible arrangements made to enable women to pray in the mosque with men.
3 Suggest one example of a Qur'anic teaching that could be used in a debate about the equality of men and women.

Evaluation practice

4 Give two reasons why some Muslims believe that women should not be Imams.
5 Explain why you agree or disagree with the reasons you have stated.

Skills practice

On these exam practice pages you will see example answers for each of the exam question types: **a**, **b**, **c** and **d**. You can find out more about these on pages 5–9.

Question (a)

*Question **(a)** tests your knowledge and understanding. You will always be asked to **define a key concept** in this question. You can find a list of the concepts at the beginning of the chapter.*

> (a)   What is meant by 'commitment'?   [2]

Student response

> Commitment is when you have strong commitments, like when you get married or when you live together with another person and you have a commitment between you both to be together.

Improved student response

> Commitment is a sense of dedication or obligation to someone or something.

🕐 **Over to You!** Have a try at answering this question:

> (a)   What is meant by 'responsibilities'?   [2]

Helpful hints

To help you answer this question effectively, you could use the check list below to make sure you include the most important things:

- Include a **synonym** for the word 'responsibilities'.
- Give an **example** of a responsibility that someone might have or carry out.

Study Challenge:

The exam board will only ever ask a question **(a)** that asks for concepts listed in the specification.

- Look back at the list of concepts at the beginning of the chapter
- Choose one from the list that has not yet appeared in the questions above
- Write your own **(a)** question using the concept you have chosen
- Now give yourself **two minutes** to answer this question by yourself!

Tip

The easiest way to make sure you get full marks for this question is to learn the definitions found on page 11.

Question *(b)*

Question **(b)** *tests your knowledge and understanding. It will always ask you to* **describe** *a belief, a teaching, a practice or an event that is included on the specification.*

> *(b)* Describe the importance of marriage ceremonies for religious believers. [5]

Student response

Marriage ceremonies are very important for religious believers. They say vows to each other in front of all their family and friends that shows how important the ceremony is. Weddings can be very expensive, and the woman wears an expensive white dress and people can sometimes spend loads of money making it a special and important day.

Improved student response

Marriage ceremonies often take place in a church for Christians because they believe that God joins the couple together. Once the marriage is official, the priest will say 'what God has joined together let no one separate.' This shows that the vows the couple have made before God are very important and permanent. The couple say vows to each other, and these are a kind of promise or covenant that is made between themselves and God. This shows that their commitment is supposed to be for life. For Orthodox Christians, they will be given lit candles to represent Christ's guiding light in the world. This shows that God is supposed to be part of the marriage all the time and it is sacred.

Over to You! Have a try at answering this question:

> *(b)* Describe the purpose of sex for religious believers. [5]

Helpful hints

Use the check list below to make sure you include the most important things:

- **Describe** one of the functions or purposes of sex according to Christians or Muslims.
- Give an **example** of a statement or story from the Bible, the Qur'an, or other Church or Islamic teaching that illustrates the importance of that function.
- Then **repeat** the above process for two more religious functions or purposes of sex for religious believers.

Now give yourself **five minutes** to answer this question by yourself:

> *(b)* Describe ways in which families are important in a faith community. [5]

What went well
The mention of the vows spoken in front of family and friend is awardable.

How to improve
You must focus on the aspect of the question that asks for the importance for religious believers.

You should mention how the rituals that are performed demonstrate an important reason for or function of marriage.

You could include specialist vocabulary from the religion you are talking about.

Tip
The best answers will show reference to all aspects of the question. Here, the candidate talks about:
- the ceremony itself
- its importance
- people who are religious.
All these things are mentioned in the question.

Question (c)

*Question (c) tests your knowledge and understanding. You need to give detailed evidence and reasoning to support your explanation of the topic. For the Themes paper, you will always be asked to **explain two different viewpoints**, but you don't need to evaluate which is the better view.*

(c) Explain from **either two** religions **or two** religious traditions, attitudes about the use of contraception. [8]

Student response

Christians do not agree with contraception at all. It is never acceptable to use contraception and so they should not do it. The Bible is clear about this and says that contraception is always completely wrong. This, though, doesn't reflect modern attitudes today. Contraception is now freely available in this country and so Christian teaching on this is out of date.

Improved student response

The Catholic Church teaches that it is not acceptable to use artificial contraception. Scripture shows this because humans were given the command in Genesis 1:28 to be fruitful and multiply but contraception violates the purpose of sex, which is procreation. Some Catholics look to Natural Law and see that the Primary Precept of 'reproduction' implies that they should never use artificial contraception.

In Islam, Muslims may use contraception to help them space out children or protect the woman's health, but it is haram to use it outside of marriage as sex is for within marriage only. However, in the Qur'an, which is the word of Allah, it tells Muslims never to kill their children for fear of poverty because Allah will provide for them. As a result, some Muslims may think that this applies to contraception too because Allah and the Ummah will provide for any children.

Over to You! Have a try at answering this question:

(c) Explain, from **two** religions **or two** religious traditions, beliefs about divorce. [8]

Helpful hints

- Include **two** beliefs either from different religions (such as Christianity and Islam) or from different traditions within a religion (for example, Catholic and Protestant).
- For each belief give an **example** from religious authority to demonstrate it (e.g. the vows, scripture, Church law, a papal statement, the hadiths).
- Explain **why** each of the religions or traditions believe this (e.g. they are influenced by other teachings on marriage, or how to treat others).
- Explain **how** people of this faith are expected to behave as a result (e.g. rules about participating in communion or remarrying in church).

What went well

This response mentions scripture very briefly and gives one possible Christian response. It also mentions that there have been some changes in modern society.

How to improve

You must stick to the requirement of the question to give two religious attitudes, not just one.

You should give some clear, specific detail of what the religious attitudes are and how they are shown in behaviour or teachings.

You could include some short quotes or examples as evidence of the attitudes you are explaining.

Tip

Question (c) never requires you to evaluate or weigh up which view is better. It only wants you to describe two different views. The evaluation comes later in question (d).

Now give yourself **eight minutes** to answer this question by yourself:

> *(c)* Explain from **either two** religions **or two** religious traditions, attitudes to same sex relationships. [8]

Question *(d)*

*Question **(d)** tests your ability to **evaluate**. This means you need to show you have considered more than one point of view and that you have referred to religion and belief. You will need to be able to make judgements that are supported by detailed reasoning and argument.*

> *(d)* 'Marriage should be for life.'
> Discuss this statement showing that you have considered more than one point of view. (You must refer to religion and belief in your answer.) [15]
> Marks for spelling, punctuation and the accurate use of grammar are allocated to this question. [6]

What went well

There is some awareness of two different points of view. The Christian viewpoint is briefly mentioned and there is some support for the idea that Christians believe that marriage is for life. There are some evaluative statements about the acceptability of divorce when the candidate mentions that society has changed, and that divorce may solve some family problems.

How to improve

You must avoid personal opinions (such as the first sentence here) unless they are supported by reasoning or evidence.

You should evaluate the ideas that are raised throughout the whole essay, avoiding simple descriptions of different views.

You could make reference to or even quote sources of wisdom or authority to support your answers.

Student response

I don't think that marriage should be for life. Sometimes people can fall out of love and they can't help it. If they stay together for the kids, then they might become very unhappy and that would make the children's lives difficult too. In the end it is not anyone else's business except the couple who are married and if they want to have a divorce then they should. It is very easy to divorce these days and lots of people do it, so there is no social stigma to it like there was in the past. If a religious person says that marriage is for life, then they are behind the times and need to catch up with society and the way that life is these days. It could be that someone will get married lots of times and have children with lots of wives.

But if they are Christians, they do believe that marriage is for life because they do make promises to stay together in sickness and in health until death do us part. This means that divorce is not allowed and so they can't do it.

Improved student response

Many Christians agree that 'marriage is for life'. Marriage is a sacrament — an outward sign of an invisible grace from God. This means once a couple are married, they are joined by God and cannot be separated. Christians show these beliefs at their weddings when they vow to one another before God and before a priest that they will stay together 'until death parts us.'

However, not all Christians agree. This is not because they value marriage less, but because they are realistic. Even Catholics, who teach that divorce is always wrong, understand that sometimes there is no choice. If a partner was abusive, or cheated on them, there is a less than ideal situation where divorce might be the only option. Therefore, it seems that whilst marriage 'should' be for life, in reality it is not. In the Church of England there is more acceptance that sometimes marriage may not be for life. This is not ideal, but since 2002 divorced people can remarry in a church in special circumstances.

This candidate has begun by using the wording in the question statement to focus their answer on the right material.

There is appropriate use of technical vocabulary.

Examples of diverse views within Christianity are given.

Supporting evidence from scripture and practice is given.

However, the Bible is quite clear that divorce is only allowed when a partner commits adultery and the Church of England Synod affirmed that marriage is supposed to be permanent and lifelong. This means that divorce should only be in exceptional circumstances and should not be the norm. Therefore, marriage 'should' be for life even if sometimes things go wrong and make it impossible.

In Islam, marriage does not have to be for life if the couple cannot live together in peace. In the Qur'an it says that the husband can release the wife with good treatment if he cannot be with her in an acceptable matter. However, the hadiths tell Muslims that divorce is 'hated by Allah' and Islam has put in place many measures to prevent divorce from happening. Counselling services, the Iddah and application via a Shariah council put up barriers to try and prevent divorce. This suggests that marriage should ideally be for life and divorce is allowed, but not welcomed. Therefore, whilst in an ideal world marriage should be for life, in the real world it may not be.

> Evidence is used from scripture and Church tradition to back up the view.

> The writing ends with a final judgement on the question statement.

(L) **Over to You!** Have a try at answering this question:

(d) 'Women and men should have equal roles in worship.'

Discuss this statement showing that you have considered more than one point of view. (You must refer to religion and belief in your answer.) [15]

Marks for spelling, punctuation and the accurate use of grammar are allocated to this question. [6]

Tip

Remember that in this question there are up to six marks attached for spelling, punctuation and grammar. Make sure you learn how to spell the key words in particular.

Helpful hints

If you find it difficult to answer this question effectively, you could try using the structure below to help you set out your paragraphs:

- **A**rgument – Clearly state a religious view about the question.
- **B**ack it up – Give some evidence or an example of teaching or behaviour that shows this view.
- **C**hallenge – Offer a counterargument that directly opposes the view you have previously stated.
- **D**ecide – Weigh up which views are the best and why.

This could be one paragraph. Repeat the formula again for a second paragraph and at the end conclude with a final decision.

Now give yourself **fifteen minutes** to answer this question by yourself:

(d) 'Sex outside of marriage is always wrong.'

Discuss this statement showing that you have considered more than one point of view. (You must refer to religion and belief in your answer.) [15]

Marks for spelling, punctuation and the accurate use of grammar are allocated to this question. [6]

Tip

You can mix up this scaffolding idea to make your answer more varied. Try A, B, B, C, D for another paragraph. This will help you to become more fluid in your writing and more independent.

Chapter 2:
Issues of life and death

Introduction

The subject of life and death is both broad and controversial. Where do we come from? What is the purpose of life? Does it matter how I live? What happens after I die? The world's religions have many ideas about the answers to these questions, but so do non-religious people and sometimes these answers conflict. In this chapter, you will consider issues of life and death from Christian, Muslim and non-religious perspectives, beginning with an understanding of different accounts of the origins of the world and human responsibility for it, the origins and value of human life, and beliefs about death and the afterlife.

Things to remember:

- Not all Christians, Muslims or non-religious people will necessarily believe or teach the same things. For example, Catholics believe in a temporary place of punishment after death known as purgatory. Other Christians do not. Different denominations may disagree with each other on the importance of these matters. Non-religious people do not necessarily conform to a particular group or system of belief.
- The relationship between religion and science is a complex one. Not all religious believers reject scientific findings, although some do. Not all scientists reject religious beliefs in their entirety. For example, Francis Collins is a well-respected scientist who led the Human Genome project and is also a religious believer.
- There is a difference between what religion teaches about life and death and what individuals believe about the issues. Sometimes an individual believer may reject a teaching from within their own faith or understand it differently. For example, Islam teaches that abortion is usually wrong, but some individual Muslims might feel that in some situations it is necessary.
- When people describe themselves as Humanists or Atheists, it is not the same thing. Atheists do not have any belief in God/gods. Humanism is a world view that emphasises compassion for people and human equality without the need for reliance on any God/gods.

Concepts

Afterlife – life after death; the belief that existence continues after physical death

Environmental sustainability – ensuring that the demands placed on natural resources can be met without reducing capacity to allow all people and other species of animals, as well as plant life, to live well, now and in the future

Euthanasia – from Greek, *eu* 'good' and *thanatos* 'death'. Sometimes referred to as 'mercy killing'. The act of killing or permitting the death of a person who is suffering from a serious illness

Evolution – the process by which different living creatures are believed to have developed from earlier, less complex forms during the history of the earth

Abortion – when a pregnancy is ended so that it does not result in the birth of a child

Quality of life – the extent to which life is meaningful and pleasurable

Sanctity of life – the belief that life is precious, or sacred. For many religious believers, only human life holds this special status

Soul – the spiritual aspect of a being; that which connects someone to God. The soul is often regarded as non-physical and as living on after physical death, in an afterlife

Non-religious views on the origins of the universe and the environment

Non-religious views of creation

Non-religious people base their understanding of the origins of the universe on different sources of authority from some religious people. Rather than trusting scripture, they are likely to rely on **scientific theories**. A scientific theory is based on observation of the world. A **hypothesis** is made and tested repeatedly to explain observations. The hypothesis is altered in response to testing until it is widely accepted.

Scientific research shows that the universe probably began about 14 billion years ago due to a dramatic cosmic event called the **Big Bang**. Non-religious people argue that this could have begun spontaneously without any need for God. Science tells us that the universe emerged from a single point of infinite density that began to quickly expand, forming particles and atoms. This happened through a combination of chance and the operation of the natural laws that began at the Big Bang, such as the law of gravity. The universe is still expanding now. It is not fixed or complete.

Some of the scientific evidence for the Big Bang includes:

- Cosmic microwave background radiation – we can measure radiation in the universe that remained after the Big Bang.
- Red shift – we can measure the wavelength of light from objects as they move away from us as the universe expands.
- Mixture of elements – the mixture of elements in the universe is exactly consistent with a huge explosion followed by rapid expansion and cooling.

Stephen Hawking's view of the Big Bang

Stephen Hawking was one of the world's leading scientists on the origins of the universe. He was an Atheist and viewed the universe as the result of a cosmic event, not a divine one. Sometimes it seems as though there is a conflict between religious accounts in scripture about the beginning of the universe and scientific theories.

Stephen Hawking's view	Christian and Islamic views
There was a beginning to the universe and it was caused by the Big Bang.	All Christians and Muslims agree that the universe began. Not all accept that the beginning was the Big Bang.
It began as a single point that rapidly expanded to form our universe.	Some Christians argue that after God created the universe, it was complete (God rested). Other Christians and Muslims see God as still involved in the continuing process of creation.
We cannot understand a time before the Big Bang since that was the beginning of everything.	There is no difficulty for Christians or Muslims in accepting that it is not possible to fully understand an infinite God who existed before the universe began.
The universe created itself due to the law of gravity.	This is wrong according to Christians and Muslims. The universe requires God to exist.
It is unnecessary to suggest that there needed to be a God involved in the creation of the universe.	Christians and Muslims agree that God caused the universe to begin, whether they accept the Big Bang or not. Only God can bring order to chaos.

Specification focus

The world: Non-religious views of creation; Stephen Hawking's view of the Big Bang. Non-religious beliefs, teachings and attitudes about dominion, stewardship, environmental responsibility, sustainability and global citizenship: 'Humanists for a Better World'.

Scientific research shows that the universe originated from a Big Bang

Useful terms

scientific theories – a hypothesis that is tested extensively and repeatedly to see if it is true or false. Theories may be altered or changed if new evidence is found

hypothesis – an explanation that has been proposed but not yet tested out

Big Bang – the idea that the universe began at a single point that quickly expanded

sustainable – causing little or no damage to the environment so that life may continue for a long period of time

global citizen – a person who understands their role and responsibilities as part of the worldwide community

Environmental responsibility, sustainability and global citizenship

Humanity currently faces problems resulting from damage to the environment, such as:

- air pollution from emissions
- land pollution from litter and physical waste
- deforestation, which damages habitats and increases carbon dioxide.

All of this contributes to the problem of global warming. Global warming or climate change is the rising of the earth's overall temperature. This is natural to some extent as part of the lifecycle of the planet, but human activity is speeding up the warming process. The likely results of global warming are:

- more extreme weather, such as storms and droughts
- faster melting of the ice caps and rising water levels, causing flooding
- some areas becoming too hot to sustain human or animal life
- an increasing cost of living.

The solutions to slowing global warming include:

- finding **sustainable** alternatives to fossil fuels such as wind, wave or solar power
- avoiding deforestation and planting more trees
- limiting our use of natural resources – reduce, reuse, recycle
- walking, cycling or using public transport, and flying less.

Many religious and non-religious people feel responsible for protecting the environment, but their motivations might differ. The Humanist or Atheist may act because their reason and empathy tells them that **environmental sustainability** is sensible as we are all **global citizens** who have a shared responsibility to care for the world and ensure human survival. The religious person may act for these reasons, but also because they believe the world belongs to God and they have a duty to protect it.

Fossil fuel emissions are one of the main causes of global warming

Read more about religious views on dominion and stewardship on pages 36–39.

Humanists for a Better World

Humanists for a Better World (H4BW) is a programme run by Humanists UK. The aim of this programme is to bring together Humanists who want to campaign on environmental issues. H4BW works to highlight environmental issues, as well as support and advise Humanist campaigners.

Humanists do not base their beliefs about climate change on scripture. They use evidence from the world, and they use their reason. They are sceptical about the existence of a supernatural being who has given humans authority or who will come to the rescue, so they say we have a responsibility to care for the environment because it is the only one we have, and it is the only way to ensure that the world is sustainable for future generations.

Knowledge recall

1 Define the following concepts: environmental sustainability, afterlife, quality of life. (You can find these definitions on page 33.)
2 List two pieces of scientific evidence for the Big Bang.
3 Give one reason why a Humanist or Atheist may choose to be environmentally responsible.

Evaluation practice

4 Give one reason why some religious believers might reject Stephen Hawking's understanding of the Big Bang and one reason why others might accept it.
5 Which of these views do you find most convincing? Give two reasons why.

Christian teachings on the origins of the universe and environmental responsibility

Christian beliefs about the origins of the universe

The main source of Christian belief about the origins of the universe is the Bible. However, there is a spectrum of belief when it comes to how Christians interpret the creation stories.

Fundamentalists/Literalists believe that scripture is the word of God dictated to humanity. The Genesis stories are literally true.	**Conservatives** accept the traditional view that the Bible is the word of God and may accept that not all passages are to be interpreted literally; there may be metaphors and stories.	**Liberals** are open to interpreting the Bible through science. They may believe Genesis shows how the writers understood God at that time.

Genesis 1 and 2

The biblical book of Genesis contains two creation stories:

Genesis 1	Genesis 2
• God created the universe in six days. • God created the universe first: day one – light; day two – sky; day three – land, sea and plants; day four – sun, moon and stars; day five – animals. • God created human beings last on day six, just by speaking. • God created men and women together. • God is powerful and distant. He creates with just a word or command.	• God created the universe over an unspecified time. • God began with a man and then created the contents of the earth around him. • God created man out of dust and his own breath. • God created woman last, after he had created everything else. • God is close and attentive, talking to humans.

Some of the differences between these two accounts are a problem for Literalists who wish to believe that both accounts are the word of God and are factually true. Conservatives and Liberals can accept both accounts without difficulty because they may understand the stories as symbolic or that they contain a different kind of truth.

The relationship between Christian views and non-religious views of creation

Literalists are **Creationists**. They argue that scripture tells us exactly how God created the universe; it was not a blind accident. There was no Big Bang.

- Young Earth Creationists believe it is possible to trace historical events back through the Bible and find that the date of God's six days of creation was 6000 years ago.
- Old Earth Creationists believe that the earth is 14 billion years old, but that God directly created it. Each 'day' of creation represents an 'age' or 'era'. There was no Big Bang.

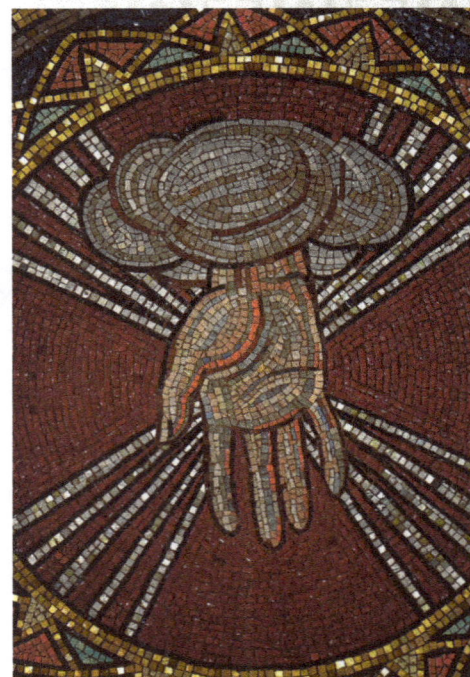

All Christians believe that God had a hand in creating the world

Conservatives accept the Big Bang theory but see God as the power behind the natural processes. They believe scripture tells us through stories and metaphors that God's creative power is responsible, but science tells us how it occurred.

Read about the Big Bang theory on page 34.

Liberals have no difficulty in accepting scientific accounts. They believe that scripture can be interpreted to allow for the insights of science. They may believe that scripture is written by humans or that it involves human cooperation with God and so it may say more about the human relationship with God rather than facts about how God brought the world into being.

Christian beliefs about dominion and stewardship

Christian scripture says that God gave human beings **dominion** over all living creatures. Over the centuries, Christians have interpreted 'dominion' in different ways.

Some have argued that it means God has given them the gift of using the world's resources however they like. In the past, the term 'dominion' was understood to be about domination, control and superiority over the rest of creation.

Most Christians today believe that humans share some of God's qualities – such as reason, morality and responsibility – because we were made in his image. Therefore, humans have been appointed **stewards** of God's creation and should care for the planet and manage its resources. Dominion is now understood as a responsibility to manage the land and the creatures within it.

All Christians believe that human life is sacred or special. Some argue that this extends to all life and so the world and all animals in it must be treated with care and respect.

> ❝God blessed them and said to them, "Be fruitful and increase in number; **fill the earth and subdue it.** Rule over the fish in the sea and the birds in the sky and over every living creature that moves on the ground."❞
> *Genesis 1:28*

> ❝**You made them rulers over the works of your hands;** you put everything under their feet.❞
> *Psalm 8:6*

Environmental responsibility, sustainability and global citizenship

The Catholic Church has spoken out in support of Christians taking environmental responsibility and living sustainable lifestyles.

- In 2015, Pope Francis called for urgent action on climate change in the encyclical 'Laudato Si' or 'Praise Be'. He suggested that caring for the planet should be a spiritual work of mercy. He described the destruction of the environment as a sin.
- In 2019, Pope Francis declared a global climate emergency and said that failure to act was an injustice against the poor and future generations. He urged Catholics to be global citizens and to join the fight against climate change.

A minority of Christians deny global warming because they do not accept that human beings have the power to destroy something that God has created, or they believe that God will intervene to prevent the destruction of his creation.

Pope Francis is the head of the Catholic Church

Knowledge recall

1 Define the following concepts: environmental sustainability, quality of life, soul. (You can find these definitions on page 33.)
2 List three differences between the creation stories in Genesis 1 and 2.
3 Suggest two different ideas about what dominion means.

Evaluation practice

4 Give two reasons why some religious people might accept environmental responsibility and two reasons why others might not.
5 Which of these views do you think is the most persuasive? Give a reason why.

Islamic teachings on the origins of the universe and environmental responsibility

Islamic beliefs about the origin of the universe

Islam teaches that Allah has absolute authority over everything in the universe and that the Qur'an is Allah's **revelation** to humankind. This means that Muslims can trust the Qur'an to be accurate in accounting for Allah's involvement in creation.

The Qur'an does not have a distinct creation story, but it contains many passages that refer to Allah's creative work. The Qur'an says that Allah:

- created the universe over six days
- formed everything from smoke, including the sun, moon, stars and planets
- made all the creatures, angels, vegetation and rain
- made Adam out of clay, and breathed life and power into him
- made Adam and Hawwa (Eve) from a single soul.

The Qur'an confirms that Allah, being **omniscient**, has the knowledge to be able to create everything, including human life. He is **eternal**, **omnipotent** and the creator of everything in the universe.

> ❝ Is **He who created the heavens and the earth** not able to create the likes of these people? Of course He is! He is the All Knowing Creator. ❞
> *Qur'an 36:81*

The relationship between Islamic views and non-religious views of creation

Some Muslims are Creationists. They believe the Qur'an has authority over human reasoning and evidence because it is factually true. Therefore, since the Qur'an seems to disagree with the Big Bang theory, they would reject scientific accounts of the origin of the universe.

Other Muslims argue that there is no contradiction between the Qur'an and modern science. While the Qur'an says that the universe was made in six days, the Arabic word used for 'day' ('yawm') means 'age' or 'eon' rather than a 24-hour period. The Big Bang is how Allah formed the universe. The scientific account is incomplete because it describes how Allah created the universe without mentioning him. The universe can't have come about by itself.

Some Muslims argue that the Qur'an is not a scientific account of the creation and existence of the universe. It is a work that encourages deep thought about the nature of Allah and human relationships with Him. There is no contradiction between science and the Qur'an.

Specification focus

The world: Islamic beliefs, teachings and attitudes about the origin of the universe: Qur'an 36:81; the relationship between Islamic views and non-religious views of creation and the extent to which they conflict; Islamic beliefs, teachings and attitudes about fitra, khalifah, environmental responsibility, sustainability and global citizenship: Qur'an 7:54. ·

Islam teaches that the Qur'an is Allah's revelation to humankind

> ❝ Then He turned to the sky, which was smoke – He said to it and the earth, "Come into being, willingly or not," and they said, "We come willingly." ❞
> *Qur'an 41:11*

Useful terms

revelation – God's direct communication to humanity
omniscient – all-knowing
eternal – with no beginning and no end
omnipotent – all-powerful or almighty
khalifah – a deputy, steward or Viceregent. Allah's representative on earth
fitra – natural disposition or in-built nature
ummah – means 'community' and refers to the worldwide community of Muslims who share a common religious identity

Islamic beliefs about fitra and khalifah

Muslims believe Allah is the omnipotent creator of everything. The world has been created by him as a place of worship and human beings are his **khalifahs**, who have been given the responsibility to govern the world on Allah's behalf. Muslims believe the world does not belong to us and we do not have the right to waste or spoil it.

> ❝Your Lord is God, who created the heavens and earth in six days, then established Himself on the throne; He makes the night cover the day in swift pursuit; He created the sun, moon and stars to be subservient to His command, **all creation and command belong to Him.** Exalted be God, Lord of all worlds.❞
> *Qur'an 7:54*

The natural disposition or **fitra** of the universe must be maintained to ensure the survival of life on it. The Qur'an instructs Muslims not to interfere with the natural balance of Allah's creation. Khalifahs must work to maintain the fitra of the world by using the earth's resources fairly and frugally.

Environmental responsibility, sustainability and global citizenship

The hadiths show that Muhammad led by example and lived a frugal life. He instructed people to preserve water, treat wildlife with respect and he ate a limited amount of meat. He gave instructions about conserving trees and avoiding wastefulness.

Muslims are commanded to treat Allah's creation with care

Muslims are commanded to act as global citizens and live sustainable lifestyles. On the Day of Judgement, Allah will punish those who have not performed their duty to the world. This is for the benefit of the **ummah** so that the world can be passed on to the next generation of khalifahs.

The Islamic Foundation for Ecology and Environmental Science (IFEES) is an international voluntary organisation dedicated to environmental protection and resource management. It argues that Muslims have a responsibility to do good and avoid evil, and that their faith commands them to treat Allah's creation with care.

The Qur'an tells Muslims that God provided all of creation for the nourishment and benefit of human life.

> ❝He has made the night and day useful to you and given you some of everything you asked Him for. If you tried to count God's favours you could never calculate them; man is truly unjust and ungrateful.❞
> *Qur'an 14:33-34*

Knowledge recall

1 Define the following concepts: environmental sustainability, euthanasia, abortion. (You can find these definitions on page 33.)
2 List three of Allah's qualities.
3 State two beliefs about the role of a khalifah.

Evaluation practice

4 Give one reason why some Muslims might reject scientific explanations regarding the origin of the universe and one reason why some Muslims might accept them.
5 Which do you think is the strongest argument and why?

Non-religious views on evolution and abortion

Specification focus

The origin and value of human life: Non-religious beliefs about evolution; Charles Darwin, Richard Dawkins; abortion.

Non-religious beliefs about evolution and Charles Darwin

Charles Darwin is credited with being the father of modern evolutionary theory. In 1859 he published his book *On the Origin of Species by Means of Natural Selection*. This book outlined the idea that human life was formed as a result of **evolution**.

The theory of evolution teaches that at an early stage in the development of life on earth, there were single-celled organisms that became more complex as they reproduced. Tiny, random variations between generations produced features that were sometimes beneficial for the organism's survival. When a feature helped survival, it could be passed on through reproduction. Features that were not beneficial died out. This is called **natural selection**. Life became steadily more complex until, after millions of years, human life was formed. This process has become known as **survival of the fittest**.

Most non-religious people interpret this evidence to mean that life evolved by chance, not because of a God or cosmic designer.

> On the Galapagos Islands, Darwin observed that some finches had long, pointed beaks that enabled them to survive by feeding on cacti. Other finches had shorter, fatter beaks that were more adapted to picking seeds from the ground. Those that caught insects had sharper, thinner beaks. This showed that the birds' beaks had adapted to the environment they lived in and these features were passed on to their offspring.

Those species with the most suitable characteristics for survival can mate and pass on those characteristics

Richard Dawkins

Richard Dawkins is an Atheist and a supporter of evolutionary theory. He argues that the scientific explanation for the origin of human life is more rational and evidenced than the religious explanation.

In addition, he argues that a process called **cumulative selection** would explain the speed at which order and complexity were produced. This means that where a feature helped the survival of an organism, it was retained and added to by other variations.

> Dawkins produced an example of cumulative selection called 'the weasel program'. A computer simulation generated random combinations of letters with the aim of recreating Shakespeare's phrase 'Methinks it is like a weasel'. Each time, the program retained the letters that worked best before generating a new combination. For Dawkins, this example shows that a combination of accident and necessity work together to bring about the world, but there is no need for a designer.

Useful terms

natural selection – the organisms that are best adapted to their surroundings are the ones that survive and reproduce
survival of the fittest – the process of natural selection
cumulative selection – favourable changes in an organism that are retained and built on

Some Christians and Muslims see the theory of evolution as a challenge to their beliefs because they feel it contradicts scriptural accounts of the creation of human life by God. Others see no challenge if evolution was God's method of creating humanity. But non-religious people argue that evolution does away with the need for a creator God because it explains the existence of human life through natural processes.

Read about religious attitudes towards the origins of life on pages 44–47.

Abortion

Abortion is the process of ending a pregnancy without it resulting in a live baby. If this happens naturally, it is called a miscarriage. However, an induced abortion, is the process of intervening in a pregnancy to deliberately end it. There can be many reasons why someone might have an abortion:

- the woman is too young to manage being a mother
- the parents cannot afford to support the baby
- the pregnancy or birth would result in health problems for the woman or baby
- the woman has been raped
- the woman does not want to be a mother.

Abortion in the UK is legal until 24 weeks; after this it is still allowed if the foetus has a severe abnormality or there is a grave risk of death for the mother.

People who are pro-choice are in favour of abortion. Some pro-choice people argue that women should be allowed to choose to have an abortion at any time for any reason. Others argue for abortion but only as an option for women in difficult situations.

People who are pro-life argue that the unborn foetus is a human life and so must be protected. They argue that it is not up to an individual person to decide whether the foetus lives or dies. All human life must be protected and respected. This is more likely to be a religious view.

Whether a person is pro-life or pro-choice can depend on their view of when a life begins. Some people say that life begins at conception. Others argue that it begins at a later stage. The development of life in the womb is gradual and there are no sudden events that can easily be called the beginning of life. Some possible suggestions for when life 'begins' are as follows:

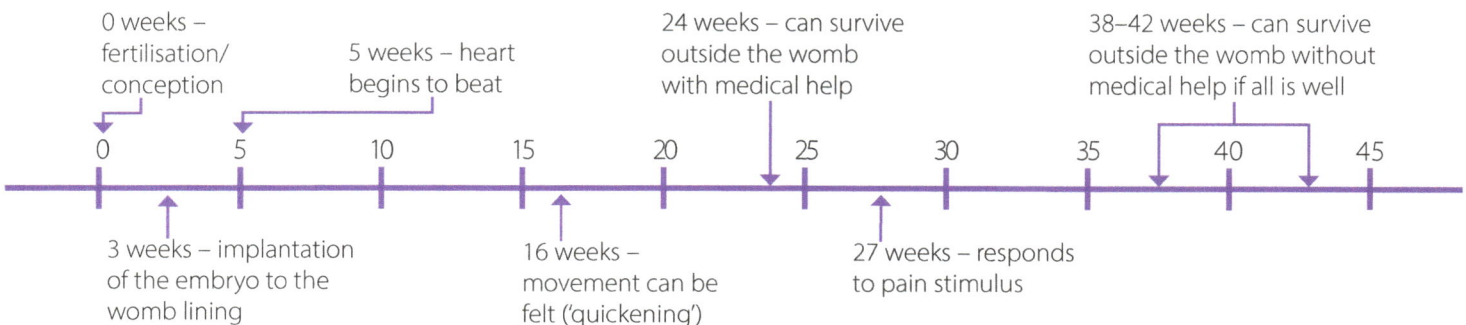

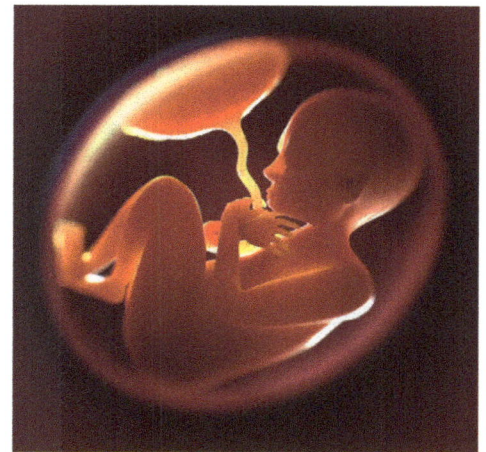

There is disagreement over when the developing foetus should be considered a 'human life'

0 weeks – fertilisation/ conception

5 weeks – heart begins to beat

24 weeks – can survive outside the womb with medical help

38–42 weeks – can survive outside the womb without medical help if all is well

| 0 | 5 | 10 | 15 | 20 | 25 | 30 | 35 | 40 | 45 |

3 weeks – implantation of the embryo to the womb lining

16 weeks – movement can be felt ('quickening')

27 weeks – responds to pain stimulus

Knowledge recall

1 Define the following concepts: abortion, sanctity of life, evolution. (You can find these definitions on page 33.)
2 Explain how the process of evolution works. (Use the terms natural selection, random variation and survival of the fittest.)
3 What is the difference between pro-choice and pro-life?

Evaluation practice

4 Give one reason why some people might take a pro-life view about abortion and one reason why someone might be pro-life.
5 Which of these views do you think is the most convincing and why?

Non-religious views on euthanasia, the value of life and funerals

Specification focus

The origin and value of human life: Euthanasia; non-religious views on the importance of human and animal life; Peter Singer's views on 'speciesism'; Humanist 'Dignity in Dying' Movement.

Beliefs about death and the afterlife: How Humanist funerals in Britain reflect beliefs about the afterlife.

Euthanasia

Euthanasia means a gentle, easy death. It is sometimes known as 'mercy killing' and involves ending a life early to avoid unnecessary suffering.

When a person is terminally ill with no hope of recovery, and the last stages of their life are likely to contain a high degree of suffering, sometimes they ask for help from a doctor to end their life early. Sometimes people want to make this last choice because they are worried that later on they will lose the ability to communicate what they want, they will experience great suffering or they will have to rely too much on others for personal care.

There are different kinds of euthanasia:

- Voluntary euthanasia is when a person has expressed a wish to die and clearly asked for help to do so. For example, sometimes people state their preference for euthanasia in a **'living will'**.
- Involuntary euthanasia is when a person cannot express a wish to die, so the decision is made for them. For example, a person is in a coma or has lost the ability to communicate.
- Active euthanasia is where the death of a person is caused through direct action. For example, through taking medication to end their life faster.
- Passive euthanasia is where treatment is removed so that death is faster. For example, by removing a feeding tube or respirator. This can be legal in the UK in some cases, since patients and doctors have the right to refuse treatment.

It is currently illegal to perform euthanasia in the UK and in many other countries around the globe. However, sometimes people travel to places like Switzerland, where clinics like Dignitas can legally allow doctors to give patients the means to administer their own medication and end their own life early. This is known as assisted suicide.

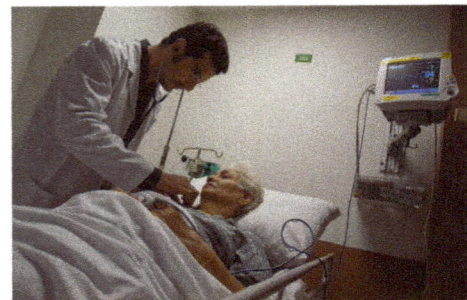

It is currently illegal in the UK for a person to receive active euthanasia

Non-religious views on the importance of human and animal life

Most religious believers argue that humans are more important to God than animals. They believe God gave humans special qualities when he created them, which animals do not share.

Atheists and Humanists do not have the same religious duty to see human life as more sacred or special than any other creature. Some non-religious people believe that although we are all products of evolution, humans are superior to animals as they are more intelligent. Other non-religious people argue that since we are all creatures, humans are of no greater worth than any other animal.

Peter Singer's views on speciesism

The Atheist philosopher Peter Singer argues that the value of life should be based on how useful that life is, or how much a living being can achieve what they are supposed to be able to achieve.

Useful terms

living will – when a person writes down their wishes for their care and whether they wish to refuse certain treatments before they lose the ability to communicate

persistent vegetative state – a continuing state of having no apparent consciousness but having a beating heart and appearance of being awake but not alert (usually with life support)

speciesism – the belief in, and practice of, treating humans as more important than animals

Singer argues that a life has value not because it is created by God but because it can perform the tasks expected of its species. Therefore, a fish that can swim is a valuable fish. A human that can move, think and communicate is a valuable human.

For Singer, abortion or euthanasia are acceptable in cases where someone does not have a valuable life. So he argues that someone with a disability that prevents them from having a good **quality of life**, or someone in a **persistent vegetative state**, should be able to be euthanised.

Singer argues that we are guilty of **speciesism** when we are prepared to test on or kill a healthy, able-bodied animal and yet will fight for the life of a foetus that is not fully formed, or for the life of someone who is barely conscious. He argues these individuals do not have personhood.

Humanist 'Dignity in Dying' movement

Humanists do not consider human life to be sacred in a religious sense, but as they believe they only have one life and there is no **afterlife**, they do consider human life to be important. Most Humanists strongly believe in personal choice, and this extends to choosing when to end their life.

The 'Dignity in Dying' movement campaigns for individual choice over when we die, who is present and how we are treated. It argues for access to information regarding our options and to good-quality end of life care. This means that a person could choose the time and manner of their death and could have their loved ones present with them.

Humanist funerals in Britain

A Humanist funeral is non-religious and so will not contain any reference to God or religion. There is often music, some thoughts on life and death from a non-religious viewpoint, a tribute to the person who has died, and non-religious poetry or other readings. Respect will be shown for the dead person but there will be no suggestion that they live on elsewhere. There will be a time for reflection when friends and family will remember the person who has died in their own way.

It is popular to dispose of the body in a way that is environmentally friendly. Many choose to have biodegradable coffins made of cardboard or wicker, while others may choose cremation or a coffin that reflects something of the person's character. Some prefer to plant a tree in the person's memory rather than have a headstone.

Many Humanists will decide to have less traditional coffins as part of their funeral services

Knowledge recall

1 Define the following concepts: euthanasia, quality of life, sanctity of life. (You can find these definitions on page 33.)
2 Define two types of euthanasia.
3 Give two reasons why Peter Singer might accuse some people of speciesism.

Evaluation practice

4 Give two reasons why some humanists might campaign for dignity in dying.
5 Do you agree with either of these reasons? Why or why not?

Christian teachings on human life, abortion and euthanasia

Diverse Christian beliefs about the origin of human life

Scripture says that God created human life on the sixth and final day of creation. For Young Earth Creationists, this means that human beings were created separately from other creatures and that there was a **fixity of species**. Humans were created perfect and complete – there was no **evolution**.

> 'God saw all that he had made, and it was very good. And there was evening, and there was morning – the sixth day.'
> *Genesis 1:31*

Christians with a conservative view would agree that the Bible, as God's word, says humans are the pinnacles of God's creation, made for a special relationship with him. In accordance with tradition, they would accept that Genesis does not need to be interpreted literally and so they may be open to accepting evolution as part of God's creative process. Liberal Christians accept scientific accounts of evolution and reinterpret scripture in a way that does not contradict modern science. They would accept **theistic evolution**. This is God creating life and working out his purpose through the process of evolution.

In 1802, the Christian minister William Paley wrote that we can see evidence in the world of an intelligent designer. He argued that there are similarities between natural items like an eye and designed items such as a pocket watch. They have four significant marks of design:

	Eye	Watch
1. **Complexity**	Lens, optic nerve, retina, cornea, etc.	Cogs, hands, springs, studs, wheels, etc.
2. **Orderliness**	Regular, predictable function	Regular, predictable function
3. **Fitting together of parts**	Each part enables the working of the other parts	Each part enables the working of the other parts
4. **Purpose**	Sight	Telling time

Paley argued this shows that just as a watch cannot have occurred by accident, items in the natural world (like the eye) cannot have occurred by accident.

In the late 1980s, the Intelligent Design (ID) movement built on Paley's design argument. This movement claims to be scientific in nature and states that there are some parts of the world that cannot have evolved slowly. They are too complex and require all the parts to be present and working together to function at all. Therefore, they must have been designed together. This argument has been rejected as **pseudoscience** by mainstream science.

Most Christian denominations have embraced the theory of evolution. In 2014, Pope Francis issued a statement on behalf of the Catholic Church declaring that evolution is not inconsistent with the idea that God created the world. He stated that God created beings and allowed them to develop according to laws given by him. Evolution is the process of God's creative work.

Specification focus

The origin and value of human life: Diverse Christian beliefs, teachings and attitudes towards the origin and sanctity of human life: Genesis 1:31, Jeremiah 1:5; diverse Christian attitudes towards abortion and euthanasia.

Read about evolution on page 40.

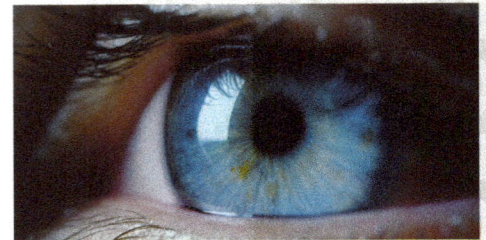

ID supporters argue that items like the eye only function when all the parts work together. They cannot have evolved from simpler structures

Useful terms

fixity of species – species remain unchanged from their initial, created state

theistic evolution – science is correct, but God is the power behind the events that science describes

pseudoscience – practice that claims to be science but is not properly following the scientific method

conception – the point at which an egg is fertilised by a sperm

double effect – when an action has two outcomes, one intended and one unintended

hospice – a place of health care that attends to the physical and emotional needs of a dying person

Diverse Christian beliefs about the sanctity of human life

Christians believe human life was created in God's image by God himself and is sacred. God has a plan for each individual person and as Jeremiah 1:5 shows, this plan can be in place before a human is even born.

Many Christians believe that because life is God-given and sacred, only God should choose when to take it away. Other Christians argue that a sacred life is not about the length of time it lasts, especially if that life contains extensive suffering. Instead, a sacred life is about the extent to which a person experiences the joy of the gift of life. God intends for Christians to show compassion to those who suffer and respect their life, but not at all costs. Therefore, **quality of life** is a vital consideration.

Diverse Christian attitudes towards abortion

Some Christians believe that since life is sacred, **abortion** is wrong.

The Catholic Church considers abortion to be a sin in any circumstance. The foetus is a person from **conception**. Abortion goes against Natural Law. The primary precepts to reproduce and defend innocent life mean that abortion is sinful. It is against the commandment that forbids murder and it disregards the **sanctity of life**. This is a pro-life position.

However, the law of **double effect** allows a doctor to act to save a woman's life even if the unwanted side effect is that the pregnancy ends, but the aim must never be to end the pregnancy.

The Church of England tries to balance compassion for the mother with responsibility towards the unborn life. It rejects abortion in place of contraception and supports alternatives to abortion, but argues that if a woman's life is at risk, the child is severely disabled or in cases of rape, abortion may be a compassionate answer. In these cases, abortion should take place as early in the development of the foetus as possible.

Diverse Christian attitudes towards euthanasia

The Catholic Church strictly forbids **euthanasia**. It violates the commandment not to murder, the primary precept to preserve life, and the principle of sanctity of life. In the eyes of the Catholic Church, anyone who assists with euthanasia is guilty of murder and anyone who performed euthanasia for themselves commits suicide, which is also a sin. Instead, the Church regards end of life care through **hospices** to be the best approach. This allows God to choose when to take life away. The Church teaches that suffering has a purpose and God does not give people more than they can bear.

Among Quakers, there is no single view on euthanasia. Some Quakers argue that if we offer the right support, euthanasia is unnecessary. Others argue that when a person is in extreme suffering or experiences a loss of dignity, it is more important that we have compassion for their situation and prioritise their quality of life, rather than the quantity of it.

> ❝Before I formed you in the womb I knew you,❞ before you were born I set you apart; I appointed you as a prophet to the nations.❞
> *Jeremiah 1:5*

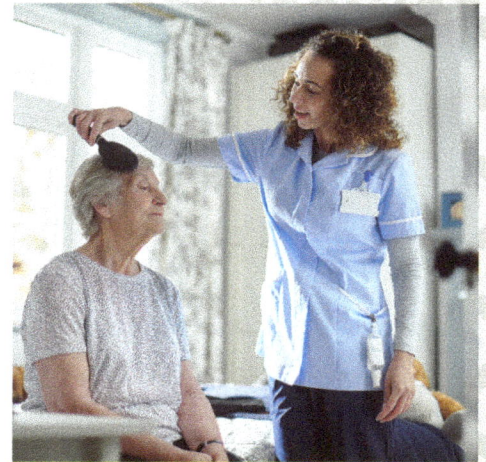

Those who reject euthanasia consider it important to offer high-quality end of life care

Knowledge recall

1 Define the following concepts: sanctity of life, evolution, abortion. (You can find these definitions on page 33.)
2 Give three reasons why some Christians are against abortion.
3 In what kinds of situations might some Christians accept abortion?

Evaluation practice

4 Give one reason why some religious believers might reject euthanasia and one reason why others may accept it.
5 Which of these views do you find most persuasive? Give two reasons for your view.

Islamic teachings on human life, abortion and euthanasia

Specification focus

The origin and value of human life: Islamic beliefs, teachings and attitudes towards the origin and sanctity of human life: Qur'an 5:32, 6:151; Islamic attitudes towards abortion and euthanasia: Qur'an 30:40.

Islamic beliefs about the origin of human life

The Qur'an teaches that Allah made human beings as the pinnacle of his creation. Adam was created as a fully formed human being. He was given knowledge and power; even angels were commanded to bow before him. Many Muslims would interpret this literally and therefore reject the idea of **evolution** because the Qur'an says that Allah created humans through a single act, not through evolution from simpler species.

At a talk called 'Have Muslims Misunderstood Evolution?' held in London in 2013, Muslim scholars also expressed more Liberal views.

The Muslim scholar Shaykh Yasir Qadhi argued that Muslims can accept evolutionary theory but with an exception for human beings. Allah is in control of the laws of nature, but can also decide when to set them aside. He created the natural world through evolutionary processes but suspended those laws to create human beings through a miracle.

The Muslim scholar Usama Hasan argued that there is no contradiction between the theory of evolution and Muslim faith. Those who agree with Hasan might argue that the Qur'an refers to Allah as both the creator (Al Kahliq) and the evolver (Al Bari). This means that Allah can be responsible for creating humankind over millions of years. These Muslims look for consistency in the words of the Qur'an and scientific teaching. For example, the Qur'an speaks of creating in stages or of Allah improving human forms.

Islamic beliefs about the sanctity of human life

The Qur'an tells Muslims that Allah is the creator who gives life and is the only one with the authority to take it away. No one else has the power to do this. Each person is created by Allah, who has made life sacred.

> **It is God who created you and provided for you, who will cause you to die and then give you life again.** Can any of your "partners" do any one of these things? Glory be to God, and exalted be He above the partners they attribute to Him.
> *Qur'an 30:40*

Islamic attitudes towards abortion

Islam teaches that **abortion** goes against Allah's plans and is always wrong. No one has the right to take their own or anyone else's life and the killing of one **ruh** (or **soul**) is as terrible as killing the whole of humanity. Those who kill will face punishment on the Day of Judgement.

Useful terms

ruh – soul
ensoulment – the point at which Allah gives the foetus a soul
zulm – depriving someone of their rights or failing to fulfil a duty towards someone
DNR – 'do not resuscitate'; an order to not try to resuscitate someone if their heart stops beating

> ❝On account of [his deed], We decreed to the Children of Israel that **if anyone kills a person – unless in retribution for murder or spreading corruption in the land – it is as if he kills all mankind, while if any saves a life, it is as if he saves the lives of all mankind.** Our messengers came to them with clear signs, but many of them continued to commit excesses in the land.❞
> *Qur'an 5:32*

The Qur'an does not explicitly refer to abortion, but it offers guidance that may be relevant. It tells Muslims not to kill their children out of poverty, so this is understood to mean that abortion is haram if it is done because the couple are poor. Allah will provide for any children who are produced.

Some Muslims believe the foetus is a person at conception. If so, an abortion cannot take place. However, many Muslims do accept that in extreme situations, an abortion can be permitted. Those who regard **ensoulment** to be the point of personhood may allow that the mother's rights are greater than the child's until this time. There is debate about when ensoulment is. Some argue it happens on the 40th day and other on the 120th day of pregnancy. Only if the mother's life is at risk can abortion be permitted as the lesser of two evils, but the further along in the pregnancy, the greater the wrongdoing.

> ❝Say, "Come, I will tell you what your Lord has really forbidden you. Do not ascribe anything as a partner to Him; be good to your parents; **do not kill your children fearing poverty – We will provide for you and for them** – stay well away from committing obscenities, whether openly or in secret; do not take life, which God has made sacred, except by right. This is what He commands you to do: so that you may use your reason."❞
> *Qur'an 6:151*

Islamic attitudes towards euthanasia

Islam teaches that no matter what state the body is in, the ruh is still perfect. While it is vital to show compassion and kindness to those who suffer, **euthanasia** is always wrong and anyone who facilitates it is guilty of the sin of **zulm**. It goes against Allah's plan.

There are some Muslims who believe that even passive euthanasia is haram and would object to **DNR** ('do not resuscitate') orders. They may argue that pain and suffering are part of Allah's plan to help them prepare for the afterlife. However, the Islamic code of medical ethics says that it is futile to try to keep someone alive when they are in a persistent vegetative state or when there is no hope of a cure. This means that for many Muslims, turning off life support is acceptable but giving medication to speed up death is haram. However, many Shi'a Muslims would not allow life support to be removed unless there is a complete death of all organs.

Muslims believe that Allah will provide for children through the ummah

Knowledge recall

1 Define the following concepts: sanctity of life, evolution, euthanasia. (You can find these definitions on page 33.)
2 Give three examples of Muslim responses to evolution.
3 Why is it haram for Muslims to perform an abortion because they may not have much money?

Evaluation practice

4 Give one reason why a Muslim might object to euthanasia and one reason why a Muslim might support it.
5 Which reason do you find most convincing and why?

Christian beliefs about the afterlife

Specification focus

Beliefs about death and the afterlife: Christian beliefs and teachings about life after death, including soul, judgement, heaven and hell: John 11:24–27, 1 Corinthians 15:42–44; diverse Christian beliefs about the afterlife; how Christian funerals in Britain reflect beliefs about the afterlife.

Christian beliefs about life after death

Christian beliefs about life after death are based on the resurrection of Jesus. Jesus' death made **atonement** for human sin, and his **resurrection** after three days defeated the power of sin and death to restore humans' relationship with God.

> ❛Martha answered, "I know he will rise again in the resurrection at the last day." Jesus said to her, "**I am the resurrection and the life.** The one who believes in me will live, even though they die; and whoever lives by believing in me will never die. Do you believe this?" "Yes Lord," she replied, "I believe that you are the Messiah, the Son of God, who is to come into the world."❜
>
> *John 11:24–27*

Many Christians believe a human being is made of two parts: a physical body and a spiritual **soul**. After death, the soul leaves the body to be united with God in heaven.

However, this is not consistent with the Bible. Some Christians believe that whilst humans have a body and a soul, they are inseparable. This means that for there to be a life after death, the soul must be housed in a body again.

Scripture and Church teaching tell Christians that death is not the end. After death, everyone can expect to be judged for how they have lived their lives. Firstly, like Christ, people will be resurrected and their souls restored to their bodies before they face judgement. Scripture suggests that at the resurrection, people's bodies will be a little different.

Many Christians believe that a human is made of both body and soul

> ❛So will it be with the resurrection of the dead. The body that is sown is perishable, it is raised imperishable; it is sown in dishonour, it is raised in glory; it is sown in weakness, it is raised in power; it is sown a natural body, it is raised a spiritual body. **If there is a natural body, there is also a spiritual body.**❜
>
> *1 Corinthians 15:42–44*

Christians believe that after resurrection everyone will be judged by God. Some believe they will be judged solely on whether they had faith in God. Others believe that moral behaviour is important too. There is disagreement over when this judgement will happen:

- Some believe they will be judged immediately after death.
- Others believe they must all wait for the Day of Judgement.
- Others believe that both judgements will occur.

The Bible teaches that if people have not been faithful to God through their beliefs and actions, they can expect to be punished in hell. Liberal Christians may see these teachings as symbolic of the truth that all actions have consequences.

Useful terms

atonement – the belief that Jesus' death on the cross healed the rift between humans and God

resurrection – the belief that Jesus rose from the dead on Easter Sunday, conquering death

mortal sin – a deliberate, serious sin against God's law

purgatory – the purification of souls still tainted by less serious sins

Other Christians may believe that heaven and hell are literal places, or that heaven is a spiritual union with God while hell is separation from him.

Diverse Christian beliefs about the afterlife

The Catholic Church teaches that at death, everyone will receive personal judgement. A Catholic who has repented of their sin can be reunited with Christ in heaven, while those who die in **mortal sin** will be punished in hell. Catholics who die but have not yet repented of their sin will continue to be purified in **purgatory**. On Christ's return, everyone will be resurrected and receive the last judgment. At this point God will restore heaven and earth to a new glory and all souls will be reunited with their bodies.

In contrast, a more diverse range of beliefs is held among Quakers:

- Some Quakers do not believe in an 'individual survival' after death but think that the good and evil people have done lives on in those who come after them.
- Others believe the soul survives after death, potentially in either heaven or hell.
- Few accept an eternal hell since they believe God is loving and wishes to save all humanity.

Christian funerals in Britain

When a Christian is close to death, they are often given the last rites. These are prayers for a dying person asking God for forgiveness for their sins. They may also be given Holy Communion to help them be united with Christ in heaven.

At the funeral, the priest will repeat the words of Jesus from John 11:25 to remind listeners that eternal life is gained through faith in Christ; 'I am the resurrection and the life. The one who believes in me will live, even though they die; and whoever lives by believing in me will never die.'

The funeral will usually be held in a church or crematorium. There will be readings, prayers, hymns, a sermon and a talk, remembering the person who has died.

Candles are lit to show that Jesus is the light of the world who guides Christians through their lives to heaven.

The priest recites the words of commendation and committal. These are prayers that represent the friends and family giving the deceased person to God, who will welcome them into heaven.

Traditionally Christians would have been buried so their bodies could await the last judgement. It is increasingly popular for Christians to choose cremation. Many believe that it is more environmentally friendly to be cremated, since the body is not needed after death and God will restore them to their spiritual bodies at the last judgement. Limited space in graveyards may also influence their decision.

At Christian funerals, a priest reminds mourners that through faith in Christ, their loved one has eternal life

Knowledge recall

1 Define the following concepts: afterlife, soul, quality of life. (You can find these definitions on page 33.)
2 Suggest two reasons why some Christians might choose to be cremated.
3 What is the difference between hell and purgatory?

Evaluation practice

4 Give one argument for beliefs in life after death being important and one argument for these beliefs being unimportant.
5 Which do you think this is the most successful argument? Why?

Islamic beliefs about the afterlife

Islamic beliefs about life after death

Akhirah is a fundamental belief for Muslims. Death is seen to be a gift as it enables a Muslim to move to the next world to be with Allah. All religious and moral behaviour (such as performing salah or donating to charity) is preparation for akhirah. Muhammad encouraged believers not to become too attached to this life and instead to focus on the next.

> ❝Those who say, "Our Lord, we believe, so **forgive us our sins and protect us from suffering in the Fire…**"❞
> *Qur'an 3:16*

Islam teaches that the earthly body is a vehicle for the ruh (**soul**). At death, the ruh is removed from the body by the angel Azrail and transferred to **barzakh**. Muslim traditions differ over what barzakh is. For some, the ruh hovers over the grave, while others say it sleeps until the last day (so barzakh seems like a brief moment between death and the last day). Others see barzakh as a place where the ruh has a glimpse of its destiny in **Jannah** or **Jahannam**.

The Qur'an says that on the Day of Judgement, a trumpet will sound that destroys all of creation. At the sound of a second trumpet, all ruhs will return to their bodies which will be resurrected. They will stand before Allah and face Allah's judgement. Each will be given a book containing their good and bad deeds. The deeds will be weighed on scales and then they will cross a bridge over the fires of Jahannam. Some will cross safely to Jannah while others will fall into the fire.

> ❝Do the disbelievers not understand that **God, who created the heavens and earth and did not tire in doing so, has the power to bring the dead back to life?** Yes, indeed! He has power over everything.❞
> *Qur'an 46:33*

Just before the Day of Judgement, Sunni Muslims believe that Mahdi ('the guided one') will appear as a saviour to rid the world of evil, followed by a time of rule by Isa (Jesus). Shi'a Muslims believe Mahdi will be revealed as the last of Allah's twelve appointed **Imams**.

Jannah and Jahannam

Most Muslims believe that Jannah and Jahannam are physical places. Jannah is a garden of contentment full of flowers, fruits and fountains. Jahannam is a state of torment and terror where the damned are separated from Allah. They face boiling water, fire and smoke.

Specification focus

Beliefs about death and the afterlife: Islamic beliefs and teachings about life after death, including soul, judgement, akhirah, heaven and hell: Qur'an 46:33, 3:16; how Islamic funerals in Britain reflect beliefs about the afterlife; diversity of views between Shi'a and Sunni Muslims regarding worship at graves.

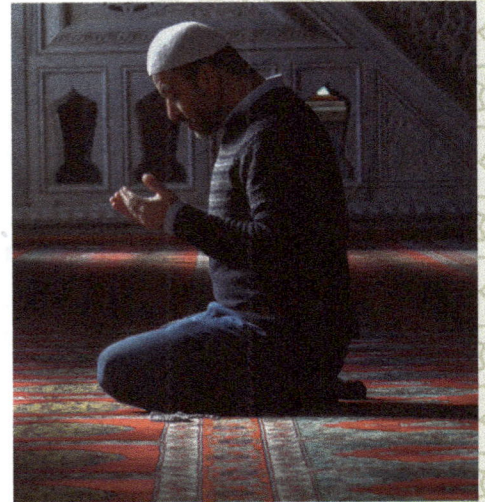

Prayer is part of a Muslim's preparation for akhirah

Useful terms

akhirah – life after death
barzakh – a state of waiting for the soul
Jannah – paradise
Jahannam – hell
Imam – for Sunni Muslims: a Muslim prayer leader. For Shi'a Muslims: one of the twelve infallible successors to Muhammad chosen by Allah to guide humans towards Him
Shahadah – the declaration of faith: 'There is no God but Allah, and Muhammad is the messenger of Allah'
tawassul – intercession or intervening on behalf of someone else
shirk – an unforgiveable sin of associating other beings with Allah (idolatry or polytheism)

The Qur'an teaches that Jahannam is eternal unless God wills it, but there is disagreement between scholars. Some argue that it is only eternal for non-believers. Some believe that Muslims who have died in a state of sin can be purified in Jahannam and then enter Jannah.

How Islamic funerals in Britain reflect beliefs about the afterlife

If possible, the bed of a dying Muslim should be turned to face Makkah with their face in the direction of the Ka'ba. Surrounded by family they should recite the **Shahadah** ('There is no God but Allah and Muhammad is the messenger of Allah'). If they cannot do this, it may be whispered into their ear just as it was at birth. This demonstrates the expectation that a Muslim will return to their creator.

After death, the body is given a ritual wash by family members. It should not be cremated, nor should any part be removed for donation, so that it is prepared for the Day of Judgement. However, growing numbers of scholars have begun to issue rulings that permit organ donation.

The dead are buried as quickly as possible after death, in clean, white sheets that cover the whole body. Coffins are not always used because Muslims believe they are created from the earth and will return to it. However, coffins are more likely to be used in Britain, when they should be very simple to emphasise that all are equal before Allah.

The funeral prayers should be performed by at least one Muslim, usually in an open space. The prayers emphasise the greatness of Allah and belief in his power to resurrect the dead.

The grave is dug parallel to Makkah and the body of the deceased is placed on their right-side, facing Makkah. The funeral should be simple to emphasise that there is no difference to Allah between the rich and the poor: everyone is the same in death.

Traditional Muslim funerals are often simple, showing that all are equal before Allah

Diverse Muslim views on worship at graves

Most Muslims believe worship at graves is wrong. It is haram to pray to the dead for help. All prayers should be addressed only to Allah.

Shi'a Muslims traditionally visit the graves of the Imams, or relatives of the Imams, but they do not worship them – they only ask for **tawassul**. This is where someone uses the dead person's name or authority to give them a higher chance of their prayer being heard by Allah. Some Sunni Muslims consider this to be **shirk**, which is a sin.

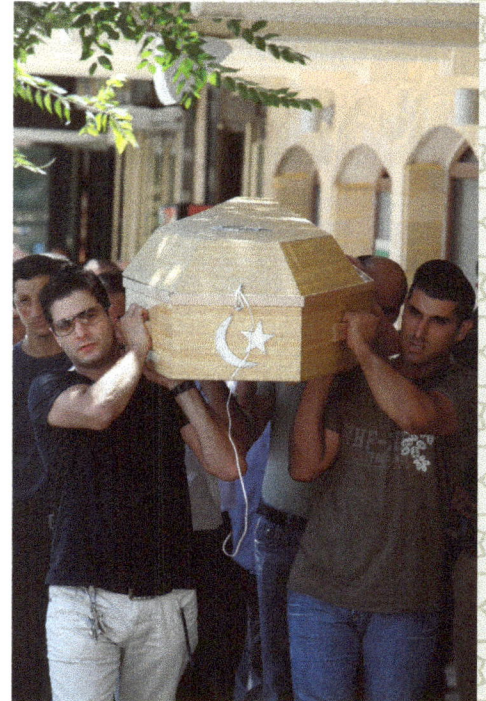

Knowledge recall

1 Define the following concepts: afterlife, soul, evolution. (You can find these definitions on page 33.)
2 List three features of a Muslim funeral and state what each feature represents.
3 Suggest two ways in which Muslim beliefs about life after death might differ.

Evaluation practice

4 Give two reasons why Muslims believe they should be more concerned with the afterlife than this life.
5 Do you agree that this life is less important than the next? Give a reason for your view.

Skills practice

On these exam practice pages you will see example answers for each of the exam questions types: **a**, **b**, **c** and **d**. You can find out more about these on pages 5–9.

Question (a)

*Question (a) tests your knowledge and understanding. You will always be asked to **define a key concept** in this question. You can find a list of the concepts at the beginning of the chapter.*

> (a)   What is meant by 'evolution'? [2]

Student response

> Evolution is when people evolve from monkeys, like Darwin said.

Improved student response

> Evolution is the process of complex organisms, such as humans, developing over a long period of time from simpler life forms, such as ape-like creatures, as they adapt to their environment or die out.

🕐 **Over to You!** Have a try at answering this question:

> (a)   What is meant by 'soul'? [2]

Helpful hints

To help you answer this question effectively, you could use the check list below to make sure you include the most important things:

- Include a **synonym** for the word 'soul'.
- Give an **example** of a situation when the soul might be active or important.

Now give yourself **two minutes** to answer this question by yourself:

> (a)   What is meant by 'sanctity of life'? [2]

What went well

The candidate has tried to give an appropriate example of evolution and made reference to an appropriate scholar.

How to improve

You must use a synonym for 'evolve' when defining evolution and try to use a full example to demonstrate the process of evolution by talking about complexity or the length of time required.

You should learn the exam board's definition of the word at the start of this chapter.

You could learn some technical vocabulary such as 'natural selection' or 'adaptation'.

Tip

In this response, the example of humans evolving from ape-like creatures is not necessarily required, since marks can be given for mentioning complexity from simplicity, the time period, and adaptation to the environment.

Question (b)

Question (b) tests your knowledge and understanding. It will always ask you to **describe** *a belief, a teaching, a practice or an event that is included in the specification.*

(b) Describe reasons why religious believers consider it important to care for the planet. [5]

Student response

We must care for the planet because it is the only one we have and because it is kind to animals to do this. It has developed over a long period of time and it is our responsibility or duty to care for it and not be irresponsible. We must make sure that we avoid pollution, try and solve the process of climate change and make sure that we live in a sustainable way.

Improved student response

Religious believers consider it important to care for the planet because God made human beings stewards. In Genesis 1:26, God created human beings on the sixth day to 'rule over' his creation. This means that it is a Christian's duty to nurture all of God's creation by cultivating and caring for it by living in a sustainable way so that the earth can be passed on to the next generation. Humans were created in God's image in Genesis 1:27 and given responsibility for maintaining his gift of creation. Therefore, Christians believe they should respect all aspects of God's creation as a gift to humans.

Over to You! Have a try at answering this question:

(b) Describe the Big Bang theory of creation. [5]

Helpful hints

Use the check list below to make sure you include the most important things:

- **Describe** what happened in the first moment of the universe.
- Give an **example** of a piece of evidence that demonstrates how we know this is what occurred.
- Then **repeat** the above process for the next events in the early moments of the universe.

Study Challenge:

The exam board will only ever ask a question **(b)** that asks you to describe an area from the specification, for example, a belief, teaching, practice or event.

- Look back at the specification focus boxes at the top of each page in this chapter.
- Choose one area from the list that has not yet appeared in the questions above.
- Write your own **(b)** question on this area that begins with the word 'Describe'.
- Now give yourself **five minutes** to answer this question by yourself!

What went well

The mention of responsibilities and duties is relevant to this answer.

How to improve

You must focus on the aspect of the question asking why *religious believers* consider this important.

You should include specialist vocabulary such as stewardship, khalifah or God's creation.

You could include examples of scripture to support the ideas raised.

Tip

The key word in this question is 'why' rather than 'how'. This means that the question wants you to consider the reasons *why* a religious believer would hold these beliefs, not *how* they demonstrate them.

Question (c)

Question (c) tests your knowledge and understanding. You need to give detailed evidence and reasoning to support your explanation of the topic. For the Themes paper, you will always be asked to **explain two different viewpoints**, *but you don't need to evaluate which is the better view.*

> (c) Explain from **either two** religions **or two** religious traditions, attitudes about abortion. [8]

Student response

Muslims believe that abortion is always wrong. They believe that it is the same as murder because you are never allowed to kill. Muslims believe that life begins at conception and that you should never take a life no matter what the circumstance. Humanists believe in abortions and the woman's right to choose. They would say that the foetus is not a human being until it is born and so a woman should be able to choose whether she kills the baby or not.

Improved student response

Generally Islam teaches abortion is wrong because Muslims believe Allah has created each person from a single clot of blood and made each life sacred. Therefore it is not our place to take a life. The Qur'an is Allah's word and it teaches that we should not kill our children out of poverty as the ummah should provide for people. Some Muslims believe the developing foetus is human from conception, so abortion is haram. However, others believer that if the mother's life is in danger, it is not sinful to use abortion to protect her if it happens before ensoulment.

Christianity generally sees abortion as a sin. Catholics believe the foetus is human from conception and killing a human violates the commandment 'Do not kill'. Also, Jeremiah 1:5 shows that all life is sacred, since God knew us before he formed us in the womb. But the Church of England understands that there can be many reasons for abortion, such as danger to the life or wellbeing of the woman. Church of England Christians would show compassion to those who feel they need an abortion.

🕐 **Over to You!** Have a try at answering this question:

> (c) Explain, from **either two** religions or **two** religious traditions, beliefs about euthanasia. [8]

Helpful hints

- Include **two** beliefs – one from one religion and the second from either a different religion or a different religious tradition.
- For each belief, give an **example** from religious authority to illustrate it (such as a quote from or reference to scripture, Shariah Law, a papal statement or the hadiths).
- Explain **why** each of the religions or traditions believe this (e.g. they are influenced by other teachings on the sanctity of life).
- Explain **how** people of this faith are expected to behave as a result (e.g. how they are expected to treat people who are terminally ill).

What went well
This response mentions Islam and gives one Muslim attitude towards abortion.

How to improve
You must stick to the requirement of the question to give two *religious* attitudes, not a non-religious attitude.

You should give some clear, specific detail of religious texts or teachings to support the points raised.

You could demonstrate understanding of how circumstances may affect a teaching or attitude.

Tip

Your answer to question (c) can mention two different religions or two different denominations. This means the candidate here could choose to write about just the Church of England and the Catholic Church for their whole answer.

Now give yourself **eight minutes** to answer this question by yourself:

> (c) Explain, from **either two** religions or **two** religious traditions, beliefs about life after death. [8]

Question (d)

*Question (d) tests your ability to **evaluate**. This means you need to show you have considered more than one point of view and that you have referred to religion and belief. You will need to be able to make judgements that are supported by detailed reasoning and argument.*

> (d) 'Religious creation stories successfully explain the origins of the universe.'
> Discuss this statement showing that you have considered more than one point of view. (You must refer to religious and non-religious and beliefs, such as those held by Humanists and Atheists, in your answer.) [15]

Student response

Religious creation stories don't make any sense. We know from science how the world began and so there is no need for these stories. Christians and Muslims believe that the world was created in six days, that humans were made on the sixth day and that woman was made from man's rib. This happened only 6,000 years ago but this makes no sense because we all know that the universe is 14 billion years old and it started off in a hot dense state and then expansion started. Scientists can tell us that this happened so I would rather believe science than a religious story. Atheists believe in science and they know that the earth was created by the Big Bang. Religious people just believe what it says in the Bible or the Qur'an. They all take all those stories literally and they don't believe the evidence they see in front of them. There is a lot of evidence for the Big Bang and this is what makes it more convincing. We know that there is red shift that we can see, and we can sense cosmic background radiation.

So therefore religious creation stories don't explain the origins of the universe because they do not agree with science.

Improved student response

Religious creation stories do not successfully explain the origins of the universe because science has shown that the events described in scriptures such as the Bible or the Qur'an are not factually accurate. The Bible tells us that God created the world in six days, instantaneously, but science tells us that it took billions of years for organisms to form. However, not all religious believers treat the scriptures as a science textbook. Conservative and liberal believers are more likely to see scripture as containing a different type of truth, symbolising God's involvement in creation, or religious believers' relationship with God. In this case, religious creation stories may be quite successful in explaining God as the origin of the universe.

Non-religious believers argue that there is no evidence that creation stories contain any explanation about the origins of the universe. They argue that the evidence of red shift and cosmic background radiation all point towards the fact of the Big Bang and therefore there is no truth in scripture. However,

What went well
There is some awareness of two different points of view, including non-religious attitudes. There is a brief reference to the content of scripture as well as the scientific evidence for the Big Bang. There is awareness shown of the conflict between religious and non-religious ideas.

How to improve
You must make sure that you present and evaluate both sides of the debate.

You should avoid long descriptions of the different views.

You could show understanding of different interpretations of religious creation stories.

This candidate has begun their first paragraph with a clear argument relating to the question.

There is appropriate evidence to back up the initial view.

Here is an appropriate counterargument that includes evidence and explanation.

modern religious believers argue that there must be a first cause, even for the Big Bang. Within the world, there is evidence of complexity and design that indicates there must be an intelligence behind the universe – it cannot be a mindless accident. Therefore, the creation stories indicate the origin as God more successfully than science does.

Religious creation stories, like Genesis 1, tell us the origin of the universe is an all-powerful being with intelligence who created deliberately. Genesis 2 tells us that the creator is capable of a relationship with his creation and so these stories can be successful even if science is true. However, as Hawking pointed out, there is no need for God to be involved. God is unnecessary as an explanation to the world, and if there is no need for God then the creation stories are also unnecessary. The universe could have created itself, doing away with any need for God. Therefore the religious creation stories do not successfully explain the origins of the universe.

Alternative religious views are given time and consideration.

Each paragraph ends with a decision based on the arguments within the text.

The conclusion uses a scholar and references his views to support the final decision.

🕐 **Over to You!** Have a try at answering this question:

(d) 'Belief in life after death is the most important belief.'
Discuss this statement showing that you have considered more than one point of view. (You must refer to religious and non-religious beliefs, such as those held by Humanists and Atheists, in your answer.) [15]

Helpful hints

If you find it difficult to answer this question effectively, you could use the A, B, C, D structure or a variation of it to help you set out your paragraphs (see page 32).

In addition, look at the wording of the question and make sure you understand what it is asking you to do. To do this well, **BUG** the question:

- **B**ox the command words.
- **U**nderline any words that give you a clue about what should be in the answer.
- **G**o back and check the question regularly as you answer.

For example:

(d) 'Belief in <u>life after death</u> is the <u>most important</u> belief.'
<u>Discuss</u> this statement showing that you have considered more than one point of view. (You must refer to <u>religious and non-religious beliefs</u>, such as those held by Humanists and Atheists, in your answer.) [15]

Now give yourself **fifteen minutes** to answer this question by yourself:

(d) 'It is a woman's right to choose abortion.'
Discuss this statement showing that you have considered more than one point of view. (You must refer to religious and non-religious beliefs, such as those held by Humanists and Atheists, in your answer.) [15]

Tip

Remember that in this question you are expected to refer to non-religious views as well as the religious ones. To get the higher marks, you need to have covered this in some detail.

Tip

Making sure that you understand what the question wants is an especially important skill. Get into the habit of looking at old exam questions and giving yourself one minute to BUG the question. Check that you understand the skill required (evaluation in question d) and check you have noticed all the different things that the question wants you to include.

COMPONENT 1:
Religious, philosophical and ethical studies
in the modern world

Chapter 3:
Issues of good and evil

Introduction

What do 'good' and 'evil' mean and where have ideas about good and evil come from? How do issues of good and evil affect people's relationship with God or with each other? In this chapter you will consider issues of good and evil through Christian and Muslim teachings, beliefs and attitudes. You will also consider moral responsibility and how far we can be held responsible for our behaviour.

Things to remember:

- Christians and Muslims may have very different understandings about the origins of good and evil, but they must all respond to the problem of crime and how to deal with it effectively.
- Christianity and Islam sometimes differ because they have developed in very different cultural and historical circumstances. It is important to try to understand some of this background to religious beliefs. For example, Islamic law covers everything from morality, criminal and civil law to manners, whereas most Christian cultures try to keep religious laws separate.
- Attitudes towards human behaviour depend on how religious people view their sources of authority such as scripture, other religious teachings and religious leaders. If an authority contains the word of God, it cannot be changed just because society is different.
- There are some very different attitudes in the world about what it means to treat people fairly. For example, some argue that fairness means everyone having the same rules and punishments, regardless of the situation. Others argue that fairness means adjusting punishments to suit the person or circumstances.

Concepts

Good – that which is considered morally right, beneficial and to our advantage

Evil – that which is considered extremely immoral, wicked and wrong

Forgiveness – to grant pardon for a wrongdoing; to give up resentment and the desire to seek revenge against a wrongdoer

Free will – the ability to make choices voluntarily and independently. The belief that nothing is pre-determined

Justice – fairness; where everyone has equal provisions and opportunity

Morality – principles and standards determining which actions are right or wrong

Punishment – a penalty given to someone for a crime or wrong they have done

Sin – deliberate immoral action, breaking a religious or moral law

Suffering – pain or distress caused by injury, illness or loss. Suffering can be physical, emotional/psychological or spiritual

Christianity, moral behaviour and crime

Specification focus

Crime and punishment: What makes an act wrong? Religious and ethical responses: relative and absolute morality, conscience, virtues, sin; beliefs and attitudes about the causes of crime.

What makes an act wrong?

A 'wrong' action can be described as an act that is against the law or that harms other people. This explanation is focused on society and human relationships with each other. However, Christians believe that a 'wrong' action is more than this. It is also a sin that harms their relationship with God.

A Christian may consider a variety of sources to help them make a moral decision. They may look to scripture, religious leaders, tradition, **conscience**, reason, the law or a combination of these.

> ❛You shall not murder.
> You shall not commit adultery.
> You shall not steal.❜
> *Exodus 20:13–15*

Some Christians might consider traditional Church teaching. Orthodox, Catholic or Church of England Christians can refer to religious leaders who they trust as experts. As God's representatives on earth, such leaders have made pronouncements on moral issues in the past.

> ❛One may not do evil so that good may result from it.❜
> *CCC1761*

The Ten Commandments are an example of absolute moral laws

CCC means 'Catechism of the Catholic Church'. It is an official document that sums up the beliefs of Catholics and gives them moral guidance.

Relative and absolute morality

Christians who believe in **absolute morality**, view **good** moral behaviour as taking actions that obey the rules.

The Catholic Church follows an ethical theory known as Natural Law, established by St Thomas Aquinas. This absolutist approach establishes rules according to primary precepts that are always wrong to break.

Christians who believe in **relative morality** think it is important to make moral judgements based on the situation. They may still value rules, but these are considered to be advisory rather than binding. This means that if a situation arises where the rule is not helpful or fair, it can and should be broken.

The Church of England teaching on remarriage after divorce is relativist. They look at the individual situation and allow some remarriages in a church, but forbid others depending on the circumstances and people involved.

Conscience

Most Christians argue that people should use their conscience when making moral decisions and that it is wrong to disobey it. However, scholars differ over what this means.

Useful terms

conscience – the ability of the mind to think about and make moral decisions

absolute morality – the belief that moral rules are the same for everyone regardless of the situation they are in or the consequence of following them

relative morality – the belief that what is right or wrong may change depending on culture, upbringing or circumstances

virtue – a positive personal quality or characteristic, often called moral excellence of character

- St Thomas Aquinas viewed conscience as using reason to make moral decisions. This means that when someone is trying to work out the rules about right and wrong behaviour, they use their conscience to make a rational decision and come up with the correct rules. Conscience must be educated and always followed.
- Cardinal John Henry Newman saw conscience as the voice of God. This idea of conscience suggests that someone senses what God wants of them as they deliberate, and they can follow their conscience because God will help them to know what the right behaviour is.

Virtues

Aquinas spoke of moral rules that people must obey. But he was also strongly influenced by the ancient Greek scholar Aristotle, who was interested in **virtue**. Aquinas incorporated Aristotle's teaching into his Natural Law, so it is now part of Catholic teaching.

Virtues are personal qualities or characteristics people should show, rather than specific rules they should follow. St Paul gives three virtues: faith, hope and love. A good moral person is one who shows these personal qualities when they go about their lives. Aquinas added four more that the Catholic Church also accepts: prudence (wisdom), fortitude (courage), temperance (moderation) and justice (fairness).

> 'And now these three remain: faith, hope and love. The greatest of these is love.'
> *1 Corinthians 13:13*

Sin

In Christianity, a **sin** is a deliberate behaviour that breaks a religious law. It is an action against God. The Catholic Church lists seven 'deadly' sins (sometimes called 'cardinal' sins or 'capital vices'). These are bad personal qualities or dispositions that lead people to act against God's law. For example, if a person is greedy, they may commit a sin by hoarding money for themselves. The seven 'deadly' sins are excesses that shift a person's attention away from God and towards the world.

1 Lust   3 Greed   5 Wrath   7 Pride
2 Gluttony   4 Sloth   6 Envy

Poverty is one of the root causes of crime in the UK

Read about the Fall on page 106.

Beliefs and attitudes about the causes of crime

Christianity teaches that everyone is capable of sin as part of their fallen human nature, but the Bible shows how to avoid sin by giving moral and spiritual guidance.

A crime is an offence against society that is punishable by law. Sins are deliberate violations against God. Some sins may also be crimes, but not all of them. It may be a sin to have an abortion or to commit adultery, but neither of these are crimes in the UK.

Christianity recognises that there are complex reasons why people commit crime. Poverty, poor education or upbringing, peer pressure, drug addiction, mental illness and abuse are all possible causes of crime. Christians recognise that law is an important part of society and St Paul teaches that it should be obeyed.

> 'Let every person be subject to the governing authorities; for there is no authority except that which God has established. The authorities that exist have been established by God.'
> *Romans 13:1*

Knowledge recall

1 Define the following concepts: good/evil, morality, sin. (You can find these definitions on page 57.)
2 Give two different ideas of what conscience might be.
3 What is the difference between relative and absolute morality?

Evaluation practice

4 Give one reason why some Christians might think that God's laws are absolute. Give one reason why others might think that God's laws are relative.
5 Which of these reasons do you find most convincing? Give two reasons why.

Islam, moral behaviour and crime

Specification focus

Crime and punishment: What makes an act wrong? Religious responses: relative and absolute morality, conscience, free will, doing the will of Allah; beliefs and attitudes about the causes of crime: Qur'an 16:90.

What makes an act wrong?

In Islam, there is no distinction between religion, ==morality== and law. All of these things are governed by **Shariah Law**. 'Shariah' literally means a clear, straight path to water. So the purpose of Shariah is to clearly set out for Muslims exactly how Allah wants them to live, so they can be close to him.

Shariah comprises laws about social, religious and personal behaviour. It has two goals: to organise and regulate society, and to help humans gain salvation by enforcing Allah's commands. Therefore, breaking Shariah Law is wrong because it goes against the will of Allah.

The rules regarding human behaviour range from compulsory duties (like prayer and charitable giving) to recommended acts that are good but not duties (like extra prayers). There are also laws regarding haram or forbidden actions (like theft) as well as discouraged acts that are not forbidden but should be avoided (like divorce).

> ❛Be a community that calls for what is good, urges what is right, and forbids what is wrong: those who do this are the successful ones.❜
> *Qur'an 3:104*

Relative and absolute morality

Islamic ethics are absolutist. The law of Allah is unchanging and Shariah Law is based on his will, not on the will of society. It covers a wide range of issues from criminal law to religious observance and personal relationships. Some areas of Shariah are fixed, such as some ==punishments== or religious rituals, but the schools of law work to try to understand the law of Allah, so they continue to develop Shariah to answer new issues in modern life. Shariah Law is based primarily on instructions from the Qur'an. However, other sources have been used as well, such as the **Sunnah**, hadiths and, where necessary, the reasoning of Islamic scholars.

Some Muslims argue that Islam has forgotten its roots and needs to be reformed. These **modernisers** tend to have been educated or raised in Western countries like the UK and are in the minority. They may try to interpret the Qur'an in a way that is compatible with modern science, or they may reject other Islamic sources of authority.

Other Muslims argue that believers should take the authority of the hadiths and the Sunnah more seriously. These Muslims are **fundamentalists** and they argue that the best way to protect and organise society is through careful obedience to the law.

Few Muslims take a relativist approach to ethics. This is because they believe the Qur'an is the word of Allah and can therefore be trusted to give accurate teaching on morality.

Conscience

The conscience is a guide for Muslims. Islam teaches that all Muslims should listen to their conscience because it is a gift from Allah that allows a believer to know the difference between right and wrong. The Qur'an and Shariah Law can usually

Useful terms

Shariah Law – the set of moral and religious rules that put the principles set out by the Qur'an and the hadiths into practice

Sunnah – examples, practices and teachings of Muhammad

modernisers – Muslims who wish for Islam to be reformed for the modern world

fundamentalists – Muslims who wish for Islam to be brought back to traditional roots

halal – actions or things which are permitted within Islam, such as eating permitted foods

zakah – compulsory annual donation for all Muslims of 2.5% of their wealth for the relief of poverty

salah – ritual prayers

khums – annual tax for Shi'a Muslims of 20% of their wealth. Half is given to religious leaders to fund education and half to the poor

sadaqah – voluntary charitable giving

instruct Muslims about how they should behave, but when there is a moral issue that has no guidance from these sources, the conscience is the best guide.

Islam teaches that the conscience can be wrong when a person has turned away from Allah and been made numb through being too focused on worldly things. However, a faithful Muslim who does everything in their power to understand Allah's will can find peace in their conscience, which will tell them what is **halal** and cause them to feel bad if they do something haram.

All Muslims have a duty to act in accordance with the will of Allah

Free will and doing the will of Allah

Islam teaches that Allah has given people the gift of **free will** so they can choose between right and wrong. When a person freely chooses to submit to the will of Allah, they are living in the best possible way. Allah has made his will clear to Muslims through the Qur'an and other sources of authority. Muslims have obligations or duties that are expected of them, such as the giving of **zakah** or performance of **salah**. But these acts are to be performed because a person freely decides to submit to Allah, not because they have been forced to.

Muslims believe Allah is omniscient. He knows what is inside the heart of every person and knows in advance the choices they will make. Therefore, he can punish or reward for good or bad intentions as well as good or bad actions.

Beliefs and attitudes about the causes of crime

There is an understanding in Islam that the causes of crime are complex, but the Muslim way of life aims to reduce or remove these causes wherever possible.

- Poverty – the poor should be provided for through zakah, **khums** and **sadaqah**.
- Poor mental health – those with some forms of mental illness are exempt from punishment and are not obliged to fulfil the five pillars of Islam.
- Poor upbringing – parents have a duty to educate their children in the faith and morality, which should prevent criminal behaviour.
- Addiction – drinking and drug use are haram in Islam so they should not be able to cause criminal behaviour.

> ❝**God commands justice**, doing good, and generosity towards relatives and He forbids what is shameful, blameworthy, and oppressive. He teaches you, so that you may take heed.❞
> *Qur'an 16:90*

Teaching and preaching from Islamic authorities regularly warn against criminal activity, which is seen as an offence against Allah.

Knowledge recall

1 Define the following concepts: good/evil, free will, morality. (You can find these definitions on page 57.)
2 Explain how or when Muslims might use their conscience.
3 State at least two examples of religious or moral duties expected of Muslims.

Evaluation practice

4 Give one reason why most Muslims believe that moral rules should stay the same and one reason why a few might argue that they should change.
5 Which of these views do you think is most persuasive? Give two reasons why.

Christianity and punishment

Specification focus

Crime and punishment: Beliefs and attitudes about the aims of punishment: justice, retribution, deterrence and reformation; the treatment of criminals and the work of prison reformers and prison chaplains; varied conservative and liberal Christian responses to the death penalty, including interpretations of Christian teachings: Exodus 20:13, Matthew 5:38–39, 43–47.

The aims of punishment

Christian teaching acknowledges that the law has a responsibility to punish criminals for their crimes. Christianity may accept several reasons for **punishment**:

- **Justice** (fairness) – most Christians agree that a person must make amends for what they have done to help restore equality and balance to society.
- Retribution (revenge) – Christian teaching rejects punishing someone to pay them back for their crime so they suffer as much as their victims. This aim lacks mercy for the criminal.
- Deterrence (prevention) – Christians may worry that punishing one person as an example to others conflicts with biblical teachings about the sanctity of life.
- Reformation (improvement) – many Christians agree that it is merciful, through education and counselling, to aim to safely release a person back into society.

There are other aims of punishment too. Sometimes people need to be punished to protect other members of society. Or the punishment proves the authority of the law and reminds people of the reasons for it (to keep order in society).

The treatment of criminals

In the UK, there are several punishments that a judge can choose from for different criminal offences. These include fines, community service and prison.

Christians differ in their views on how criminals should be treated. Those who see punishment as retribution or a deterrent may want criminals to experience **suffering** for their crimes. They may disagree with criminals receiving 'privileges' in prison, such as access to televisions or computers.

Those who see punishment as rehabilitation believe it is vital for criminals to receive whatever they need to equip them for a crime-free life. They argue that God requires Christians to care for criminals, who are more likely to respond positively if they are treated fairly.

The work of prison reformers and prison chaplains

Christianity has inspired many to work for prison reform. While imprisonment is one way to ensure justice and protect society, it does not always support rehabilitation. Prison reformers campaign to improve conditions in prisons so they are more humane and promote rehabilitation.

In the nineteenth century, Elizabeth Fry was a Quaker prison reformer. She thought that locking people away was not consistent with Christian mercy. She visited prisons in the UK, held Bible readings and taught women skills they could use to earn money on their release. She sent care packages of clothes, Bibles, equipment and food to prisoners. She campaigned against the transportation of prisoners to Australia and against **capital punishment**.

> 'They also will answer, "Lord, when did we see you hungry or thirsty or a stranger or needing clothes or ill or in prison, and did not help you?" He will reply, "Truly I tell you, whatever you did not do for one of the least of these, you did not do for me." Then they will go away to eternal punishment, but the righteous to eternal life.'
> *Matthew 25:44–46*

Useful terms

capital punishment – the death penalty; execution as punishment for a criminal offence

pastoral care – help with personal problems

A prison chaplain's role is to provide **pastoral care** for inmates. This means they offer counselling and spiritual or emotional help to prisoners and support their rehabilitation. Christian chaplains may offer Bible studies, religious services and contact with those outside of prison to reduce their isolation and the chance of reoffending. Chaplains often work alongside parole officers, helping prisoners to get ready to go back into the community.

Varied Christian responses to the death penalty

The UK abolished the death penalty in 1969. However, it is still legal in many countries, 30 of which have used it within the last 10 years to deter crime and punish the most serious criminal behaviour. Modern methods usually aim to make the process quick and painless, with the most common being a lethal injection.

Not all Christians agree with the use of capital punishment. Some argue that it was an accepted, or even commanded, punishment in the Bible for crimes such as blasphemy or murder. They may argue that it promotes public order and the cost to society is less than life imprisonment. Many others argue that it violates the sanctity of human life and provides no opportunity for repentance.

The Catholic Church previously took a Conservative view. Aquinas saw punishment as having two aims: protecting society and reforming the sinner. The death penalty helped to protect society, so Aquinas was in favour of it. In 1997, Pope John Paul II confirmed this as the Church's position, but only in extremely rare cases if there was no other way to protect society. However, in 2018 Pope Francis declared the death penalty 'inadmissible' and something that should be abolished worldwide.

Jesus appeared to revise the Old Testament command that required revenge when a person committed a crime. Instead, he taught that Christians should show compassion.

Quakers have argued for an end to the death penalty as far back as 1818. They believe that punishment should only be used to reform, to bring healing and change for the criminal. Capital punishment does not enable this. Many argue that it is simply state-sanctioned murder.

> '[You shall not murder.]'
> *Exodus 20:13*

> 'You have heard that it was said, "Love your neighbour and hate your enemy." But I tell you, **love your enemies and pray for those who persecute you**.... If you love those who love you, what reward will you get? Are not even the tax collectors doing that? And if you greet only your own people, what are you doing more than others? Do not even pagans do that?'
> *Matthew 5:43–47*

> 'You have heard that it was said, "Eye for eye, and tooth for tooth." But I tell you, do not resist an evil person. **If anyone slaps you on the right cheek, turn to them the other cheek also.**'
> *Matthew 5:38–39*

Prisoners can often feel very isolated from their families or church communities when in prison

Knowledge recall

1 Define the following concepts: forgiveness, justice, punishment. (You can find these definitions on page 57.)
2 List four purposes of punishment.
3 State two examples of how Christians think prisoners should be treated.

Evaluation practice

4 Give two reasons why some Christians might support the death penalty and two reasons why other Christians might reject it.
5 Which of these views do you think Christians would find most persuasive? Give a reason why.

Islam and punishment

The aims of punishment

Shariah Law outlines the rules that Muslims are expected to live by. There are prescribed punishments set out in the Qur'an and by Muhammad. These are known as **hudud**. Hudud crimes include things like murder, **apostasy**, theft, adultery, slander and drinking alcohol. These may require **corporal punishments** such as lashings or amputation, or capital punishment.

Other crimes may be condemned but have no fixed punishment. In these cases, the punishment must be determined by the state on a case by case basis. This means that punishment can be flexible and take the society or individual situations into account. Punishments where Shariah Law is applied at the discretion of a judge are known as **ta'zir**.

While Shariah Law sees community service as being too weak a punishment to protect the ummah or act as an efficient deterrent, for ta'zir crimes it can play a role since service to the ummah is a fundamental part of Islam.

Islam sees punishment as having a range of aims:

Justice – punishments must be fair and they must protect the ummah from harm. The Qur'an teaches that punishment should be in proportion to the crime that was committed, and that where the punishment is severe there must be enough evidence to remove any doubt surrounding the accusation.

Retribution – **qisas** is retaliation in proportion to the crime that was committed. The intention is not revenge, but a fair consequence to restore balance. In this instance, some Islamic punishments can be chosen by the victims or their families. For example, if the criminal has deliberately harmed someone, the victim can ask that the criminal receives the same harm in return. **Diyah** is another form of retribution under Shariah Law. It means the victim or their relative can accept financial payment instead, to compensate them for the harm that was caused.

Deterrence – punishment is supposed to protect the ummah from crime so that society can be peaceful and orderly. Punishment is often administered publicly in Muslim countries so that everyone can see the consequences and be put off from performing the same actions.

Reformation – Islam does not favour reformation as a replacement for punishment but hopes that it will happen as a consequence of punishment. The punishment itself is intended to prevent the same crime from being committed again. The community then has a duty to help the criminal to become a better member of society.

Useful terms

hudud – punishments that are fixed by Allah

apostasy – abandoning or turning away from Islam

corporal punishment – physical punishment intended to cause pain

ta'zir – punishment that has not been fixed by the Qur'an

qisas – a law that allows retribution for certain crimes to ensure justice. For instance, a life for a life

diyah – a financial compensation to a victim or their family in cases of murder or harm

'Let harm be requited by an equal harm.'
Qur'an 42:40

Muslim moral, social and religious laws are based on teachings from the Qur'an

The treatment of criminals and the work of prison reformers and prison chaplains

Some Islamic scholars argue against imprisonment as it is a financial burden on the ummah, and in Muslim countries prisons are usually for those awaiting trial or punishment.

Islam teaches that human life is sacred and therefore prisoners should be treated fairly and humanely, no matter what crime they committed. They have the right to a fair trial, food and drink, medical attention and good hygiene. This is true even if corporal punishment is received.

Some Muslim organisations run projects to ensure fair treatment for Muslim prisoners. They provide prayer mats, literature and halal food for prisoners who could not otherwise practise their faith. Some work to ensure justice for Muslim prisoners who may be treated more harshly by the prison system.

In the UK, there are many Muslim prison chaplains who provide counselling and spiritual guidance for prisoners. Chaplains also support prisoners when they are released so they do not reoffend.

Muslim prison chaplains aim to prevent reoffending to protect the ummah

Varied Islamic responses to the death penalty

Most Muslim countries use the death penalty as the ultimate punishment for the most severe crimes. The death penalty is prescribed by the Qur'an and the hadiths for two types of crime: murder and spreading mischief. 'Spreading mischief' tends to include crimes like apostasy, adultery, rape, homosexuality, piracy or terrorism.

The death penalty is supposed to act as a deterrent and executions are often held in public as an example to others. Strict laws are in place to ensure that no one is unjustly executed. For example, there must be four eyewitnesses who can confirm that adultery has taken place.

Not all Muslims agree that the death penalty is appropriate for crimes such as apostasy. This is because faith is a matter for the individual and Allah, and cannot be forced. In practice, people are often declared insane for deserting Islam and are therefore not executed.

Some Muslims, especially those raised in the West, argue that the death penalty was appropriate to society when the Qur'an was revealed, but is not applicable today. They may argue that the death penalty is inhumane and adds nothing good to society, or that it is possible accused people may be executed by mistake. In these cases, if more evidence comes to light, that person can never be pardoned in a meaningful way.

Other Muslims argue that it is against the law of Allah to fail to punish a guilty criminal in the way that Shariah Law prescribes.

Knowledge recall

1 Define the following concepts: justice, morality, punishment. (You can find these definitions on page 57.)
2 Give three examples of hudud crimes.
3 Suggest three roles that a Muslim chaplain might perform.

Evaluation practice

4 Give two reasons why some Muslims may agree with the death penalty and two reasons why some might object to it.
5 Which of these views do you find the most convincing? Give a reason why.

Christianity and forgiveness

Specification focus

Forgiveness: Christian teachings about forgiveness, including interpretations of teachings: Matthew 18:21–22, Matthew 6:14–15; examples of forgiveness arising from personal beliefs.

Christian teachings about forgiveness

Forgiveness is an important part of Christian teaching, which says that it is *not*:

- letting someone off their **punishment**
- agreeing with or condoning a terrible deed
- forgetting about what someone has done wrong.

Forgiveness is when someone chooses to change the way they view another person who has caused them harm. It involves letting go of anger, resentment and a desire for revenge. The victim no longer feels the need for payment or compensation for the offence against them and the people involved can move on without bitterness or ill will. Forgiveness is difficult but is said to help victims deal with what has happened to them.

Christian teaching says no one is completely innocent as everyone **sins**. But Christians believe that God forgives everyone who **repents** of the things they have done wrong. Christian tradition says that when Adam ate the forbidden fruit in the Genesis account, he caused all humans to be in a state of **Original Sin**. Some Christians believe this means Adam's sin damaged human nature for all human beings so that they are weakened and as a result they have a natural tendency to behave in sinful ways. Humans need God's help for sin to be forgiven.

> ❝For all have sinned and fall short of the glory of God.❞
> *Romans 3:23*

Just as God forgives those who are sorry, scripture requires believers to also forgive each other when they sin or make mistakes. The Lord's Prayer contains the lines: 'And forgive us our debts, as we also have forgiven our debtors' (Matthew 6:12). Just as Christians hope for God's forgiveness when they sin, they believe they should treat people who wrong them with the same kind of compassion.

> ❝Then Peter came to Jesus and asked, "Lord, how many times shall I forgive my brother or sister who sins against me? Up to seven times?" Jesus answered, "I tell you, **not seven times, but seventy-seven times.**"❞
> *Matthew 18:21–22*

In Matthew 18:21–22, 'seventy-seven times' means an unlimited amount. Jesus tells his followers there is no maximum number of times a person should be forgiven. Christians believe that God's forgiveness is unlimited and they should try to follow his example.

Jesus continues by telling the parable of the unmerciful servant. In the story, a slave owed his master money but could not repay. He was to be sold, but he begged the master for mercy and was forgiven. He immediately went out and asked a fellow slave for money he was owed. That slave begged for mercy but was thrown in prison. When the master heard of this, he handed the unmerciful slave over to be tortured until he repaid the money he owed. Christians cannot expect forgiveness from God unless they show the same behaviour to each other.

Useful terms

repent – to be sorry for or to regret a past action

Original Sin – a tendency to sin that is human nature as a result of the actions of Adam and Eve in the Garden of Eden

sacrament – an outward sign of an invisible and inward blessing by God. For example, Baptism, the Eucharist

confession – admitting wrongdoing and saying sorry to God. For Catholics this may be done through a priest

reconciliation – bringing people back into a good relationship with God

penance – demonstration of remorse for sin through the performance of prayer, good works or sacrifice

In the Gospels, Jesus repeatedly demonstrated an ability to forgive sins. Even on the cross, he prayed to God: 'Father, forgive them, for they do not know what they are doing' (Luke 23:34).

Jesus' parable of the prodigal son in Luke 15:11–32 shows the unlimited forgiveness offered by God to humans. In this story, a son (who represents human beings) asked for his inheritance before the death of his father (who represents God). The son left home and spent all his inheritance on wild living. When a famine swept the land, he had nothing left and was starving. He decided to go back to his father and ask to be hired as a servant, but his father forgave him and celebrated the return of his son.

> ❝ **For if you forgive other people when they sin against you, your heavenly Father will also forgive you.** But if you do not forgive others their sins, your Father will not forgive your sins. ❞
> *Matthew 6:14–15*

Forgiveness in worship

Forgiveness plays an important part in Christian worship. For many Christians, God's forgiveness is celebrated in services of Baptism. Baptism is performed as a sign of God's promise that their sins are forgiven. For Catholic and Anglican Christians, it is a **sacrament** that removes Original Sin, although it does not prevent someone from sinning again.

Confession is also important in Christian worship. A Christian may confess their sins to God in private prayer or during a church service and ask God for his forgiveness. For Catholics, **reconciliation** is a sacrament through which people can be forgiven by God for their sins. Catholics are expected to visit the confessional box regularly to have their confessions heard by the priest and are asked to perform acts of **penance** to show sorrow for their actions.

> ❝ Repent and be baptised, every one of you, in the name of Jesus Christ for the forgiveness of your sins. ❞
> *Acts 2:38*

Examples of forgiveness arising from personal beliefs

In 2015, nine members of a Bible study group from the Emanuel African Methodist Episcopal Church in Charleston, South Carolina, were shot and killed by 21-year-old Dylan Roof. He was a white supremacist targeting members of the church because of its civil rights history. He had written that he was not sorry and did not regret his actions. He was sentenced to death. At the hearing, relatives of the victims were able to speak directly to Roof. All those who chose to speak offered Roof forgiveness. Nadine Collier, who lost her 70-year-old mother, asked God to have mercy on Roof's soul.

In 2005, Anthony Walker was 18 years old, aspiring to be a lawyer and living in Merseyside. He was murdered by Paul Taylor and Michael Barton, who attended the same school. They struck him on the head with an ice axe in a racially motivated attack. His mother, Gee Walker, forgave the killers, saying that God gave her the ability to cope. Her daughter, Dominique, also forgave the killers. She said that she was taught to forgive seventy-seven times and that while it was hard, it eases the bitterness and the anger. Walker's girlfriend Louise, who was with him when he was killed, said she would never forgive, adding that she hated them for what they had done.

Nadine Collier was able to rely on her Christian faith to help her to forgive

Knowledge recall

1 Define the following concepts: forgiveness, sin, suffering. (You can find these definitions on page 57.)

2 List three reasons why Christians think it is good to forgive.

3 Give three different ways that a Christian might seek or receive forgiveness from God.

Evaluation practice

4 Give one reason why a Christian might forgive someone who has done something wrong and one reason why they might not.

5 Which view do you consider most reasonable and why?

Islam and forgiveness

Specification focus

Forgiveness: Islamic teachings about forgiveness: Qur'an 42:30, 64:14; examples of forgiveness arising from personal beliefs.

Islamic teachings about forgiveness

Islam teaches that there are two types of **forgiveness**: forgiveness from Allah and forgiveness from each other.

Muslims are reminded throughout the Qur'an that Allah is merciful and compassionate. He gave them the responsibility to be khalifahs of the world, but as they are imperfect humans they will sometimes fail in this duty. Muslims are taught that Allah is merciful and if they are truly sorry and ask for forgiveness then he will forgive them.

Allah can forgive people without punishing them as he is merciful. But when a person does something wrong out of malice, then they can expect Allah's **punishment**. However, Allah recognises that people are weak and if they try hard then he will wipe out minor misdeeds. There is no limit to Allah's capacity for forgiveness.

Hajj is one opportunity for a Muslim to repent of any of their **sins**. On the second day, all pilgrims must stand in front of the hill of Arafat and confess their sins to Allah. Arafat is believed to be where Adam confessed his sins and was forgiven by Allah. Repentance ensures the believer's sins are forgiven by Allah.

> 'Whatever misfortune befalls you [people], it is because of what your hands have done – **God forgives much...**'
> *Qur'an 42:30*

Forgiveness from other people

Islam teaches that if a Muslim has harmed or wronged another person, they must ask forgiveness from that person before they seek forgiveness from Allah. A sin against another person is also a sin against Allah. Forgiveness is an important value and the hadiths say that people should forgive if they can. However, this is not always easy.

Islam allows qisas as retribution in Shariah Law when a person has been the victim of an intentional personal injury or even been murdered. However, while the family can decide what punishment should happen to the criminal, they are limited to like for like. So if someone has murdered another person, the victim's family can request the death penalty. Or they can choose to pardon the crime if they wish.

Forgiveness is thought to be greater than revenge, and those who forgive are promised a reward in the afterlife. However, it is not required of a victim and they may feel unable to forgive. Those who forgive do something difficult that may have to be repeated whenever they are reminded of the pain that was caused them. For the offender, forgiveness allows them to move forward and repair the damage they have done to others as well as themselves. Often those who forgive say they too can move on and feel relief rather than continued anger.

When a person asks for forgiveness, they should intend to never commit the sin or crime again. If they do unwittingly repeat their action, Muslims should ideally forgive them again, following the example of Allah (whose forgiveness is unlimited).

Muslims are expected to copy the example of Muhammad. There is a traditional story in which Muhammad was the target of an old woman who repeatedly threw rubbish and brushed dirt on him as he passed her house to visit the mosque each day. One day as he passed, she was not there, so he enquired

Hajj is an opportunity for Muslims to seek forgiveness from Allah

and found that she was sick. He helped to care for her until she was well, despite her prior actions.

> ❝Believers, even among your spouses and your children you have some enemies – beware of them – but **if you overlook their offences, forgive them, pardon them, then God is all forgiving, all merciful.** ❞
> *Qur'an 64:14*

Examples of forgiveness arising from personal beliefs

In 2004, Ameneh Bahrami was leaving work in Tehran when she was confronted by a fellow student she had repeatedly refused to marry. Majid Movvahedi threw acid in her face leaving her blind and disfigured, then remained in the crowd watching as she screamed for help. She was unable to continue with her studies or work as a medical engineer. The judge intended to give him a death sentence, but Bahrami requested qisas. She wanted Movvahedi to lose his sight as well. As he was prepared for the punishment he showed no remorse, but Bahrami pardoned him, saying that she knew she would have suffered and burned twice if she had done it. Some argue that this was an injustice and there was no deterrent for others; he paid no compensation for her losses, and was released and pardoned after 10 years in prison. Others argue that she was a hero and a statue was erected in her honour.

In 2016, Abraham Davis vandalised the Al Salam Mosque in Fort Smith, Arkansas with one of his friends. They drew swastikas and curses over the windows and doors as an act of bigotry and hatred. Later, while awaiting his trial in prison, Davis wrote a letter to the mosque apologising for what he had done. The mosque leaders immediately forgave him, refused to press charges and produced evidence in his defence, asking for leniency and mercy. Despite the mosque's efforts, Davis ended up with a felony conviction, community service and $3200 in fines. Attending his community service meant he had no paid work and risked a six-year prison sentence for failing to pay the fines. Hisham Yasin, the social director and co-founder of the mosque, paid off Davis' court fines.

In 2020, Raafat Magald, the **muezzin** at London Central Mosque in Regent Park, was stabbed in the neck several times as he led the afternoon prayers. Magald told reporters that he felt sorry for his attacker. He did not hold any hatred against the man who attacked him and forgave him because of his faith.

Raafat Magald relied on his faith and recognised that forgiveness can be beneficial but that sometimes it can be hard

Knowledge recall

1 Define the following concepts: forgiveness, punishment, sin. (You can find these definitions on page 57.)
2 List three things that a Muslim could do if they wish to be forgiven for wrong actions.
3 State three ways that a Muslim could respond to someone who has harmed them.

Evaluation practice

4 Give one reason why forgiveness is a useful thing for Muslims and one reason why it is not.
5 Which is the stronger of these two reasons and why?

Christian beliefs about good, evil and suffering

Philosophical challenges posed by the existence of evil and suffering

When people talk about 'evil' in the world, they are usually referring to one of two things:

- Moral evil – actions deliberately performed (or omitted) by people that cause suffering, e.g. war, murder, abuse or neglect.
- Natural evil – events that cause suffering but occur as part of the natural working of the world and cannot be controlled by human behaviour, e.g. volcanoes, earthquakes, sickness and death.

Christianity teaches that God has many qualities. Some people argue that these qualities are incompatible with the existence of evil and suffering in the world. For example:

- Omnibenevolent – God is all-loving. He should hate seeing people suffer and want it to stop.
- Omnipotent – God is all-powerful. He has the power to stop evil and suffering in the world.
- Omniscient – God is all-knowing. He knows that evil and suffering happen and understands people's experiences of it.
- Creator – God made everything that is in existence.
- Miracle worker – God can suspend the laws of nature to act as he wishes. For instance, he can heal in an instant and turn water into wine.
- One – There is only one God. There is no other being of equal power, authority and qualities.

Since everyone can see the existence of evil and suffering in the world, some people think that at least one of these divine qualities must be false.

The problem of evil can be expressed as the **logical problem of evil**. An ancient Greek scholar named Epicurus claimed that if God is all powerful and all good, then it does not make sense that evil should exist. Either God wants to help us but cannot; this would make him **impotent**. Or, he can help us but will not; this would make him **malevolent**.

In more recent times this has been restated by J. L. Mackie as an **inconsistent triad**. This means that only two points on the triad can logically be true. God can only be both omnipotent and omnibenevolent if evil does not exist. However, evil does exist, so either God is omnipotent but is not good, or he is omnibenevolent but is powerless to stop it. If either of these solutions is true then God is not the God of Christianity, since the religion teaches that God has both qualities.

Christianity teaches that humans have **free will**, which they often use to make evil choices. For example, war and neglect are evils that humans perform, not God. As a result, some argue that evil is a fair punishment that humans deserve or that suffering can teach someone how to be a better person.

Specification focus

Good, evil and suffering:
Philosophical perspectives on the origin of evil: Original Sin (free will) and 'soul-making' (Irenaeus and John Hick); philosophical challenges posed by belief in God, free will and the existence of evil and suffering.

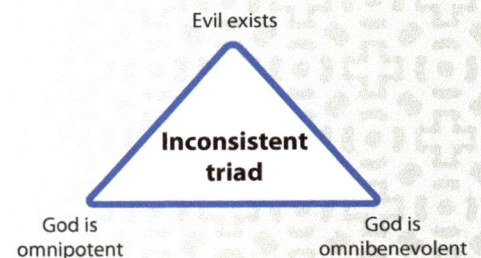

Evil exists

Inconsistent triad

God is omnipotent

God is omnibenevolent

Only two points on the inconsistent triad can logically be true at the same time

Useful terms

logical problem of evil – the attempt to show that it is logically impossible for God and evil to exist at the same time

impotent – powerless or weak

malevolent – wishing others harm

inconsistent triad – three ideas are possible but only two of them can be true at the same time

theodicies – attempts to justify the existence and qualities of God in the face of evil

epistemic distance – a distance from full knowledge of God

Others disagree and point out that:

- humans cannot be held responsible for natural evils
- good and innocent people suffer as well as bad people
- when babies die or animals suffer, they cannot learn from it
- the amount of evil in the world is too great to be fair or worthwhile.

Original Sin (free will)

To answer the problem of evil, Christian philosophers must account for how evil has come about without compromising God's qualities. The attempts to do this are known as **theodicies**.

One theodicy originates from Genesis 3. In this account, Adam and Eve are the originators of evil, not God. They lived close to God in his perfectly good creation and were given one instruction – not to eat fruit from the tree of knowledge of good and evil. God had given Adam and Eve free will so they could choose to obey him. Adam and Eve freely ate the fruit that God had warned them against. This was the first sin.

Their sin brought disorder into the world and removed their innocence. They were left with a tendency to sin that has been passed to all of their descendants. Therefore, evil exists as a result of Original Sin because now all humanity is infected with a natural inclination to do evil things. Humans began perfect but used their free will to become damaged and imperfect. This explanation is accepted in some form by most Christian denominations.

'Soul-making' (Irenaeus and John Hick)

Another suggestion regarding the origin of evil begins in the philosophy of Irenaeus of Lyons (130–202 CE). He argued that God created the ability for evil to exist in the world and he is partially responsible for its existence. Irenaeus took a quote from Genesis:

> 6 So God created mankind in his own image. 9
> *Genesis 1:27*

Irenaeus understood this to mean that God made humans incomplete and the process of being like God is a gradual one. Humans have the potential to become more like God if they freely make good moral choices. To be able to make meaningful free choices, it must be possible to choose evil. As people make choices, they 'make' their souls. When they make good choices, they make themselves better and fit to be in God's presence in heaven. Those who choose evil make their souls imperfect.

John Hick (1922–2012) agreed with Irenaeus. Hick argued that if the purpose of this world is happiness, it is not an effective creation. But if it is to make souls, it is perfect. Hick claimed that the only way people can be free and responsible for their actions is if there are real consequences to them. That means that evil must be a possibility. Humans have been created at an **epistemic distance** from God so they can make truly free decisions that are not influenced by knowledge of him. In this account, humans began imperfect and then used their free will to make themselves, through trial and error, into God's perfect image and likeness.

Some argue that evil was the fault of Adam and Eve, not God

Knowledge recall

1 Define the following concepts: good/evil, free will, suffering. (You can find these definitions on page 57.)
2 Suggest three reasons why the existence of evil is a problem for Christians.
3 Explain two ways that the problem of evil can be answered.

Evaluation practice

4 Give an argument for and an argument against evil being the fault of God.
5 Which argument do you think is the strongest and why?

Islamic beliefs about good, evil and suffering

Specification focus

Good, evil and suffering: Philosophical perspectives on the origin of evil: The Devil tests humans: Quran 2:34, 155; the belief in predestination (Al-Qadr) in relationship to free will.

Philosophical perspectives on the origin of evil

Muslims believe that Allah is:

- One (**tawhid**) – there is only one God who has no equal
- Omnipotent – Allah is all-powerful
- Omniscient – Allah is all-knowing
- Creator – Allah made everything
- Just – Allah is fair
- Merciful – Allah is omnibenevolent; he loves humans and has compassion for them.

But if these are some of Allah's qualities then the existence of evil and suffering in the world can seem problematic, as it is not clear how Allah – the one, merciful, all-powerful creator of everything – can allow humans to suffer.

The Devil tests humans

The Qur'an says that Allah made the first man, Adam, from dust. Allah appointed him as a khalifah and gave him knowledge of the created world, the ability to reason and free will. Allah tested Adam in front of all the angels and Adam was able to answer all of Allah's questions. Allah then asked all of the angels to bow down to Adam in respect.

Iblis (Shaytan), a **jinn**, refused to bow down to Adam and so was expelled from paradise. Iblis believed he was superior to Adam because he was made of fire rather than dust. Iblis was to be punished but begged Allah to postpone his punishment. So Allah allowed Iblis to remain to tempt humans. Iblis caused Adam and Hawwa's (Eve's) sin in **Jannah** and he tempts humans today. Muslims need to show self-control to resist him.

This means that for Muslims, the origin of evil is a mixture of the work of powerful evil beings and of human weakness. It is not the fault of Allah. On the Day of Judgement, Iblis will be punished, as will those who have rejected Allah and failed to resist Iblis.

Islam teaches that good can come from suffering as it enables humans to prepare for the next life. Someone living a life of challenge or struggle has the chance to develop their patience and trust in Allah's mercy and justice. Someone living a life of wealth and advantage has the chance to help those less fortunate. In this way, suffering enables human spiritual development and preparation for the Day of Judgement.

Predestination (Al-Qadr) in relationship to free will

Islam requires Muslims to choose to behave according Allah's will. Those who choose not to live according to the will of Allah can expect to be punished on the Day of Judgement. A good Muslim will follow the Qur'an, the hadiths and Shariah Law when making moral choices.

> 'When We told the angels, "Bow down before Adam," they all bowed. But not Iblis, who refused and was arrogant: he was disobedient.'
> *Qur'an 2:34*

> '**We shall certainly test you** with fear and hunger, and loss of property, lives, and crops. But [Prophet], give good news to those who are steadfast...'
> *Qur'an 2:155*

Useful terms

tawhid – 'oneness' in reference to God and is the basic Muslim belief in the oneness of Allah

Iblis – (Shaytan) the devil/Satan

jinn – a spirit made from smokeless fire (e.g. a demon)

Jannah – paradise

predestination – the belief that all actions are willed by Allah in advance and that he has already chosen some for Jannah and some for Jahannam

Al-Qadr – predestination; one of the Six Articles of Faith in Sunni Islam

Adalat – belief in Allah's justice; one of the Five Roots of Usul ad-Din in Shi'a Islam

However, this raises some problems when it comes to the nature of Allah:

- If people are free beings, then they can control their behaviour and make their own decisions. How then can Allah be said to be in complete control?

- If Allah is all-powerful and all-knowing, then he has supreme control over all that happens. How then can people make free decisions and perform free acts?

- If Allah is the one powerful being in full control of all things, he must have set out people's behaviour and decisions in advance. How then can he be fair and merciful when he hands out **punishment** or reward for behaviour people cannot control (as Allah has already decided it in advance)?

Islam teaches that **free will** must exist because otherwise humans could never show real faith in Allah and all of their actions would be meaningless. Humans would just be robots, doing what they have been programmed to do. However, Allah is the one who has complete control and knowledge over the universe, so **predestination** must be in place, governing all events including human decisions.

On the Day of Judgement, those who obey Allah's will shall be rewarded in Jannah, which is often thought of as a beautiful garden

In the Middle Ages, different schools of Islam argued over the extent to which humanity could be described as free or predestined. Some chose one to the exclusion of the other, but more orthodox theologians tried to combine both positions. Not all Muslims agree, but the generally accepted views held today are outlined below.

The Sunni tradition emphasises **Al-Qadr**, which is one of the Six Articles of Faith. This is because they wish to emphasise Allah's omnipotence. Allah has power over everything in his creation, including all human action. Human beings are both free and predestined because they can choose their actions for themselves, but they can only do so because Allah creates in them the power to act, the choice to act and then the action itself. He is in complete control. Muslims must have faith that Allah is just when he judges them on the Day of Judgement. Muslims cannot understand Allah's plan for themselves.

The Shi'a tradition emphasises the **Adalat** of Allah, which is one of the Five Roots of Usul ad-Din. This is because they believe Allah cannot be blamed for the evil that people do, and they do not accept that Allah will punish people for actions they cannot control. Therefore, Shi'a Muslims believe that Allah will punish or reward people based on the moral choices they freely make for themselves. Although Allah has foreknowledge of the choices people will make and has already decided their fate, people choose for themselves whether to follow Allah's moral guidance in the Qur'an and through the prophets, or whether to ignore it. Therefore, they are punished or rewarded for their free choices.

Read more about predestination on pages 154–155.

Knowledge recall

1 Define the following concepts: free will, suffering, justice. (You can find these definitions on page 57.)
2 List the two sources of evil in the world according to Islam.
3 State two Muslim views on the relationship between free will and predestination.

Evaluation practice

4 Give one reason why some Muslims argue that Allah is in control of human actions and one reason why some argue that humans are in control of themselves.
5 Does it make sense to believe in both reasons at the same time? Explain why/why not.

Skills practice

On these exam practice pages you will see example answers for each of the exam question types: **a**, **b**, **c** and **d**. You can find out more about these on pages 5–9.

Question *(a)*

*Question **(a)** tests your knowledge and understanding. You will always be asked to **define a key concept** in this question. You can find a list of the concepts at the beginning of the chapter.*

(a)	What is meant by 'morality'?	[2]

Student response

Morality is good behaviour.

Improved student response

Morality is about both right and wrong behaviour. For example, rules or principles about whether it is acceptable to kill.

🕐 **Over to You!** Have a try at answering this question:

(a)	What is meant by 'suffering'?	[2]

Helpful hints

To help you answer this question effectively, you could use the check list below to make sure you include the most important things:

- Include a **synonym** for the word 'suffering'.
- Give an **example** of suffering that we see in the media or in general life.

Now give yourself **two minutes** to answer this question by yourself:

(a)	What is meant by 'sin'?	[2]

Question *(b)*

*Question **(b)** tests your knowledge and understanding. It will always ask you to **describe** a belief, a teaching, a practice or an event that is included on the specification.*

(b)	Describe what religions believe makes an act 'wrong'.	[5]

What went well

The candidate has shown appropriate understanding of part of what morality is concerned with.

How to improve

You must show that morality concerns both good and bad (or right and wrong) behaviour.

You should learn the exam board's definition of the word at the start of this chapter.

You could use an example or a synonym for the word 'morality'.

Tip

In this response, adding the words 'rules' and 'principles' shows a deeper understanding of what morality is.

Student response

Christians believe that morality is very important. You should make sure that you obey all the rules of your religion and you should obey the Ten Commandments and the Beatitudes of Jesus. Christians also think that you should use your conscience and that you should be guided by the Holy Spirit. The Pope also teaches Catholics what the rules of their religion are. Christians often disagree about this. For example, some Christians think it is right to perform capital punishment. Others say it is wrong. It is very subjective and there is no right answer to this. Christians often believe what they are told by their priest or vicar and so if they are taught it is wrong, then that is what they believe.

Improved student response

Some Christians believe it is wrong to disobey religious rules as they are absolute and should never be broken. For example, the Ten Commandments say that killing is always wrong. Other Christians believe it is wrong to go against your conscience or the Holy Spirit, so what is wrong is relative to the situation you are in. The Pope's pronouncement and the Catechism teach Catholics what is wrong. They think it is wrong to go against Church tradition but are taught to follow conscience above all else. Therefore, if the Church taught that capital punishment is acceptable, it is wrong to do anything different. However, other Christians may believe that it is always wrong to disrespect God by destroying life because scripture says that all people are made in his image.

Over to You! Have a try at answering this question:

(b) Describe the work of prison chaplains. [5]

Helpful hints

Use the check list below to make sure you include the most important things:

- **Explain** one role or task that prison chaplains do.
- Describe an **example** of how they might perform that role or what acts they might carry out as part of that role.
- Then **repeat** the above process for two more roles or tasks that are performed by chaplains.

Now give yourself **five minutes** to answer this question by yourself:

(b) Describe religious views about the death penalty. [5]

Question (c)

*Question (c) tests your knowledge and understanding. You need to give detailed evidence and reasoning to support your explanation of the topic. For the Themes paper, you will always be asked to **explain two different viewpoints,** but you don't need to evaluate which is the better view.*

(c) Explain, from **two** religions **or two** religious traditions, beliefs about the death penalty. [8]

What went well

The mention of being influenced by a religious authority such as a priest or vicar is important because it gives a reason why someone would consider an act to be wrong.

How to improve

You must focus on the aspect of the question that asks for what makes an act 'wrong'.

You should turn the response around so that it addresses the specific reasons why acts are considered 'wrong' as opposed to 'right'.

You could develop the example so it demonstrates why some might think capital punishment is wrong.

Tip

The best answers will give plenty of evidence or reasoning to support any statements about what makes an act wrong. This candidate talks about and gives examples for:
- absolute rules/laws
- conscience and the Holy Spirit/ relative morality
- Church tradition
- moral principles such as sanctity of life.

Student response

All Muslims agree with the death penalty. They all think that if you have committed a crime then you should pay for it in the same way. So if you have killed someone then you should be killed too. This is the only way for it to be fair. If someone has killed another person then they deserve the death penalty. If they just get life in prison, but then life only means a few years, especially if they are well-behaved in prison, then it is not fair and so there is not much point in the punishment.

Christians do not agree with the death penalty. They don't think that we should ever kill because the Ten Commandments say, 'you shall not kill'. This means that even if one person has killed another person, the state can't kill that other person because it is wrong and against God's law.

Improved student response

Most Muslim countries have the death penalty for the most severe crimes. This is because teachings in the Qur'an and the hadiths support it for crimes like murder or terrorism. The Qur'an teaches that if you have committed a crime then you should pay for it in the same way. 'And the retribution for an evil act is an evil one like it.' So if you have killed someone then you should be killed too. It acts as retribution and a deterrent to stop others doing the same. Some Western Muslims argue punishment should be for reformation and that only Allah can decide when a person should die.

Many Christians do not agree with the death penalty. The Ten Commandments say, 'you shall not kill'. This rule is absolute and can never be broken. Until recently the Catholic Church allowed capital punishment to protect society in accordance with Natural Law. However, the Pope recently pronounced that this is not allowed. Most Christians believe Jesus revised the Old Testament command that we should take revenge by taking an 'eye for an eye', because he said we should 'turn the other cheek.' These Christians argue we should reform rather than take revenge.

Over to You! Have a try at answering this question:

(c)   Explain from **either two** religions **or two** religious traditions, teachings about forgiveness.   [8]

Helpful hints

- Include **two** beliefs – one from one religion and the second from either a different religion or a different religious tradition.
- For each belief give an **example** from religious authority to illustrate it (such as a quote from or reference to scripture, Natural Law, Shariah Law, a papal statement or the hadiths).
- Explain **why** each of the religions or traditions believe this (e.g. they are influenced by beliefs about the sanctity of life or rewards for behaviour in the afterlife).
- Explain **how** people of this faith are expected to behave as a result (e.g. rules about when religious believers should forgive).

What went well

This response addresses two religions as expected in the question. It also talks about the correct material and broadly understands some reasons why a religious person might respond in this way.

How to improve

You must give plenty of evidence from the religion, rather than an opinion, to support the view that is described.

You should make statements that recognise there can be diversity in religious beliefs, e.g. not all Muslims will agree on this matter.

You could include teachings from scripture or other sources of authority.

Tip

Always split your response into two paragraphs for a question (c). This will help to remind you to include **two** religions or traditions.

Study Challenge:

The exam board will only ever ask a question **(c)** in the Themes paper, that asks you to explain two different religious viewpoints on an issue from the specification.

- Look back at the specification focus boxes at the top of the each page in this chapter.
- Choose one area from the list that has not yet appeared in the questions above.
- Write your own **(c)** question on this area that begins with the word 'Explain' and asks for the views of two religions or two religious traditions.
- Now give yourself **eight minutes** to answer this question by yourself.

Question (d)

*Question (d) tests your ability to **evaluate**. This means you need to show you have considered more than one point of view and that you have referred to religion and belief. You will need to be able to make judgements that are supported by detailed reasoning and argument.*

> (d) 'Reform is the main aim of punishment.'
> Discuss this statement showing that you have considered more than one point of view. (You must refer to religion and belief in your answer.) [15]

Student response

Reform means that someone will be made into a better person so they are not likely to sin or commit crime again in the future. The way that criminals are reformed in the UK is by prison or community service. Criminals can be reformed in prison if they can have jobs to do or take education programmes or get counselling. Prison chaplains can help a person in prison to reform and so Christian or Muslim prison chaplains agree that we should try to reform prisoners. If the crime committed by the criminal was not that bad, they might be allowed to do community service instead. This would be through picking up litter or working for a charity. This helps them to pay for the crime they did, but also see why it is important to help people instead of hurting them.

Christians believe that reformation is the main aim of punishment. They teach that Jesus said we should turn the other cheek. Therefore, they know we should show love and forgiveness to people, even if they have done something wrong. They do not believe we should take revenge and so they argue that we should try our best to reform people. Muslims do not believe that reformation is the main aim of punishment. The main aim of punishment for Muslims is retribution or deterrence. It is important that punishments should be as harsh as possible so that people do not want to do the crimes. Therefore, if someone has stolen something, Shariah law would have their hands cut off so they cannot steal again. It is very difficult to reform if the punishment is this harsh. Some Muslims do look at the teaching in the Qur'an that allows them to forgive if they want to. That is up to individual Muslims.

Improved student response

Reform is one aim of punishment that religious people may value, but deterrence, retribution, justice and protecting society are also important to many. God requires justice and it is only fair that if someone has committed a crime then they should receive like for like. The Old Testament requires 'an eye for an eye'. This is nothing to do with reform. However, in the New Testament, Jesus revises this harsh idea of punishment. He says we should turn the other cheek and sends an adulterous woman away saying she should 'sin no more'. Therefore, people should be able to have a new start and reform

What went well

The candidate talks about the correct subject material through most of the response. There is a reasonable, broad understanding of how punishment can be used, and the candidate shows knowledge that some people might see a different purpose for punishment beyond reform. They also attempt to give reasons why some argue that we should reform prisoners, and they give examples of punishment that can be used to aid reform.

How to improve

You must remember that this is an evaluation question rather than one that asks for simple presentation of knowledge and understanding.

You should weigh up the value of the different ideas that are presented to assess whether they are strong or weak ideas.

You could consider how to conclude an answer so the essay ends by responding directly to the question.

Quotes from scripture are incorporated and blended into the writing.

can help them to do this. While reform is important, some people do not want to change. It is important that the victim and the whole society is considered.

Some argue that the main aim for punishment is to protect society. People who follow Natural Law accept that a primary precept is to order society. Reform can be part of that, but it is more important to make sure no one suffers as a victim of crime. The golden rule to love your neighbour includes the victim and we should protect innocent people from criminal activity. However, the best way to protect people is by making sure that criminals stop being criminals, so reforming them helps society more. Many people who commit crimes are themselves victims of poverty or abuse. It is more in line with Jesus' example to show agape and this helps society. Reform and protection of society are both vital aims of punishment and go hand in hand with each other.

The Qur'an says the maim aims for punishment are retribution and deterrence. Reform is too soft, and besides, many punishments are hudud, set by Allah to ensure justice. This is fairer for victims, protects the ummah and is in accordance with Allah's will. However, in countries that have the death penalty or corporal punishment, crime still happens. Punishment as a deterrent does not seem to work, no matter how harsh it is. Reform goes back to the root of the problem and looks at how to solve it. Reform is an aim for punishment, but not the only one. However, it should be the main aim if we want a more compassionate society that upholds religious ideals of peacefulness and love.

A mini judgement is made at the end of each paragraph to refocus on the question.

Possible alternative answers are considered throughout this response.

A range of religious moral principles are considered, e.g. the golden rule and agape.

Good use of specialist vocabulary throughout.

The answer ends with a small conclusion that helps to decide on a judgement and gives a reason for that judgement.

🕐 **Over to You!** Have a try at answering this question:

(d) 'It is impossible to forgive.'
Discuss this statement showing that you have considered more than one point of view. (You must refer to religion and belief in your answer.) [15]

Helpful hints

Think about ways that you can back up your arguments with evidence or examples. The types of sources you can use are:

- The Bible, Church teaching or the creeds (e.g. Jesus' teaching on forgiveness).
- The Qur'an or the hadiths (e.g. Shariah Law that enables forgiveness).
- Anecdotes from 'real life' stories you have learned (e.g. a religious person who forgave).
- Brief fictitious examples that demonstrate a general principle, e.g. the welfare of a victim may come before the welfare of an assailant. Therefore, it may be unfair to expect a victim to forgive if it causes them distress or harm to do so.

Now give yourself **fifteen minutes** to answer this question by yourself:

(d) 'The existence of suffering proves there is no God.'
Discuss this statement showing that you have considered more than one point of view. (You must refer to religion and belief in your answer.) [15]

Tip

A good starting place for answering an evaluative question is to consider what you think about it. Once you have an opinion, you can think about why you have that opinion, and then why the religions you have studied might agree or disagree with you.

Tip

Blending quotes into your writing to use as evidence to back up a statement is a very sophisticated way of writing. It is a great way of backing up an argument and showing your understanding at the same time.

Chapter 4:
Issues of human rights

Introduction

Human rights are the things that we are all entitled to simply because we are human. Throughout history, people have disagreed over who qualifies for these basic rights and how they should be protected. This chapter considers issues of human rights from Christian and Muslim perspectives. It focuses on wealth, poverty and race as areas in which people may experience injustice, prejudice and discrimination. It also considers how conflicts may arise between people and the state in which they live.

Things to remember:

- Both Christian and Muslim teachings have been interpreted to be prejudiced against certain groups of people at different times in history, or by particular groups or denominations. For example, some have believed their faith teaches that women or people of colour are not entitled to the same rights as men or white people.
- Both Christian and Muslim groups have been active in battles against prejudice at various times in history. Some have fought against social injustice because of their faith, such as Martin Luther King Jr.
- Prejudice involves the inner thoughts that we have, while discrimination is about the actions that we perform. Prejudiced ideas often lead to discriminatory behaviour. For example, if a person believes that other faiths are somehow bad, they may support action to restrict them, such as forcibly removing a hijab.
- There is a delicate balance between the rights of individuals and the protection of society. For example, it is important that we can speak freely and publicly. However, it is also important that we stop the spread of hate. These two values may conflict and we must decide how to manage them effectively.

Concepts

Censorship – the practice of suppressing and limiting access to material considered obscene, offensive or a threat to security. People may also be restricted in their speech by censorship laws

Discrimination – acts of treating groups of people, or individuals differently, based on prejudice

Extremism – believing in and supporting ideas that are very far from what most people consider correct or reasonable

Human rights – the basic entitlements of all human beings, afforded to them simply because they are human

Personal conviction – something a person strongly feels or believes in

Prejudice – pre-judging; judging people to be inferior or superior without cause

Absolute poverty – an acute state of deprivation, whereby a person cannot access the most basic of their human needs

Relative poverty – a standard of poverty measured in relation to the standards of a society in which a person lives, for example living on less than X% of average UK income

Social justice – promoting a fair society by challenging injustice and valuing diversity. Ensuring that everyone has equal access to provisions, equal opportunities and rights

Christianity and human rights

Christian beliefs about the dignity of human life

Christians believe that all human life is created by God and is therefore sacred. This means that all human beings, regardless of their skin colour, gender, or any other aspect of their being, are equally valued in God's sight.

The Bible teaches that human beings were made *imago Dei*. Being made in God's image means that some of God's characteristics are reflected in human beings. Distinct from other animals, humans have the capacity for morality, rational thought, personal relationships and free will. This is what gives humans individual worth and value.

Christianity also teaches that Jesus Christ died and rose again for the forgiveness of sin for all human beings, regardless of their social status or the colour of their skin. The Bible teaches that Jesus frequently aligned himself with the poor, the outcasts, the sick, and people of different social, racial and religious groups.

However, it should be recognised that the Church has not always taught or acted in such a way as to treat every human life with dignity. Some Christians have interpreted the Bible in ways that enable or encourage **prejudice** and **discrimination**.

For many Christians, the Universal Declaration of Human Rights is a reflection of the principle of human dignity. It was proclaimed by the United Nations General Assembly in 1948 as a collection of 30 protected **human rights** for all people in all nations. It recognises the inherent dignity of all members of humanity and is seen as essential in guarding against the mistreatment of people based on their race, religion or social status.

> 'All human beings are born free and equal in dignity and rights. They are endowed with reason and conscience and should act towards one another in a spirit of brotherhood. '
> *Article 1, Universal Declaration of Human Rights (UDHR)*

Agape in action

Christians believe they should reflect the behaviour of Jesus in their everyday lives. Jesus is shown in the Bible healing the sick, eating with the poor and preaching that people should care for each other.

Underlying any Christian belief in moral behaviour is the teaching of **agape**. Agape is unconditional love or care for other people, and many Christians believe they should act in a way that shows agape to all people.

Putting agape into action means doing something practical to help people whose human rights are not being respected. For example, different Christian denominations have spoken out to condemn governments or institutions that fail to treat people equally. They also work to change their own discriminatory practices.

There has been significant work within various branches of the Christian church to promote human rights. The World Council of Churches supports its member

Specification focus

Human rights and social justice: Christian beliefs, teachings and attitudes towards the dignity of human life: Genesis 1:26–27; Christian practices to promote human rights including equality: agape in action.

> 'Then God said, "Let us make mankind in our image, in our likeness, so that they may rule over the fish in the sea and the birds in the sky, over the livestock and all the wild animals, and over all the creatures that move along the ground." So God created mankind in his own image, **in the image of God he created them; male and female he created them. '**
> *Genesis 1:26–27*

> 'Love your neighbour as yourself. '
> *Mark 12:31*

Useful terms

imago Dei – a Latin term that means 'in the image of God'
agape – a Greek word that translates as 'unconditional love' or 'charity'
segregation – laws enforcing white and black people to be separated, e.g. on buses or at school

churches in working together, through conferences and missionary activity, to support people exposed to injustice. The Catholic Church has a body of doctrine called Catholic Social Teaching that concerns social justice, wealth and oppression. It was the basis for a movement known as Liberation Theology in Latin America in the 1960s.

Read more about the World Council of Churches on page 139.

Martin Luther King Jr was a Baptist minister who grew up in the USA at a time when there was **segregation** between black and white people in many areas of life. He led the Civil Rights Movement by campaigning peacefully for a change in law to give black people equal rights. King led protests such as the Montgomery Bus Boycott after Rosa Parks was arrested for refusing to give up her seat to a white passenger on a bus. He gave sermons and spoke at demonstrations that resulted in the Civil Rights Act being passed in 1964, bringing an end to legal segregation and allowing black Americans to vote. His work caused him to be stabbed, arrested and eventually assassinated in 1968. He put his own wellbeing to one side to show agape because he believed that all people were created equal.

> ❛He has shown you, O man, what is good. And what does the Lord require of You? To act justly and to love mercy and to walk humbly with your God.❜
> *Micah 6:8*

Oscar Romero was a Roman Catholic priest who lived in El Salvador, in Latin America during a time of political unrest. The poor were oppressed by the government who censored the press and persecuted the poor. The movement known as Liberation Theology arose from a belief that Christians have a responsibility to help the poor and free them from oppression. Romero supported Liberation Theology as liberation for the poor. When he saw a friend assassinated by the government for creating self-reliance groups for the poor, he began to speak out. He held meetings and broadcast sermons that spoke out against the oppression. He listed names of people who had disappeared and then returned, or who had been tortured or killed by the government. He wrote to world leaders asking for them to withdraw support for the government. The government began encouraging the killing of priests as an act of patriotism. In 1980, soldiers shot and killed Romero as he celebrated the Eucharist.

In May 2020, Christian groups joined other religious and non-religious organisations and individuals to participate in **Black Lives Matter** protests. These protests were provoked by the public killing of George Floyd, a black man who was arrested in Minneapolis by a police officer who pinned him to the ground by his neck. Prominent Christians across the world, including Pope Francis, spoke out publicly against the treatment of black people within systems of white privilege and advantage. The Catholic bishop Mark Seitz kneeled alongside other priests for eight minutes in prayer, holding signs reading 'Black Lives Matter'. Faith leaders conducted silent walks to the spot where George Floyd was killed and prayed in silence. Other Christians joined in marches or gave food and medical supplies to protesters outside St. John's Church near the White House.

In 2020, Christian groups joined with other organisations to join the Black Lives Matter protests

Knowledge recall

1 Define the following concepts: prejudice, discrimination, human rights. (You can find these definitions on page 79.)
2 Give two reasons why many Christians believe that all people are equal.
3 State two examples of how different Christians have worked to put agape into action.

Evaluation practice

4 Give one reason why some Christians might think it is best to fight injustice by protesting and one reason why others might prefer to give to charities that support the fight against injustice.
5 Which of these views do you find most persuasive? Give two reasons why.

Islam and human rights

Islamic beliefs about the dignity of human life

The Qur'an teaches that all humans are created and loved by Allah. Allah has created all the children of Adam as equals and appointed them to be his khalifahs or representatives on earth. All humans are therefore granted dignity and honour by Allah himself.

Islam teaches that since all the children of Adam are given honour, **discrimination** based on race, religion and gender should be rejected. All humans are in the family of Allah and all human life is sacred and to be protected. **Human rights** are therefore for all human beings, for the protection of their dignity and freedom. The Qur'an states this clearly.

Muslims believe human rights have been granted by Allah himself and it is a religious duty to protect them, so that each person can live their life and fulfil their own duty to Allah.

In 1990, several Muslim countries signed the Cairo Declaration on Human Rights in Islam. This declaration differs from the Universal Declaration of Human Rights because it is written in accordance with Shariah Law instead of Christian principles. It declares all humans are sacred and of equal status as descendants of Adam, subordinate only to Allah. It forbids discrimination based on things like race, belief, gender, religion or social status. It stipulates that human life should be protected, including civilians in times of war.

The Cairo Declaration has been criticised for giving men different rights and responsibilities to women in marriage and law, and for failing to guarantee religious freedom to reject Islam. Conversely, Muslim countries challenge the Universal Declaration for its acceptance of homosexuality.

Ummah in action

The ummah is the Muslim community. This extends across the whole world. When Muslims pray, fast or celebrate festivals, they all do so together. In the ummah, all Muslims are supposed to be equal regardless of wealth or skin colour. This means that all Muslims have a duty to care for all members of the ummah.

Islam makes it a duty to support the poor. The third pillar of Islam is zakat (or zakah), which is commanded by the Qur'an. This is the duty for all Muslims to give 2.5% of their surplus income each year to charity. In Muslim countries it is taken as a tax that is given to the poor and needy, converts who are starting a new way of life, prisoners of war and people in debt.

> ❝Alms are meant only for the poor, the needy, those who administer them, those whose hearts need winning over, to free slaves and help those in debt, for God's cause of Allah and for travellers in need. This is ordained by God; God has the knowledge to decide.❞
> *Qur'an 9:60*

Specification focus

Human rights and social justice: Islamic beliefs, teachings and attitudes towards the dignity of human life: Qur'an 5:32; Islamic practices to promote human rights including equality: ummah in action.

> ❝We have honoured the children of Adam and carried them by land and sea; We have provided good sustenance for them and favoured them specially above many of those We have created.❞
> *Qur'an 17:70*

> ❝On account of [his deed], We decreed to the Children of Israel that **if anyone kills a person – unless in retribution for murder or spreading corruption in the land – it is as if he kills all mankind,** while if any saves a life it is as if he saves the lives of all mankind. Our messengers came to them with clear signs, but many of them continued to commit excesses in the land.❞
> *Qur'an 5:32*

Useful term

Taliban – a political and military fundamentalist movement that has been condemned for its harsh interpretation of Shariah Law

Sadaqah differs from zakah because it is voluntary rather than compulsory and no fixed amount is required. It is considered a sign of true faith and honourable behaviour to keep the ummah healthy. It is not just financial giving but includes kind words or compassion. The purpose of sadaqah is to help people in need, but this is not limited to the poor.

Giving sadaqah might include volunteering for or supporting organisations that help others in need. The Islamic Human Rights Commission (IHRC), based in London, is one such organisation. It runs campaigns for justice for members of the ummah across the world. This includes advocating for people who have been subject to discrimination or hate crimes and protesting human rights abuses around the world.

> **'** A kind word and forgiveness is better than a charitable deed followed by hurtful [words]. **'**
> *Qur'an 2:263*

> **'** Why should you not fight in God's cause and for those oppressed men, women, and children who cry out, "Lord, rescue us from this town whose people are oppressors! By Your grace, give us a protector and give us a helper!?" **'**
> *Qur'an 4:75*

Malala Yousafzai was 12 years old when she became an advocate for human rights. The **Taliban** had banned girls from attending school in her home of Swat Valley, Pakistan. But Malala's father, a social activist who ran the school she attended, encouraged her to join his fight for girls' education. Malala began blogging for BBC Urdu under a false name about life under the Taliban. She gave talks, appeared on television, and continued to attend school when it was open. In 2012, when she was 15, gunmen boarded her school bus and shot her three times for her activist work. After recovering, Malala continued her education in the UK and worked to raise the profile of human rights issues around the world by speaking, writing, and starting the Malala Fund to open schools for girls.

Muslim charities like Islamic Relief and Ummah Relief International encourage Muslims to give their zakah or sadaqah to help people in extreme need. They provide emergency relief and humanitarian services to vulnerable people around the world. Inspired by their Islamic faith, these charities value the sanctity of all human life and promise relief for humans regardless of their race, religion or gender by providing water, food, shelter, health care and education.

Malala is famous for her work promoting the education of all girls

Knowledge recall

1 Define the following concepts: discrimination, human rights, relative/absolute poverty. (You can find these definitions on page 79.)
2 List three reasons why Islam rejects discrimination against any other human being.
3 State two different ways in which Muslims might show the ummah in action.

Evaluation practice

4 Give one example of how Muslim law and behaviour defends human rights and one example of how they may not according to a Western perspective.
5 Which is the strongest piece of evidence to show Muslim belief about equality? Why do you think this is strongest?

Christianity and social justice

Specification focus

Human rights and social justice: An example of conflict between personal conviction and the laws of a country; censorship, freedom of religious expression and religious extremism.

An example of conflict between personal conviction and the laws of a country

The Bible indicates that Christians should obey the laws of their country. Christians living in a **democracy**, may experience no conflict between the law and their faith when freedom and equality are encouraged by both. However, if laws are passed that conflict with religious laws, the believer must make a choice between following their **personal conviction** and following the law of the land. By following the laws of their country, they may violate their faith and do something they believe is wrong. By following their faith, they may risk punishment within the legal system.

On page 81 you read about Martin Luther King Jr and Oscar Romero, who broke or challenged the law and were punished for promoting human rights in accordance with their faith. Here are some more examples:

Corrie ten Boom lived in the Netherlands during World War II. She said she was forced to decide how a Christian should act when evil was in power. She and her family were Christians who turned their home into a hiding place for Jewish people fleeing the Nazis. She and her family were captured and arrested, but the Nazi soldiers were unable to find the people she had hidden, and they were rescued.

In 2019, Christian Climate Action joined with Extinction Rebellion to disrupt rail travel in London. They climbed onto the roof of a train in Canary Wharf, sang hymns and prayed to protest climate change. Their protest was peaceful, but it broke the law and so the group was arrested. Members of the group argued that lawful methods of protest had been ineffective, and that their actions were an example of Christian love towards future generations who would be affected by climate change.

> 'Let everyone be subject to the governing authorities, for there is no authority except that which God has established.'
> *Romans 13:1*

Some see groups like Christian Climate Action as extremists, but not everyone agrees

Censorship

In the UK, the law is designed to balance the desire for freedom of religious expression with the requirement to control **extremism**. Part of creating that balance involves placing restrictions on what people can say and when or how they say it.

Censorship involves suppressing or controlling materials and information that some people find offensive or which might be dangerous. This might mean restricting people's access to certain books or films, or regulating what they say publicly. Some social media platforms remove images that they think might be offensive. UK law punishes speech that is designed to stir up violence. This is censorship.

- Censorship is useful when it protects society against the spread of racist or sexist violence.
- Censorship is harmful when it takes away people's freedom to express their desires for political, religious or moral change.

Useful terms

democracy – a system of government, elected or run by the people
secular – non-religious; having no relationship to religion
evangelism – preaching the gospel to others with the intention of converting them to the Christian faith

Freedom of religious expression

Freedom of religious expression is the ability of a religious person or organisation to share what they believe in public. This means that a Christian could wear a cross as a sign of faith, or a church could advertise their faith on posters in the street. Some countries prefer society to be **secular**. Others have a religious government that wishes for the whole society to observe their religious laws. In some cases, religious expression may sometimes be restricted by laws that ban religious advertising or the wearing of religious symbols.

- Freedom of religious expression is helpful when it allows individuals the freedom to choose from a variety of options concerning their own beliefs, or helps give people a sense of belonging to their faith.
- It is unhelpful when it upsets others. For instance, Christians protesting outside abortion clinics have been accused of upsetting vulnerable women who need help.

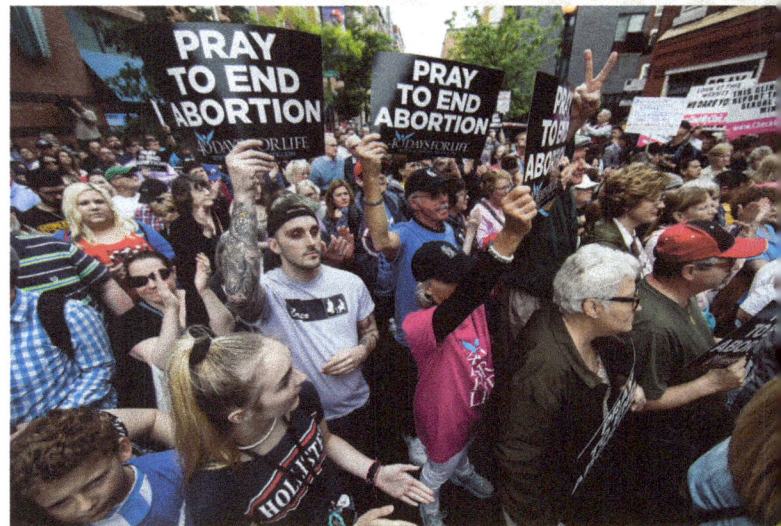

Anti-abortion protesters exercise their freedom of religious expression but can cause distress to vulnerable women

Religious extremism

Religious extremism involves views or behaviours that are not consistent with commonly held beliefs about what is reasonable and what may cause violence or harm. For some religious people, their beliefs are so important to them that they feel the need to take extreme action to maintain their beliefs or encourage others to do the same. For instance, people who have violently attacked mosques because of their own religious beliefs could be considered to be terrorists or extremists.

- Extremism is a problem when it disrupts society or harms other people. Christian extremists, such as the organisation 'Army of God', fight abortion with violence by using bombs or kidnapping medical professionals.
- Groups like Christian Climate Action are not terrorists but some have labelled them as extremists. Others argue they are needed to fight injustice and that they work to improve the world.

In the UK, people are legally allowed to follow any religion or denomination they like without fear of persecution. If someone is targeted for their religious beliefs then they are protected by law. It is a criminal offence (a 'hate crime') to attack or harm someone because of their religion.

Article 18 of the Universal Declaration of Human Rights states that everyone has the right to freedom of thought, conscience and expression. This allows people to do whatever their religion requires, alone or as part of their community.

Christians are taught they should share their faith in the salvation of Christ with other people, in the hope that they become Christians too. This is known as **evangelism** and it requires freedom of expression. Non-Christians may find this annoying or even offensive. Most Christians argue that evangelism should be done with kindness, but some extremist groups, like the Westboro Baptist Church in the USA, express their beliefs through actions like picketing funerals.

If freedom of expression is restricted in some cases to protect against offence, people must accept that their own freedom might be affected by these restrictions. Some worry that this means people like Corrie ten Boom or Martin Luther King Jr could be viewed as extremists.

Knowledge recall

1 Define the following concepts: censorship, extremism, personal conviction. (You can find these definitions on page 79.)
2 Choose one example of a Christian whose personal conviction has conflicted with the laws of their country. List two ways that they challenged the laws of their country.
3 State two examples of how Christians might want to demonstrate their faith in a public way.

Evaluation practice

4 Give one reason why censorship might be a good thing and one reason why it might be a bad thing.
5 Which of these views do you think is the most persuasive? Give a reason why.

Islam and social justice

Specification focus

Human rights and social justice: An example of conflict between personal conviction and the laws of a country; censorship, freedom of religious expression and religious extremism (including Islamophobia).

An example of conflict between personal conviction and the laws of a country

Many Muslims live in countries that are not governed by Shariah Law and sometimes they may experience a clash between their religious faith and the expectations of society. When this occurs, a Muslim risks punishment for observing their faith. This is especially challenging for Muslims who live in Western societies that are secular or Christian in outlook.

Shariah Law is the basis of the legal system in many Muslim countries, and so religious law and the law of the land are the same. Here there may be difficulties for Muslims who feel the interpretation of the law in their country is too severe. On page 83 you read about Malala Yousafzai, whose personal convictions about the education of girls conflicted with the laws of the Taliban. Below are some more examples of people who have experienced conflict between their faith and the law.

Manal al-Sharif is an observant Muslim woman who considers herself to be 'Liberal'. She became widely known in 2011 when she cofounded and led the 'Women2Drive' movement, challenging the ban on women driving in Saudi Arabia, where she lived. She uploaded films to social media that showed her driving a car, and was arrested and imprisoned several times as a result. After a long campaign, in 2017 Saudi women were given the right to drive.

France is a secular society that does not welcome visible signs of religious belonging. In 2004, a law was passed forbidding the wearing of any obvious religious symbols in public schools. This led to many girls protesting by refusing to remove their **hijab** and being expelled as a result. In 2011, a further law was passed banning the **niqab** and the **burqa** in public places. This led to peaceful protests in Paris by veiled Muslim women who were arrested, detained and even fined for breaking the law.

Wearing the hijab, burqa or niqab in France conflicts with the laws of the country but is an important part of faith for some Muslim women

Censorship

Shariah Law means that in some Muslim countries there is **censorship** of materials that are deemed offensive to Islam. Some hadiths prohibit the use of visual images of the prophet Muhammad. Therefore, some countries ban films or images that depict him.

In the UK, Muslims must navigate both Shariah Law and the law of the country. This means there may be times when they come across material offensive to Islam. For example, UK law requires sex education to be taught in schools but in 2019, some Muslim families protested outside their children's primary school in Birmingham because they were concerned that the lessons went against Islamic teaching about homosexuality.

Freedom of religious expression

Shariah Law allows non-Muslims who live in Muslim countries to be protected from abuse or ridicule, and to follow their own religion within the laws of the

Useful terms

hijab – a scarf that covers the head and neck but not the face

niqab – a veil for the face that leaves the eyes clear and is paired with a full head and body covering

burqa – a one-piece veil that covers the face and body with a mesh screen to see through

revert – when a non-Muslim becomes a Muslim; they 'revert' because they return to the state that Allah created them in

jihad – to struggle or strive for Allah. The lesser jihad is the outward struggle to remove evil from the world and has been used to justify some military or even terrorist activity

country. No one should ever be forced to believe in Allah. This is confirmed in the Cairo Declaration of Human Rights in Islam, which prohibits any use of force to change a person's faith.

However, Muslims believe that while other religions are to be tolerated, they are not correct. Muslims want to encourage non-Muslims to **revert** to Islam and so they share their beliefs with other people. This requires freedom of religious expression.

In Islam, apostasy is a sin that Allah will punish in the afterlife. However, there is disagreement over whether there should be a punishment for it in this life too. Some Muslims argue that people should be free to leave Islam if they wish. Others point out that some hadiths say an apostate should receive the death penalty.

In the UK, religious belief is a protected characteristic. This means that no one should suffer **discrimination** for their religion and so Muslims should be able to follow their faith freely. In practice, many Muslims do experience abuse from people who do not understand their faith or are fearful of it.

Religious extremism and Islamophobia

Religious **extremism** involves having religious views that are very different from most believers. Islamic extremists have had a great deal of attention in the media since the 9/11 attacks in 2001, followed by smaller incidents in London, France and other places around the world. Moderate Muslims firmly condemn these actions and the Muslim Council of Britain makes it clear that extremist action does not represent the views of British Muslims.

Some extremist Muslim groups have argued that their duty to perform **jihad** means they should take up arms in their struggle to remove evil from society. Extremist groups like Al Qaeda or Boko Haram say they must fight to create an Islamic state governed by Shariah Law. Western governments and mainstream Muslims view these groups as terrorists.

Islamophobia describes a **prejudice** against Muslims that result in harmful actions against them. Some people have blamed all Muslims for the extremist attacks that have occurred around the world. It can often result in Muslim people being insulted, intimidated or even physically attacked. In 2019, a gunman committed a terrorist attack at two mosques in Christchurch, New Zealand, killing 51 people and injuring another 50 in an attack on Muslim migrants. He was sentenced to life in prison without parole.

Many Muslim organisations have arranged activities to try to educate people about Islam so they will feel less fearful. The Muslim Council of Britain has helped over 250 mosques hold open days to welcome people from all faiths and none, to build relationships in the community.

In 2019, New Zealand Prime Minister Jacinda Ardern vowed to work to end extremism after the Christchurch attacks

Knowledge recall

1 Define the following concepts: censorship, extremism, prejudice. (You can find these definitions on page 79.)
2 Choose an example of one Muslim whose personal conviction has conflicted with the laws of their country. List two ways that they challenged their country's laws.
3 State two different examples of how Islam allows freedom of religion.

Evaluation practice

4 Give two reasons why some people might argue that religious people should break a country's laws when they conflict with their faith, and two reasons why some think they should not.
5 Which of these views do you find most persuasive? Give two reasons why.

Christianity, prejudice and discrimination

Specification focus

Prejudice and discrimination: Christian beliefs, teachings and attitudes towards prejudice and discrimination: Galatians 3:27–29; Christian beliefs, teachings and attitudes towards racial prejudice and discrimination, including Martin Luther King's teachings on equality.

Christian attitudes towards prejudice and discrimination

Christians believe that all people are created by God and all human life is sacred. This means that no one is more important or special than anyone else, so there is no basis for prejudice. This view is supported in scripture:

> ❛For all of you who were baptised into Christ have clothed yourselves with Christ. **There is neither Jew nor Gentile, neither slave nor free, nor is there male and female, for you are all one in Christ Jesus.** If you belong to Christ, then you are Abraham's seed, and heirs according to the promise.❜
> *Galatians 3:27–29*

- Being 'baptised into Christ' suggests having a close personal relationship with him.
- Clothing 'yourself' with Christ is like being adopted, taking on his appearance.
- 'All' Christians are given this gift, no matter their race, social status or gender.
- To be 'one' is to be like a single person. There is no distinction between people in the Christian faith.
- To be 'heirs' is to take a privileged position, but this is available to everyone who has accepted Christ.

In the UK there are laws that prevent people from discriminating against others based on **protected characteristics** such as race, gender, sexuality, disability, age and religion. However, despite the teaching in Galatians, some would argue that Christians still discriminate against others. For example, the Bible says that women can never have authority over men. Therefore, women in the Catholic and Orthodox Churches are not allowed into the priesthood. In the Church of England women can now be vicars and bishops, but this was not always the case.

Christians today can be the victims of **discrimination** and are persecuted in some countries. For instance, in North Korea, an Atheist country, it is illegal to be a Christian and those who are may be held in detention camps.

Christian attitudes towards racial prejudice and discrimination

There are some passages in the Bible that have been used to justify racist behaviour and slavery. For example:

- The Ten Commandments do not forbid slave ownership. They only forbid people from being jealous of their neighbour's slave.
- St Paul returned a runaway slave to his master. He did not condemn slavery and neither did Jesus.

However, Jesus did not endorse racism. The story of the Good Samaritan instructs Christians to love their neighbour regardless of racial origins. Samaritans and Jews were enemies, but in the story help was given anyway.

Many Christians today follow the loving approach of Jesus by working against racism. For example, the World Council of Churches is an **ecumenical** organisation that challenges its member churches to address racism and spearheads campaigns against racism.

In 2020, the Archbishop of Canterbury said he was ashamed of the Church of England's history of racism. The General Synod backed a motion to apologise for racism in the Church of England and to stamp out conscious or unconscious racism.

> ❛I do not permit a woman to teach or to assume authority over a man; she must be quiet.❜
> *1 Timothy 2:12*

Useful terms

protected characteristics – a quality of a person that the law keeps safe from harm

ecumenical – encouraging the different Christian churches to unite

non-violent direct action – using civil disobedience that causes no harm to people or property to bring about political change, e.g. sit-ins, strikes and blockades rather than petitions or negotiation

Organisations like the Committee for Minority Ethnic Anglican Concerns (CMEAC) and the Catholic Association for Racial Justice (CARJ) work to support black, Asian and minority ethnic (BAME) people in their churches. They aim to increase their inclusion of BAME people, eliminate racism and support cultural understanding.

Racial Justice Sunday is an annual event that is observed by British Christian churches on the second Sunday in February. It focuses on services, fundraising events and prayers that support inclusion and racial equality.

Martin Luther King's teachings on equality

Martin Luther King Jr was an American Baptist minister and civil rights activist who fought against racism in the 1950s and 60s.

One of King's teachings was **non-violent direct action**. King founded the Southern Christian Leadership Conference, a group committed to achieving full equality for African Americans through non-violent protest. Its motto was 'Not one hair on one head of one person should be harmed'.

Read more about Martin Luther King Jr on page 81.

King wrote the civil rights manifesto known as 'Letter from Birmingham Jail' while in prison for his non-violent campaigning. This letter particularly addressed a group of white clergymen who had argued he should be patient rather than disrupt society in his fight for equality. King taught that Christians should take action rather than be passive witnesses to injustice.

King was motivated by the love of Christ. He taught that the loving thing to do was to fight injustice with love rather than hate. He was accused of being an **extremist** but argued that Christ too was an extremist. He wrote: 'The world is in dire need of creative extremists' and 'Will we be extremists for hate or for love?'

King taught that people should act in accordance with their conscience, even if it means breaking the law. He quoted Augustine, saying 'an unjust law is no law at all.' He claimed that Christians should break a law like segregation if conscience tells them it is unjust. They must also accept the punishment to raise people's awareness of the need for **social justice**.

King led the 1963 march on Washington that helped to bring about the Civil Rights Act and the Voting Rights Act. It ended with his most famous speech, which showed his motivation for equality for all: 'I have a dream that one day this nation will rise up, live out the true meaning of its creed: we hold these truths to be self-evident, that all men are created equal.'

King argued that one of the biggest problems for black people were Christians who prefer to wait peacefully rather than strive for justice

Knowledge recall

1 Define the following concepts: discrimination, human rights, social justice. (You can find these definitions on page 79.)
2 List three reasons why Christianity believes all people have equal status.
3 State two examples of Christian individuals or organisations working to end racism in today's society.

Evaluation practice

4 Give one reason why some Christians might support Martin Luther King's approach of non-violent direct action and one reason why some might argue for taking a different approach (e.g. patience or even violent action).
5 Which reason seems to be more consistent with Christian teaching and why?

Islam, prejudice and discrimination

Specification focus

Prejudice and discrimination: Islamic belief, teachings and attitudes towards prejudice and discrimination: Qur'an 5:8, 49:13; Islamic beliefs, teachings and attitudes towards racial prejudice and discrimination, including the actions of the Christian/Muslim Forum.

Islamic attitudes towards prejudice and discrimination

Islam teaches that all human beings are created by Allah from the same substance and deserve equal treatment. Any differences between individuals are a sign of Allah's creative power. Some hadiths suggest that Allah sent his angels to collect different types of soil to create humans, implying that diversity was part of Allah's plan.

The ummah is the worldwide community of Muslims. Members of the ummah are expected to perform the same religious responsibilities regardless of race, social status or gender, such as the performance of salah. When Muslims perform Hajj, they all wear the same simple white robes that show they are all equal before Allah. The Cairo Declaration on Human Rights in Islam states that every human being is equal.

> ❛People, **We created you all from a single man and a single woman, and made you into races and tribes so that you should get to know one another.** In God's eyes, the most honoured of you are the ones most mindful of Him: God is all knowing, all aware.❜
> *Qur'an 49:13*

- Allah points out that everyone's origins are the same.
- Division of people into families and nations is natural, but this does not demand inequality or **discrimination**. It is a way of cooperating together.
- The only basis for superiority is moral excellence.

Islam teaches that moral excellence is the only basis for one person being superior to another. This must be earned through correct behaviour, not through skin colour, gender or social status. Muhammad taught that those of other faiths, such as Christians and Jews, should be treated with tolerance and respect.

> ❛You who believe, be steadfast in your devotion to God and bear witness impartially: **do not let hatred of others lead you away from justice,** but adhere to justice, for that is closer to awareness of God. Be mindful of God: God is well aware of all that you do.❜
> *Qur'an 5:8*

- This verse is about being fair-minded regardless of personal feelings.
- Bearing witness is about Muslims offering their own honest accounts in a court of law.
- There is no room for bias in the treatment of others.

However, Muslims today are often accused of **prejudice** and are the victims of it. For example, Islam teaches that men and women, while equal, are created for different roles. This means Westerners sometimes feel that Islam discriminates against women. Muslim countries may have laws that govern women's clothing or their voting rights, yet men do not experience the same restrictions. Women may be attacked in some countries or imprisoned for not wearing a hijab or burqa. However, in the West, many have been attacked or arrested for wearing it.

Statistics about hate crime show that many Muslims suffer abuse as a result of people associating them with extremist groups such as **ISIS**. Muslim organisations have had to work hard to try to educate people about Islam to combat Islamophobia. 'Visit My Mosque' is an annual event organised by the Muslim Council of Britain. Mosques open and provide activities to give people the chance to ask questions and understand the role that the mosque plays in the local community.

Read about more examples of discrimination against Muslim women on pages 86–87.

Useful terms

ISIS – a terrorist military group that has been condemned for their harsh interpretation of Shariah Law and violent attacks

muezzin – the person appointed to recite and lead the call to prayer at a mosque

Islamic attitudes towards racial prejudice and discrimination

Islam condemns racism in the same way that it condemns any other form of discrimination. There is a story from the hadiths in which Muhammad was angry with an associate, Abu Dhar, for having made racist comments to Bilal ibn Rabah about his Ethiopian heritage. Muhammad reminded Abu Dhar that the only way for one person to be superior to another is through moral excellence.

Muhammad selected Bilal ibn Rabah as his first **muezzin**. Bilal was a former slave who had refused to renounce Islam under torture and had the responsibility of distributing funds to those in need, thus showing his moral excellence.

In Muhammad's last sermon it is believed he said:

Open days are a good opportunity for mosques to interact positively with non-Muslim members of the community

> ❝ An Arab has no superiority over a non-Arab nor a non-Arab has any superiority over an Arab; also a white has no superiority over a black nor a black has any superiority over a white except by piety and good action. ❞

There are many Muslim individuals and organisations that work to combat racism in society.

Malcom X was an African American civil rights leader in the 1950s and 60s. He originally promoted black supremacy and even urged his followers to use violent resistance. However, he experienced a change of outlook while on Hajj, when he felt able to share his thoughts and ideas with Muslims of all races. This caused him to campaign for integration as a solution to racial problems in America. He founded the Organisation of Afro-American Unity to help highlight the importance of **human rights** for black people all over the world and respect between people regardless of skin colour.

The Christian Muslim Forum was founded in London in 2006. The aim of the forum is to build inter-faith relationships and work for a greater understanding between religions. While there are differences between Christians and Muslims, the forum recognises that they also have a lot in common. Both faiths regard the freedom of religion as vital and consider themselves to have a duty to show love to others and to build peace.

The forum is run by representatives from different traditions of both faiths. They aim to stand together in times of need, such as after violent attacks on mosques. They run church and mosque twinning programmes, women's and youth activities, and residential trips for believers from both religions.

Knowledge recall

1 Define the following concepts: prejudice, personal conviction, censorship. (You can find these definitions on page 79.)
2 Give two examples of Muslim teaching about equality.
3 Describe two different ways in which Muslims might work to help fight prejudice.

Evaluation practice

4 Give one reason why some people think Islam discriminates against some groups of people, and one reason why Muslims argue that Islam does not.
5 Which of these is the strongest argument and why?

Christian attitudes to poverty and wealth

Ethical considerations about acquisition and use of wealth

Christian teaching says that wealth is not the most important thing in life, and that those who are too attached to their wealth will find it hard to prepare for God's kingdom.

Christian teaching also says that if a person has wealth, they must use it for the benefit of those who have little. Jesus taught his followers that the rich should use their wealth to help those in need and that the poor would be rewarded in paradise. It is greed and love of money that causes social injustice, not money itself. Wealth among the early Christians was shared voluntarily among the community in accordance with Jesus' teachings.

In the Gospel of Luke, the story of the rich man and Lazarus is a parable that was told by Jesus to a large crowd containing Pharisees (who had been said to 'love money'). Here is a summary of the parable:

> There was a rich man living in luxury while a beggar, Lazarus, lay at his gate. When the rich man died, he was sent to hell. He looked up and saw Lazarus, far away in heaven at Abraham's side. The rich man called for Lazarus to bring water. Abraham refused, saying "In your lifetime you received your good things, while Lazarus received bad things, but now he is comforted here, and you are in agony." The rich man asked that Lazarus be sent to warn his brothers so they would not meet the same fate. Abraham again refused since the brothers could listen to the teachings of Moses. The rich man argued that the brothers would be more likely to believe if Lazarus rose from the dead. Abraham answered: **"If they do not listen to Moses and the prophets they will not be convinced even if someone rises from the dead."**
> *Luke 16:19–31*

Many Christians believe it is important to gain wealth ethically, not through exploitation of others or illegal activity. It is also important to use wealth ethically. So it is not acceptable to spend money on things that harm or exploit other people.

For example, Christians may buy **Fairtrade** products or support food banks. Many food banks are coordinated by The Trussell Trust, which is a Christian charity that supports 1200 food banks in the UK. Food banks provide emergency food and practical support to people in need, and campaign for **social justice** for people in **relative poverty**. Christians may volunteer, donate food or fundraise.

Specification focus

Issues of wealth and poverty: Ethical considerations about acquisition and use of wealth: Luke 16:19–31; the actions and attitudes of Christian charities in twenty first century Britain whose aim is to alleviate poverty: Christian Aid.

'Do not store up for yourselves treasures on earth, where moths and vermin destroy, and where thieves break in and steal. But store up for yourselves treasures in heaven... For where your treasure is, there your heart will be also.'
Matthew 6:19–21

- The rich man had a responsibility to be generous to the beggar but was not.
- Their roles are reversed after death. Lazarus is given luxury in heaven and the rich man is reduced to begging in hell.
- The rich man attempts twice to use Lazarus as his servant, still struggling to understand that worldly wealth does not make a person superior.

Useful term

Fairtrade – products that are produced by workers in the developing world who are ensured a fair wage and decent working conditions

Christian charities in Britain that aim to alleviate poverty

Many Christians believe it is important to use any wealth they have to try to relieve the sufferings of those who have none. They may do this by donating their time or wealth to support those who are poor.

The Salvation Army is a Christian church and a charity. It was founded in 1865 by William and Catherine Booth, who decided to take the church to the people rather than expecting the people to come to church. They set up shelters and soup kitchens for homeless people, ran a family tracing service for missing persons, and helped those living in slums or fleeing domestic abuse. Today the Salvation Army is particularly known for its extensive work with the homeless, but it also offers services and support to other poor or vulnerable people.

The Salvation Army runs 'Lifehouses', which are supported housing services to try to help those who are homeless. When it is very cold, they work with local councils to keep people safe in communal spaces and they operate night shelters for those who are sleeping rough.

CAFOD is the Catholic Agency for Overseas Development. Founded in 1960, CAFOD helps people all over the world who are in the greatest need by giving money and aid to those in **absolute poverty**. It also trains and equips people to begin providing for themselves. The charity encourages Catholics to give their own wealth and time to support those who are poor by volunteering, donating and praying.

Christian Aid

Christian Aid was founded in 1945 by British and Irish churches to help refugees following World War II. Since then, it has aimed to provide humanitarian relief and long-term development support for poor communities around the world.

One of its best-known projects is Christian Aid Week. This is an annual charitable week of giving where volunteers from local churches take envelopes around their communities for people to donate money towards projects that help and support the poorest people. The money is used to respond to humanitarian emergencies, as well as to campaign for change and help people claim the rights they are entitled to.

A specific campaign run by Christian Aid is the Syria Crisis Appeal. After years of conflict in Syria, Christian Aid is providing support to the most vulnerable refugees. The money raised helps to educate refugee children, provide counselling, and give vocational training to refugees so they can work. It also provides hot meals, blankets, fuel, shelter and hygiene kits to the recently displaced. Christian Aid encourages churches to have collections and individuals to donate as well as to pray.

> ❝All the believers were together and had everything in common. They sold property and possessions to give to anyone who had need.❞
> *Acts 2:44–45*

Christian Aid runs the Syria Crisis Appeal to support the most vulnerable refugees

Knowledge recall

1 Define the following concepts: relative/absolute poverty, social justice, personal conviction. (You can find these definitions on page 79.)
2 List three examples of actions taken by Christian charities that work to end poverty.
3 Suggest two different biblical teachings about what Christians should do with their wealth.

Evaluation practice

4 Give an argument for and an argument against the idea that money is not important.
5 Which argument do you think would be the most appealing to Christians and why?

Islamic attitudes to poverty and wealth

Ethical considerations about acquisition and use of wealth

Islam teaches that wealth is a blessing from Allah for the benefit of humanity, allowing people to provide for themselves and their families. The Cairo Declaration of Human Rights in Islam states that it is a basic **human right** for every person to have access to clothing, food, water and shelter. Therefore, Muslims have a duty to share their wealth with those who have none so that everyone's human rights are fulfilled.

> ‘Goodness does not consist in turning your face towards East or West. The truly good are those who believe in God and the Last Day, in the angels, the Scripture, and the prophets; who give away some of their wealth, however much they cherish it, to their relatives, to orphans, the needy, travellers and beggars, and to liberate those in bondage; **those who keep up the prayer and pay the prescribed alms; who keep pledges whenever they make them; who are steadfast in misfortune, adversity, and times of danger. These are the ones who are true,** and it is they who are aware of God.’
> *Qur'an 2:177*

Sharing wealth is compulsory for Muslims. Zakah or khums are part of worship to Allah and paying these alms is a religious duty. The giving of zakah began as a way to care for orphans and widows after Muslim soldiers were killed in battle. It is now also used to provide for the poor, the homeless, those who administer the tax, and to build Muslim schools or mosques.

There are clear laws that instruct Muslims how to earn wealth ethically. **Usury** and gambling are haram. This means Muslim charities cannot accept lottery funding which has been gained from gambling. Muslim banks or money lenders are forbidden from charging or giving **riba**. Instead they have systems in place so they can share profits and pool savings so that new businesses can operate, and families can buy houses.

> ‘God blights usury but blesses charitable deeds with multiple increase.’
> *Qur'an 2:276*

Islamic charities in Britain that aim to alleviate poverty

In addition to zakah, Muslims are invited to give sadaqah. This is voluntary giving to charity and will be rewarded in the afterlife by Allah. Charitable giving is important for Muslims because it is seen to protect human dignity. No one should

Specification focus

Issues of wealth and poverty: Ethical considerations about acquisition and use of wealth: Qur'an 2:177; the actions and attitudes of Islamic charities in twenty first century Britain whose aim is to alleviate poverty: Islamic Relief.

- While prayer and fasting are important, they are not all there is to being a good Muslim.
- This verse talks about the moral virtue or character of a good Muslim: one who is patient and generous, and who keeps promises and has faith.
- It also talks about the actions that are required in the real world: paying zakat, giving sadaqah, praying to Allah and working to help those in need.

Islamic Relief provides emergency help for the poor as well as long-term aid to create social justice

ever have to resort to begging or crime because of poverty. When these things do occur, it is seen as a failure of the ummah to protect its members. This means that Muslims may be involved in the development of projects to support those in **absolute** or **relative poverty**.

The Penny Appeal is a Muslim charity that is marketed as an affordable way to give to charity. It was set up in 2009 to provide poverty relief across the world by offering water solutions, sustainable food projects, soup kitchens, orphan care and medical aid. The idea is to take small change that many people do not value highly and make a difference with both short- and long-term projects.

There are many Muslim food banks in the UK organised by mosques or individuals, such as the Salma Food Bank in Birmingham. Founded on the idea that no Muslim goes to bed satisfied while his neighbour is hungry, these food banks do not only provide for Muslim people but aim to serve the whole community. Muslims may volunteer alongside non-Muslims to drive delivery vans to take food parcels to doorsteps.

Islamic Relief

Islamic Relief is a UK-based charity that works in more than 40 countries across the world. It pledges to give help to whoever is most in need, based on the principle that all human life is sacred regardless of gender, race or religion.

Founded in 1984, Islamic Relief provides emergency relief for those who have suffered catastrophes. In the 2020 COVID-19 pandemic, they appealed for donations so they could distribute food to the most vulnerable in quarantine. They also aim to relieve poverty in the long-term by providing water, food, shelter, health care and education to children and families. The charity campaigns for social justice by encouraging people to sign petitions or write to their MPs about topics like the unjust debt of poorer countries, or intervention for peace in countries affected by war.

An example of one Islamic Relief project is 'Hunger No More'. This project targets those in absolute poverty in the world's poorest communities. It aims to provide sustainable long-term solutions by distributing seeds and training people in agricultural production. The project has introduced small-scale fisheries and run food banks, school gardens and irrigation schemes. It provides emergency feeding centres for those needing immediate help, and distributes fresh meat during **Ramadan** and **Qurbani** to malnourished families.

Useful terms

usury – earning or charging high rates of interest on money that is borrowed

riba – the term used for usury in Islamic banking

Ramadan – the ninth month of the Muslim year in which fasting is performed during daylight hours

Qurbani – the sacrifice of an animal to Allah during the festival of Id-ul-Adha. A third of the meat is then given to the poor

Zakah is used for a range of purposes, including the building of Mosques and schools

Read about Qurbani on page 180.

Knowledge recall

1. Define the following concepts: relative/absolute poverty, social justice, extremism. (You can find these definitions on page 79.)
2. List three ways that Muslims are expected to acquire and use their wealth ethically.
3. Give two examples of projects or actions performed by Muslim charities to alleviate poverty.

Evaluation practice

4. Give two reasons why Muslims would agree they have a duty to share their wealth with the poor. Give two reasons why some people would disagree with this practice.
5. Which do you think is the most convincing reason and why?

Skills practice

On these exam practice pages you will see example answers for each of the exam question types: **a**, **b**, **c** and **d**. You can find out more about these on pages 5–9.

Question (a)

*Question (a) tests your knowledge and understanding. You will always be asked to **define a key concept** in this question. You can find a list of the concepts at the beginning of the chapter.*

(a) What is meant by 'relative poverty'?	[2]

Student response

Relative poverty is when you have got enough for some basic needs like a bit of food, but you haven't got enough for luxuries like a car.

Improved student response

Relative poverty is when you have less income than the average person in the society where you live, e.g. you earn less than the minimum wage but others around you might earn more.

Over to You! Have a try at answering this question:

(a) What is meant by 'prejudice'?	[2]

Helpful hints

To help you answer this question effectively, you could use the check list below to make sure you include the most important things:

- **Synonym** – Include a synonym for the word 'prejudice'.
- **Example** – Give an example of a prejudice that some people might hold.

Now give yourself **two minutes** to answer this question by yourself:

(a) What is meant by 'discrimination'?	[2]

Question (b)

*Question (b) tests your knowledge and understanding. It will always ask you to **describe** a belief, a teaching, a practice or an event that is included in the specification.*

(b) Describe the actions of **one** religious charity to reduce poverty.	[5]

What went well

The candidate has given an example which shows an understanding that there might be degrees of poverty.

How to improve

You must show understanding of the word 'relative' by making a comparison.

You should learn the exam board's definition of the word at the start of this chapter.

You could use a more accurate example that shows a person's wealth in relation to other people.

Tip

In this response, the candidate has used the words 'less than' to show a comparison. They also use an example that shows wealth *in relation* to others.

Student response

The charity Islamic Relief believes it is a Muslim's responsibility to help other members of the ummah because Allah gave us wealth and we have a duty to be his khalifahs by sharing that wealth. They also think all human life is sacred and so they will help to look after other people who are in need, even if they are not Muslim. For example, there are some Muslim food banks that give out food even to non-Muslims. The Qur'an tells all Muslims to look after people who are in need and this is the mark of a good Muslim if they do this.

What went well
The mention of food banks is a good example of the actions of a Muslim charity, and there is also the mention of a specific charity.

Improved student response

Islamic Relief is a charity in the UK that provides emergency relief for people who have suffered catastrophes. For example, during the COVID-19 crisis in 2020 they asked for zakah or sadaqah donations so that food could be delivered to vulnerable people. They also work on sustainable projects by providing water, food, shelter, health care and education in the world's poorest communities. Projects like 'Hunger No More' teach people how to grow and sell their own vegetables or run a small fishing business. They also share out fresh meat from Qurbani to hungry families. They run social justice campaigns that appeal for change to the structures in society that keep poor people poor, by asking people to sign petitions or write to their MPs.

How to improve
You must focus on the aspect of the question that asks for actions rather than beliefs.

You should include several examples of the type of work that the religious charity does.

You could include specific examples of projects or campaigns that are run.

🕐 **Over to You!** Have a try at answering this question:

> (b) Describe why some religious believers agree with censorship.　　　[5]

Tip
The best answers will give lots of examples to illustrate their points. Here, the candidate talks about:
• emergency relief in catastrophes
• sustainable projects.
• social justice campaigns.
And for each of these, the candidate has given examples of what the charity does.

Helpful hints
Use the check list below to make sure you include the most important things:

- **How/Why** – Explain one positive aim of censorship (e.g. protection of a group in society).
- **Example** – Give an example of something that might be censored for this reason (e.g. a film, book, picture or news story that is sensitive for this reason).
- **Repeat** – Then repeat the above process for two more aims of censorship.

Now give yourself **five minutes** to answer this question by yourself:

> (b) Describe **one** example of when personal religious conviction has conflicted with the laws of a country.　　　[5]

Question (c)

*Question **(c)** tests your knowledge and understanding. You need to give detailed evidence and reasoning to support your explanation of the topic. For the Themes paper, you will always be asked to **explain two different viewpoints**, but you don't need to evaluate which is the better view.*

> (c) Explain, from **two** religions **or two** religious traditions, how personal conviction may conflict with the laws of a country.　　　[8]

Student response

Some Catholics have a personal conviction that abortion is wrong, but it is acceptable in UK law. This means that Catholics don't have abortions, but other people often do. This is because in the Bible it says 'do not kill'. So, Catholics want to do what the Bible says. The Bible also says that we should love our neighbour and Catholics do not think it is very loving to kill an unborn baby.

Some Church of England Christians have a personal conviction that abortion is wrong, but they might allow it because they think that sometimes people have special situations that make it a very difficult decision. They think we should be loving like the Bible says and so we should show love to the mother rather than the baby.

Improved student response

Catholics have a personal conviction that abortion is wrong because the Bible says 'do not kill', yet it is acceptable in UK law. Therefore, a Catholic may campaign to end abortion in the UK. Some Catholics might join groups who offer services to support pregnant women so they can have the baby instead of an abortion. They believe the Bible tells us to show agape, so they do this for the baby and the mother. They act within the law to get the law to be changed.

Other Christians argue that if our beliefs conflict with the law, we should fight against it. Martin Luther King Jr was a Baptist Christian who was involved in Civil Rights protests against segregation in America. He believed that everyone should be treated the same, whereas segregation treated black people as inferior. He organised rallies, a bus boycott and other civil disobedience, breaking the law to force change. He argued for non-violent direct action because Christ directed his love to all people, regardless of race or religion. He argued people should even be prepared to face punishment, like Jesus, to make their point heard if the law is unjust.

Over to You! Have a try at answering this question:

(c) Explain from **either two** religions or **two** religious traditions, attitudes to wealth. [8]

Helpful hints
- Include **two** beliefs – one from one religion and the second from either a different religion or a different religious tradition.
- For each belief give an **example** from religious authority to illustrate it (such as a quote from or reference to scripture, Shariah Law, a papal statement or the hadiths).
- Explain **why** each of the religions or traditions believe this (e.g. they are influenced by other teachings on life after death, or how to treat others).
- Explain **how** people of this faith are expected to behave as a result (e.g. rules about giving to charity, gambling, interest or taxation).

What went well
This response begins well by showing a conflict between what some Christians believe and what UK law says. The candidate also gives an example of where the belief comes from. There is an attempt to give examples from two traditions.

How to improve
You must stick to the focus of the question, which is conflict not beliefs about abortion.

You should give examples of other conflicts and/or the actions of people whose beliefs conflict with law.

You could include examples of real people who have acted on their beliefs and how they have done this.

Tip
Question (c) allows you to write about two religious traditions. This means you don't have to talk about two different religions; you can use views from different denominations within the same religion.

Now give yourself **eight minutes** to answer this question by yourself:

(c) Explain from **either two** religions or **two** religious traditions, attitudes to gaining and using wealth. [8]

Question *(d)*

*Question **(d)** tests your ability to **evaluate**. This means you need to show you have considered more than one point of view and that you have referred to religion and belief. You will need to be able to make judgements that are supported by detailed reasoning and argument.*

(d) 'It is up to you what you do with your money.'
Discuss this statement showing that you have considered more than one point of view. (You must refer to religion and belief in your answer.) [15]

Student response

It is up to you what you do with your money because it is yours, you have earned it and therefore it is not up to anyone else to tell you what you can or cannot do with it. A religious person might agree with this because they would say that wealth is a gift from God and therefore it is yours. Some religious people might disagree with this because they say that we have to give our wealth away to other people. The best argument is the one that says it is ours.

It should not be completely up to you to decide what to do with your money. This is because some people might want to do something illegal with it, like pay for an assassin. A religious person would agree with this because they would say it is wrong to kill. Some other religious people might disagree because they would say that what we do with our money is a private thing. Jesus said that we should give away money in secret, so no one can tell us what to do. The best argument here is the one that says we should not be allowed to do something illegal.

It is up to you what you do with your money, but you will pay the price in the afterlife when God judges you. Muslims and Christians would agree with this because they say that God knows everything that we do. However, some religious people say that we should have our money controlled because it is better for society. The best argument here is the one that says we can do what we want and then God can judge us later.

What went well

There is an awareness of the need for a structure in this answer, and the candidate has used it to help them write different points of view and relate them to religious belief. There is some reference to specific religious ideas or religious figures and some real-life issues concerning wealth.

How to improve

You must give reasoning to support why one view is better than another.

You should expand on ideas, such as how or why it is better for society to have rules or controls in place.

You could refer to or even quote sources of wisdom and authority to support your answers.

Improved student response

It is not up to you what you do with your money because all religions give guidance about how we should use our wealth. Matthew's Gospel says 'do not store up treasure on earth' and the story of Lazarus says that God will punish those who do not share. Conversely, some argue that these directions are not laws. Jesus did not force people to give up their wealth or say rich people were immoral. He left it to us to decide whether we want to share, and sometimes rich people choose not to give everything away. Therefore, it is up to us what to do with our money, but we must accept there could be consequences if we do not follow scripture.

It should not be completely up to us to decide what to do with our money because people have a natural tendency to be greedy. In Islam, it is compulsory to share wealth through zakah or khums, which benefits society, and earns approval from Allah in the afterlife. However, compulsory laws do not show what is in a person's heart and do not really help the person in the afterlife. Giving should be from the heart, like at

There is reference to religious teaching and tradition in every paragraph.

This candidate has understood the question and focuses on choice as well as wealth.

The candidate has shown contrasting views in each paragraph.

Ramadan, when people understand what it is to be hungry. Then we would deserve paradise. Yet society in this life needs to be provided for. There must be a limit to how much people can choose what they do with their own money so that society can run and the poor do not starve. Taxes are vital to help the poor, so we should not be able to choose completely.

In conclusion, we should be free to decide what to do with our own money, but only to an extent. It is important that society can function and some do not suffer while others are very rich. On the other hand, if someone has earned money by working hard, they should be able to choose what they do with it. Taxing some of a person's wealth to provide for society is a good idea, but choosing to give to charity shows what is in our hearts. Therefore, the best society seems to be the one after Jesus' death when the Christian community shared everything, so no one suffered, but they were not forced to do this, so they deserved their reward in heaven after death.

Each paragraph ends with a statement of decision that is supported with reasons.

The candidate has understood that the answer may not be a simple yes or no.

There is a clear conclusion at the end of the final paragraph that gives a judgement.

🕐 **Over to You!** Have a try at answering this question:

(d) 'Everyone should obey the laws of a country.'
Discuss this statement showing that you have considered more than one point of view. (You must refer to religion and belief in your answer.)   [15]

Helpful hints

You should consider what vocabulary you can use to help you evaluate effectively. See how many of the following words you can use in your arguments:

To add more information:	To show a different view:	To conclude:
• In addition	• However	• Therefore
• Moreover	• Conversely	• Consequently
• Furthermore	• On the other hand	• In conclusion

Study Challenge:

The exam board will only ever ask a question **(d)** that gives you a statement to discuss based on the content of the specification and then asks you to discuss it from different viewpoints, referring to religion and belief.

- Look back at the specification focus boxes at the top of each page in this chapter.
- Choose one area from the list that has not yet appeared in the questions above.
- Create a statement that you can debate.
- Write your own **(d)** question on this area that begins with this controversial statement and asks you to discuss it, using the wording from the questions you can see above.
- Now give yourself **fifteen minutes** to answer this question by yourself!

Tip

Remember that when you write a question (d) response, there are many possible conclusions. It might be that the best response is not a simple 'agree' or 'disagree' with the question, but instead it might be a partial agreement. It might depend on the situation and you can explain this.

Tip

The best answers often use more sophisticated language, but only use it if you understand what it means. Otherwise your answers may come across as confused.

Tip

Remember, if you decide to repeat this challenge for any of the material on life after death, this is the only question that requires you to include non-religious beliefs as well as religious ones.

Chapter 5:
Christianity: Beliefs and teachings

Introduction

Christianity is the largest world religion and the main religion of Great Britain. In this chapter, you will study the beliefs and teachings of Christianity, which primarily come from the Bible. The largest section of the Bible – the Old Testament – is scripture shared with Judaism. The reason for this is that Jesus was Jewish, and Christianity was originally a Jewish sect. The New Testament consists of stories about Jesus' life and teachings along with letters and stories of his early followers. However, you will see that there are different ways of understanding scripture and sometimes Christians disagree. Christian beliefs have been formed over 2000 years of thinking and some of them are very complex. You will find that it has been necessary for other sources of teaching to evolve, so you will learn about teachings from creeds and tradition as additional ways of explaining what Christians believe.

Things to remember:

- Christianity has split over the centuries into different denominations. This means that Christians sometimes disagree on aspects of doctrine or belief. For example, whilst all Christians believe in Jesus Christ, they may not agree on exactly how salvation is gained or the relationship between the three persons of the Trinity.

- In the past, some Christian teachings have been so important to people that they have been prepared to die rather than reject them. While this might seem extreme to some, it shows that these beliefs cannot be easily dismissed for a Christian.

- Society has changed a lot since the Bible was written. This means that there are some teachings in it that are a little more difficult for us to understand. For example, modern society is more secular and is more likely to see belief as a choice, whereas belief in God was taken for granted in the past.

- While the Bible is the most vital source of Christian authority, it is not the only authority. For example, when Christians are making decisions about matters of faith and belief, they will also refer to Church teaching, conscience, tradition, key religious leaders, creeds and scholars. If the Bible is unclear about a religious matter, it is likely that Christians will look to these other sources to tell them what to believe.

Concepts

Omnipotent – the all-powerful, almighty and unlimited nature of God

Omnibenevolent – the state of being all-loving and infinitely good – a characteristic often attributed to God

Trinity – the three persons of God; God the Father, Son and Holy Spirit

Incarnation – God becoming human in the form of Jesus

Atonement – the belief that Jesus' death on the cross healed the rift between humans and God

Resurrection – the belief that Jesus rose from the dead on Easter Sunday, conquering death

Sacraments – an outward sign of an invisible and inward blessing by God. For example, Baptism, the Eucharist

Evangelism – preaching the gospel to others with the intention of converting them to the Christian faith

The nature of God

Specification focus

The nature of God: Omnipotent: Exodus 7–11, Exodus 14:21; Omnibenevolent: Psalm 86:15, John 3:16, Romans 8:37–39; evil and suffering: quote on God and evil from Epicurus, Book of Job 1:8–12, 42:1–6.

God's qualities

Christians are monotheists. This means they believe there is only one God and he has certain key qualities. For example, God is omnipotent (all-powerful) and omnibenevolent (all-loving).

Omnipotent

The Old Testament emphasises God's complete power over everything. This power is both frightening and exciting as God uses it to both punish and protect. One of the best-known stories of God's power is in the book of Exodus, chapters 7–11.

The Israelites were slaves in Egypt. God commanded Moses, with the help of his brother Aaron, to tell the Pharaoh to release the Israelites. The following sequence of events emphasises God's absolute power over every aspect of the journey to freedom, even to the point of working **miracles**:

- Moses asks for the Israelites' freedom. The Pharaoh refuses as God has hardened his heart.
- God transforms Aaron's staff into a snake that swallows the staffs of the court magicians.
- God sends ten plagues against Egypt, each more destructive than the last. No plague affects the Israelites.
- God's tenth plague causes every firstborn in Egypt to die except the Israelites.
- The Pharaoh sends them out of Egypt. God guides their way with pillars of cloud and fire.
- God hardens the Pharaoh's heart so he gives chase with his army.
- God uses Moses to part the Red Sea so the Israelites can cross safely. He then sweeps back the sea to drown the entire pursuing army.

In the Bible, God's power is absolute – he can even suspend the laws of nature

> ❛Then Moses stretched out his hand over the sea, and **all that night the Lord drove the sea back with a strong east wind and turned it into dry land**. The waters were divided…❜
> *Exodus 14:21*

Omnibenevolent

Christians believe that God is all-loving. He is compassionate, kind and merciful to his whole creation. Scripture repeatedly emphasises God's loving nature throughout the Old and New Testaments.

> ❛**But you, Lord, are a compassionate and gracious God,** slow to anger, abounding in love and faithfulness.❜
> *Psalm 86:15*

This song or prayer is thought to be from David, worshipping God who will protect him from harm.

> ❛**For God so loved the world that he gave his one and only Son,** that whoever believes in him shall not perish but have eternal life.❜
> *John 3:16*

God's love for humans is so great that God will do whatever it takes to protect and save them.

Useful term

miracles – a wonder or marvel that occurs in the physical world, as a direct work of God

'No, in all these things we are more than conquerors through him who loved us. **For I am convinced that neither death nor life, neither angels nor demons, neither the present nor the future, nor any powers, neither height nor depth, nor anything else in all creation, will be able to separate us from the love of God** that is in Christ Jesus our Lord.'
Romans 8:37–39

The love of God is believed to be absolute. It extends to all beings and cannot be diverted or damaged.

Evil and suffering

Some people question how God can be an omnipotent and omnibenevolent being who still allows evil to exist. He must lack one of the qualities that have been traditionally assigned to him. Alternatively, either God or evil do not exist. This is the problem of evil.

This was first stated by the ancient Greek philosopher Epicurus (341–270 BCE), who is believed to have said: 'is God willing to prevent evil, but not able? Then he is impotent. Is he able, but not willing? Then he is malevolent. Is he both able and willing? Whence then is evil?'

This problem is highlighted in the Bible in the Book of Job, when God seems to allow evil to take place. God allows Job, a faithful believer, to be tormented by Satan as a test to see if Job is only faithful because God protects him or if his motivation is pure.

Job experiences extreme suffering and his wealth, health and even his children are taken from him. His wife suggests he should curse God. Three friends come to comfort him and suggest that he or his children in some way deserved their fate, so he should work harder to earn God's approval. Job rejects all this advice and continues to trust in God, whose ways he does not understand.

Christians conclude that they, like Job, should trust that God's reasons are beyond their understanding. At the end of the story of Job, his faithfulness is rewarded with wealth, health and more children. Christians believe that their faith will be rewarded in the end.

'Then the Lord said to Satan, "Have you considered my servant Job? There is no one on earth like him; he is blameless and upright, a man who fears God and shuns evil." "Does Job fear God for nothing?" Satan replied. "Have you not put a hedge around him and his household and everything he has? You have blessed the work of his hands, so that his flocks and herds are spread throughout the land. But now **stretch out your hand and strike everything he has, and he will surely curse you to your face**." The Lord said to Satan, "Very well, then, everything he has is in your power, but on the man himself do not lay a finger."'
Job 1:8–12

Read about the problem of evil on page 70.

'Then Job replied to the Lord: "**I know that you can do all things; no purpose of yours can be thwarted**. You asked, 'Who is this that obscures my plans without knowledge?' Surely, I spoke of things I did not understand, things too wonderful for me to know. You said, 'Listen now, and I will speak; I will question you, and you shall answer me.' My ears had heard of you but now my eyes have seen you. Therefore, I despise myself and repent in dust and ashes."'
Job 42:1–6

Knowledge recall

1 Define the following concepts: omnipotent, omnibenevolent. (You can find these definitions on page 101.)
2 List three ways that God shows his power in the Exodus stories.
3 Give one example of how Christians think God shows his love for all people.

Evaluation practice

4 Give one reason why some Christians might see the existence of evil as a problem and one reason why some might argue it is not a problem.
5 Which of these views do you think is most reasonable? Give two reasons for your view.

The Trinity

Specification focus

The nature of God: The Trinity, beliefs and teachings about the oneness of God: Father, Son and Holy Spirit: John 10:30, John 14:6–11.

Beliefs and teachings about the oneness of God

Christians are monotheists, so they believe there is only one God. No other being is equal to God in power or authority. There are clear rules in the Bible about the importance of worshipping only God and no other being.

> 'This is what the Lord says – Israel's King and Redeemer, the Lord Almighty: I am the first and I am the last; apart from me there is no God. '
> *Isaiah 44:6*

Christianity also teaches that God has a **Triune** nature. This means that God is God the Father, God the Son and God the Holy Spirit. This is known as the **Trinity**.

As early Christians tried to understand who Jesus was and what his relationship with God was, some teachings started to spread that were thought to be **heresy**. For example, some thought Jesus was an ordinary man or that he was God pretending to be human. In response, early Christian leaders constructed the **Nicene Creed**, which was finalised in Western churches in 381 CE. This Creed is still recited in many churches today as a way for Christians to affirm what they believe.

The Nicene Creed teaches that all three parts of the Trinity or **Godhead** are equal and are God. There is no difference between the three parts of God and yet each part is distinct. Christianity clearly states that this is not the same as believing in three gods.

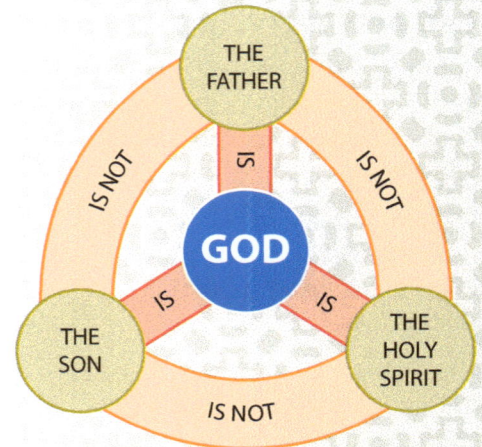

Christians believe that there is one God with a Triune nature

God the Father

God the Father is referred to throughout the Bible, including in the New Testament. God the Father is the creator of all things; the **omnipotent**, **omnibenevolent** being who nurtures and interacts with his creation. This belief is shown in the Nicene Creed.

> 'We believe in one God, the Father, the Almighty, maker of heaven and earth, and of all that is, seen and unseen. '
> *The Nicene Creed*

God the Son

God the Son refers to Jesus. Christians believe that Jesus is God **incarnate**. Jesus was not conceived in the same way as other humans, since he was not a result of sexual intercourse. Therefore, he is free of sin. He is both fully human and fully God. In the words of the Nicene Creed:

> 'We believe in one Lord Jesus Christ…God from God, Light from Light, true God from true God, begotten, not made, of one Being with the Father. Through him all things were made… '
> *The Nicene Creed*

Useful terms

Triune – three in one

heresy – a teaching that is against accepted doctrine

Nicene Creed – a formal statement of the main Christian beliefs, initially adopted by the first Council of Nicaea

Godhead – another name for the one God in three persons of the Trinity

incarnate – made flesh

Paraclete – Holy Spirit

World Council of Churches – an organisation that coordinates hundreds of Christian churches so they can work together

Christians can worship Jesus without sinning because they believe he is an aspect of the one God. The title 'Son of God' does not mean that Jesus is literally God's son. It is an indication that Jesus shares God's divinity.

> ❝I and the Father are one.❞
> *John 10:30*

> ❝Jesus answered, "I am the way and the truth and the life. No one comes to the Father except through me. **If you really know me, you will know my Father as well. From now on, you do know him and have seen him**." Philip said, "Lord, show us the Father and that will be enough for us." Jesus answered: "Don't you know me, Philip, even after I have been among you such a long time? Anyone who has seen me has seen the Father. How can you say, 'Show us the Father?' Don't you believe that I am in the Father, and that the Father is in me? The words I say to I do not speak on my own authority. Rather, it is the Father, living in me, who is doing his work. Believe me when I say that I am in the Father and the Father is in me; or at least believe on the evidence of the works themselves."❞
> *John 14:6–11*

God the Holy Spirit

God the Holy Spirit, or **Paraclete**, refers to God as humans experience him today. The Bible says Jesus was touched by the Holy Spirit at his Baptism. Jesus also taught that he would send his Holy Spirit to be with the disciples after his ascension to heaven. The Holy Spirit gives Christians wisdom and inspiration in their prayers, when reading and understanding scripture, and guides them in worship. The Nicene Creed states:

> ❝We believe in the Holy Spirit, the Lord, the giver of life, who proceeds from the Father and the Son. With the Father and the Son he is worshipped and glorified.❞
> *The Nicene Creed*

Belief in the Trinity is held by almost all people who call themselves Christians. The **World Council of Churches** requires churches to believe in the Trinity if they wish to join. The Council is:

> ❝A fellowship of churches which confess the Lord Jesus Christ as God and Saviour according to the scriptures, and therefore seek to fulfil together their common calling to the glory of the one God, Father, Son and Holy Spirit.❞
> *The World Council of Churches*

Christians accept that the teaching of the Trinity is a divine mystery. God is beyond human understanding and so Christians do not need to understand the Trinity; they only need to have faith.

Knowledge recall

1. Define the following concepts: Trinity, sacraments. (You can find these definitions on page 101.)
2. List two sources of authority which tell Christians that there are three persons in one God.
3. State three functions of the Holy Spirit in the world today.

Evaluation practice

4. Give one reason why some people might reject the Church teaching of the Trinity and one reason why Christians might accept it.
5. Which of these views do you think is the most convincing religious argument? Give a reason why.

Creation

Specification focus

Creation: Genesis 1–3; nature and role of humans, literal and non-literal ways of interpretation; the role of Word and Spirit in creation: John 1:1–5.

The nature and role of humans in Genesis 1–3

Genesis 1–3 are the opening chapters of the Bible. They set out the creation story for Jews and Christians.

Chapter 1 – God creates everything *ex nihilo* in six days:
- Day 1 – light, day and night
- Day 2 – sky and water
- Day 3 – land, sea and vegetation
- Day 4 – sun, moon and stars
- Day 5 – birds and fish
- Day 6 – animals and humans. Humans are created *imago Dei*, commanded to reproduce and given vegetation for food.
- Day 7 – God rests because his creation is complete.

Genesis 1 is a methodical account, whose authors were most interested in the organisation of religion and the sequence of events. Humans are the most important part of creation. They are made last, in God's image, with free will and the capacity for moral decision making. Humanity is told to 'fill the earth and subdue it'. They must reproduce and have dominion over God's creation. Each day in the account ends with 'God saw that it was good', implying that God's creation was perfectly made.

Chapter 2 – God begins to create the earth. He starts by making a man from dust and breathing life into him.
- God plants a garden in the East (Eden) and puts the man there.
- He gives the man plants for food and beauty. He creates four rivers.
- He tells the man to cultivate the garden and to eat anything except the fruit from the tree of knowledge of good and evil.
- God creates animals as helpers for Adam, who names them. They are not suitable helpers.
- God puts Adam to sleep, removes a rib and creates a woman from it to be his helper.
- They are naked and feel no shame. They are husband and wife.

Genesis 2 describes a different order of events. This account was written earlier than Genesis 1 and is less organised. Humans are still most important; man is created first and everything else is made for him. He is given responsibility to act as a steward, caring for Eden and everything in it. Man is made lovingly by God, who is **anthropomorphised** to show their close relationship.

Genesis 3 describes the Fall. Humans were created with free will and used it to commit Original Sin. Once they ate the forbidden fruit, their nature changed. They were no longer innocent and they hid from God, showing that their relationship with him had been damaged. Adam and the woman, now named Eve, both have distinct roles in which they suffer as punishment for their sin.

Chapter 3 – The serpent tempts the woman to eat from the tree.
- The fruit is beautiful, good for food and something that brings wisdom, so the woman eats it.
- She gives some to Adam and he eats it.
- Both realise they are naked and hide from God when he calls them.
- When God challenges their disobedience, they try to blame each other or the serpent.
- God curses the serpent to crawl in the dust as an enemy of humans.
- God curses the woman to have pain in childbirth and be ruled over by her husband.
- God curses Adam to work the ground for food until death.
- God makes them clothes and banishes them from the garden.

Useful terms

ex nihilo – out of nothing
imago Dei – a Latin term that means 'in the image of God'
anthropomorphised – given human characteristics, such as walking or speaking
inerrant – cannot be wrong
myth – a fictional story that contains truths expressed as symbols to explain the world view of that religion
theistic evolution – science is correct, but God is the power behind the events that science describes

Literal and non-literal ways of interpretation

Christians understand the Genesis stories in a range of different ways. Some consider them to be literally true. They believe the world was created in six days by God, in the order stated. Christians who believe this are called Creationists. They believe scripture is **inerrant**, so it cannot contain mistakes. This brings some challenges:

- It contradicts scientific understanding about the origins of the world and human life.
- The two stories say different things, yet Creationists believe both are literally true.

Other Christians do not take these stories literally. Some, like Catholics, take a conservative approach. They believe Genesis contains **myths** that teach Christians about God and his relationship with humanity. Science gives facts about *how* the world began, while Genesis explains its purpose: *why* it began. This is **theistic evolution**, where God created the world as explained by science, for a reason. Humans are vital to that purpose and have a role to fulfil.

Liberal Christians may think that the Bible is written about God and that writers, although inspired by God, interpreted God's message from their perspective in history. They may say that Genesis is not literally true but is still valuable for teaching about human experience through the ages.

The Role of Word and Spirit in creation

In Genesis 1, God is the creator of all things and his Holy Spirit was present in the creative process from the beginning. Christians believe that God's Triune nature means that Christ was also intrinsically involved in creation.

> ❛In the beginning was the Word, and the Word was with God, and the Word was God. **He was with God in the beginning. Through him all things were made**; without him nothing was made that has been made. In him was life, and that life was the light of mankind. The light shines in the darkness, and the darkness has not overcome it.❜
> *John 1:1–5*

Christians believe that God the Father, Son and Holy Spirit were involved in creation

- The 'Word' is Christ, who Christians believe is God's message to humanity.
- John's reference to the creation of 'all things' shows Christ was an essential part of the creative process.
- Humanity is in the 'darkness' of sin from the Fall.
- Jesus is God's eternal Word made flesh, bringing light or understanding to everything that God made.

Knowledge recall

1 Define the following concepts: omnipotent, incarnation. (You can find these definitions on page 101.)
2 List three things that Genesis 1–3 teaches Christians about humans.
3 State two things that John 1:1–5 says about creation.

Evaluation practice

4 Give one reason why some Christians believe Genesis to be literally true and one reason why some other Christians think it is not.
5 Which of these views do you think is the most convincing religious argument? Give a reason why.

The incarnation of Jesus

Specification focus

Jesus Christ: Beliefs and teachings about Jesus' incarnation: John 1:14, Luke 1:28–33.

Beliefs and teachings about Jesus' incarnation

The gospel of John begins by setting out clearly who Jesus is according to Christian teaching:

> '**The Word became flesh and made his dwelling among us.** We have seen his glory, the glory of the One and only Son, who came from the Father, full of grace and truth.'
> *John 1:14*

John states that the 'Word' or **revelation** of God became a human being and lived here on earth. This is what is known as the **incarnation**. God was literally made flesh so that people could see, speak to and even touch him.

Belief in the incarnation is a vital part of the Christian story:

- God created human beings to be in a close relationship with him.
- Humanity sinned against God through Original Sin, which means that human nature now tends towards personal sin.
- Sin causes distance from God, which is against his plan for humanity.
- God tried to bring human beings back to him, for example through a covenant made with Abraham and ethical rules given to Moses and the prophets.
- Humanity continued to break away from God's plan through sin. Distance from God prevented people from having faith and so God intervened.
- God himself became flesh so that humanity could see him, hear his teaching and follow his example.

The gospel of Luke says that Mary was told she would give birth to the Son of God

The incarnation in the gospels of Matthew and Luke

The story of Jesus' birth is told in the gospels of Matthew and Luke. Their accounts focus on different parts of the story. Matthew tells how an angel visited Joseph and told him:

> '"The virgin will conceive and give birth to a son, and they will call him Immanuel" [which means "God with us"].'
> *Matthew 1:23*

The use of the name **Immanuel** clearly sets out who Jesus was believed to be: God incarnate. Luke's gospel focuses more on Mary's story:

> 'The angel said to her, "Do not be afraid, Mary, you have found favour with God. You will conceive and give birth to a son, and you are to call him Jesus. He will be great and will be called the Son of the Most High.'
> *Luke 1:28–33*

Useful terms

revelation – God's direct communication to humanity
Immanuel – 'God with us'
doctrine – a set of teachings accepted by the Christian Church
monogenes – an Ancient Greek word translated as 'begotten', meaning 'one of its kind'
hypostatic union – the one personality of Christ in which his human and divine nature are united

The gospel of Luke makes Jesus' nature very clear. He was not conceived in the usual way, from sexual intercourse. Mary is believed to have been a virgin when she gave birth to Jesus. This miracle pregnancy was performed by God because Mary was virtuous enough to carry the Son of God.

The Nicene Creed

After Jesus' death, at the start of the early Church, there were lots of unofficial teachings that tried to explain who Jesus really was. Some people argued that Jesus was just an ordinary human being. Others saw him as a puppet that God controlled to do his bidding. Still others thought he was not human at all, but was God just pretending to be human or that he was a human who was adopted as God's son.

Early Church leaders gathered to form the Council of Nicaea in 325 CE and the Council of Constantinople in 381 CE, to work out the official Church **doctrine** that is known today as the Nicene Creed. Jesus is believed to be fully human and fully God at the same time:

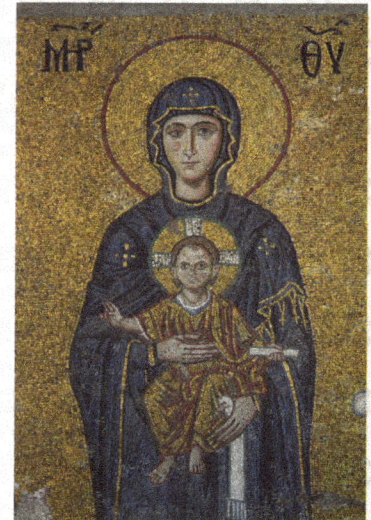

> ❛We believe in one Lord, Jesus Christ,
> the only Son of God,
> eternally begotten of the Father.
> God from God, Light from Light,
> true God from true God,
> begotten, not made, one in Being with the Father.
> Through him all things were made.
> For us men and for our salvation
> he came down from heaven:
> by power of the Holy Spirit, he was born of the Virgin Mary,
> and became man.❜
> *The Nicene Creed*

Jesus is believed to be fully human and fully divine

'Begotten' comes from the Greek word 'monogenes'. This means that Jesus is unique – the only legitimate son (not an adopted son).

Jesus was not created; he is an eternal being, not a creature made by God.

Jesus came down from heaven, so is from God and has divine power and authority.

Yet he was born from a human and so is human himself, with humility and fragility. He has not inherited Original Sin, being born of a virgin, but understands suffering and mortality.

Jesus is the second person of the **Trinity**. He has both a divine and human nature. This is not the same as being half God and half human. It is also not the same as having two separate identities within one body. Instead, this is known as the **hypostatic union**. Jesus is fully human and fully God, so when Jesus preaches, it is the word of God that he speaks. When a person has seen Jesus, they have seen God.

Knowledge recall

1 Define the following concepts: Trinity, incarnation. (You can find these definitions on page 101.)
2 List the steps in the Christian story that lead up to the incarnation of Christ.
3 State one teaching that tells Christians Jesus is both human and divine.

Evaluation practice

4 Give one reason why a Christian might accept the hypostatic union and one reason why someone might reject this teaching.
5 Do you think any of these views are reasonable? Give a reason why or why not.

The crucifixion of Jesus

Specification focus

Jesus Christ: Crucifixion: Matthew 27:28–50; salvation and atonement: Matthew 26:26–29, Leviticus 16:20–22, Isaiah 53:3–9.

Crucifixion

Crucifixion was a Roman method of capital punishment reserved for political or religious agitators and for slaves. It involved being **scourged**, stripped and nailed or bound to a crossbeam. This crossbeam was then fixed to an upright shaft and the feet bound or nailed in place. A sign was placed above the head to indicate the crime that had been committed.

Christians believe that Jesus was innocent of all sin so he did not deserve to be crucified. The leaders of the **Sanhedrin** had accused Jesus of blasphemy as they saw him as a threat to Jewish authority. They put Rome under pressure to have him crucified and so Pontius Pilate reluctantly agreed to have him executed.

Most Christian denominations believe that Jesus' death happened just as the Bible describes in Matthew 27:28–50:

- Jesus is mocked, spat on and repeatedly beaten over the head by the centurions.
- They force a passer-by, Simon of Cyrene, to carry Jesus' crossbeam to Golgotha when Jesus is too exhausted to do it himself.
- Jesus is offered bitter wine to help numb his pain, which he refuses to drink.
- The guards cast lots for his clothes.
- They crucify him between two thieves with the sign 'This is Jesus, the King of the Jews' above his head.
- Passers-by, chief priests, elders, teachers of the law and those executed with him all mock him and tell him to save himself if he really is the Son of God.
- At the ninth hour Jesus cries out 'My God, My God, why have you forsaken me?'
- Jesus cries out again and then dies.

Christians believe that Jesus' crucifixion was not an accident. They believe that Jesus is the **Messiah**. The Messiah expected by the Jews was going to be a powerful ruler to save them from political oppression. However, when Jesus died as a vulnerable human being, Christians came to understand that he died to save them from eternal punishment for their sin.

Salvation and atonement

In the gospel accounts of the Last Supper, the writers make it clear that Jesus expected to be killed. As they celebrated the Passover, Jesus told his disciples that the purpose of his death, symbolised in the bread and the wine, is for the forgiveness of sin. So Christians believe that his death served to offer them **salvation** from the punishment they deserve.

Crucifixion was a gruesome and humiliating Roman method of capital punishment

Read more about the practice of sharing bread and wine in the Eucharist on pages 128–129.

Useful terms

scourged – whipped/flogged
Sanhedrin – an ancient Jewish council of judges or elders
Messiah – another word for 'Christ'; a saviour or liberator
salvation – being rescued or saved from the punishment for human sin
agape – a Greek word that translates as 'unconditional love' or 'charity'
scapegoat – one that is made to bear the blame of others

Christianity teaches that humans have inherited Original Sin and so have a tendency to make sinful choices. Sin has destroyed the relationship between God and humanity, creating distance between them. Justice requires that sin is punished, but Jesus, in the ultimate act of **agape**, took on the punishment himself so that humanity can go free. This idea of transferring the effect of sin to another being is not new. The Old Testament talks of a religious tradition of setting the punishment for sin upon a sacrificial **scapegoat**.

Like the goat, Christ took upon himself all the sin and rebellion of the world and carried it with him into death. As God made flesh, he had the power to do this for all of humanity. In the Old Testament, the Hebrew prophets predicted that someone would come who would do this. The prophet Isaiah predicted that one would come who would be humiliated and rejected for humanity's **atonement**.

> ❝He was despised and rejected by men,
> a man of suffering, and familiar with pain.
> Like one from whom people hide their faces
> he was despised, and we held him in low esteem.
> Surely, he took up our pain
> and bore our suffering,
> yet we considered him punished by God, stricken by him, and afflicted.
> But **he was pierced for our transgressions,
> he was crushed for our iniquities;**
> the punishment that brought us peace was on him,
> and by his wounds we are healed.
> We all, like sheep, have gone astray,
> each of us has turned to his own way;
> and the Lord has laid on him the iniquities of us all…
> …for the transgression of my people he was punished.❞
> *Isaiah 53:3–8*

Christians believe that Isaiah is talking about Jesus in this song. They believe that Jesus died to atone for humanity's sins and bring salvation from sin. Jesus has taken the punishment and by doing so the sins have been paid for. The thing that was keeping humans separate from God has been removed, allowing Christians to spend eternity in heaven with God.

> ❝When Aaron has finished making atonement for the Most Holy Place, the tent of meeting and the altar, he shall bring forward the live goat. He is to lay both hands on the head of the live goat and confess over it all the wickedness and rebellion of the Israelites – all their sins – and put them on the goat's head. He shall send the goat away into the wilderness in the care of someone appointed for the task. **The goat will carry on itself all their sins to a remote place;** and the man shall release it in the wilderness.❞
> *Leviticus 16:20–22*

> ❝While they were eating, Jesus took bread, and when he had given thanks, he broke it and gave it to his disciples, saying, "Take and eat; this is my body." Then he took the cup, and when he had given thanks, he gave it to them, saying, "Drink from it, all of you. **This is my blood of the covenant, which is poured out for many for the forgiveness of sins."**❞
> *Matthew 26:26–29*

Knowledge recall

1 Define the following concepts: incarnation, atonement. (You can find these definitions on page 101.)
2 List two reasons why human beings might deserve to be punished by God.
3 State two reasons why Jesus could act as a scapegoat for human sin.

Evaluation practice

4 Give one reason why Jesus' death is a suitable payment for human sin and one reason why it is not.
5 Which of these views is the most convincing? Give two reasons for your answer.

Jesus' resurrection and ascension

Specification focus

Jesus Christ: Resurrection: Luke 24:1–9, 1 Corinthians 15:3–8, 12–14; ascension: Luke 24:50–53.

Key events in the resurrection of Jesus Christ

Christians believe the death of Jesus meant that he paid the price for human sin. All four gospels tell how three days after his death, Jesus was resurrected. Both Fundamentalist and Conservative Christians believe this event really happened. However, there are some differences in the gospel accounts.

- All the gospels report that Jesus' body was given to Joseph of Arimathea by Pilate and placed in a tomb on Friday night, before the Sabbath. In John's gospel, Jesus' body is prepared for burial, but the other gospels indicate this could not be done because the Sabbath laws prevented work.
- In all of the gospels, Mary Magdalene visits the tomb to finish preparing the body. The accounts disagree over which women may have gone with her. In Matthew's gospel, an angel appears and rolls the stone back from the tomb. The others say it was already removed when the women arrived.

> ❝… In their fright the women bowed down with their faces to the ground, but the men said to them, "Why do you look for the living among the dead? **He is not here; he has risen!** Remember how he told you, while he was still with you in Galilee: 'The Son of Man must be delivered into the hands of sinners, be crucified and on the third day be raised again.'" Then they remembered his words. ❞
> *Luke 24:5–9*

> ❝…Christ died for our sins according to the Scriptures, that he was buried, that **he was raised on the third day according to the Scriptures**, and that he appeared to Peter, and then to the Twelve. After that, he appeared to more than five hundred of the brothers at the same time, most of whom are still living, though some have fallen asleep. Then he appeared to James, then to all the apostles, and last of all he appeared to me also, as to one abnormally born. ❞
> *1 Corinthians 15:3–8*

- In all of the gospels except Luke, Jesus appears to women first. John says Mary mistook Jesus for a gardener and when she recognised him, he told her not to touch him. In Luke, Jesus appears first to two disciples on the road to Emmaus; they do not initially recognise him.
- All the gospels report that Jesus appeared to the disciples. In Mark and Luke this was while they were eating. For Luke, they recognised him the moment he broke bread. In John, he appeared twice while they hid from authorities in a locked room. In Luke and John, the disciples were able to touch Jesus and his wounds.

The differences in these accounts need not be a problem for Christians. Some Christians try to **harmonise** these stories. Others believe that the details reflect the interests of the writer, but the fundamental truth of Jesus' **resurrection** is more important.

The importance of the resurrection

Paul teaches that there is no doubt that Jesus returned from death. He cites many meetings between Jesus and others after his resurrection, including his own experience, offering them as evidence. He reminds the church in Corinth that all of this was prophesied in scriptures.

Useful term

harmonise – fit together, expanding or completing the story

Christians believe that only one who is truly God has power over life and death, so this event confirms Jesus' divine nature and his victory over sin and death. They also believe that death is no longer something to be feared. On the Day of Judgement, God will resurrect them so they can participate in the close relationship with him for which they were created. Paul states that Christ's resurrection is evidence for this.

Challenges to the resurrection

Some people argue there are other explanations for Jesus' reappearance that seem more likely than his resurrection. Maybe:

- the women went to the wrong tomb
- the disciples stole his body and lied about it
- Jesus was not dead and just needed time to recover
- it was just wishful thinking from his followers.

Others argue that Mary had accompanied Jesus' body to the tomb, so knew where it was. The disciples had little motive to risk arrest from the guards after what had happened to Jesus. The Romans were experts at killing people, and a guard had checked Jesus was dead by piercing his side with a spear. A man so seriously injured is unlikely to recover enough to move a giant boulder and escape. Finally, the disciples had to be reminded of Jesus' teaching. They were not expecting him to rise again.

The ascension of Jesus Christ

Luke reports that the ascension of Jesus happened 40 days after his resurrection. After Jesus met with his followers and showed them his power over sin and death, he ascended or was raised up into heaven to be with God. Christians believe that Jesus is still alive today.

> 'But if it is preached that Christ has been raised from the dead, how can some of you say that there is no resurrection of the dead? **If there is no resurrection of the dead, then not even Christ has been raised.** And if Christ has not been raised, our preaching is useless and so is your faith.'
> *1 Corinthians 15:12–14*

All the gospels report women finding the tomb empty

> 'When he had led them out to the vicinity of Bethany, he lifted up his hands and blessed them. **While he was blessing them, he left them and was taken up into heaven.** Then they worshipped him and returned to Jerusalem with great joy. And they stayed continually at the temple, praising God.'
> *Luke 24:50–53*

Some Christians understand the story of the ascension literally, believing that Jesus rose into the sky to be in heaven with God. Others interpret this symbolically: the story shows that Jesus has triumphed over evil and resides with God.

Knowledge recall

1 Define the following concepts: atonement, resurrection. (You can find these definitions on page 101.)

2 List three events from the gospel stories which indicate that Jesus was resurrected from the dead.

3 State two reasons why Jesus' resurrection is so important to Christians.

Evaluation practice

4 Give two reasons why some people might deny Jesus' resurrection and two reasons why others might accept it.

5 Which do you think is the most persuasive reasoning and why?

Salvation

Specification focus

Salvation: Law: Word of God; inspiration and revelation: differing ways of interpreting biblical writings; Bible in relation to other sources of authority; sin as preventing salvation; grace and the Spirit: Acts 2:1–6; the role of Holy Spirit in Evangelical worship.

Law

The Bible contains several different kinds of writings, including poetry, prophecy, letters, history and law. Law is described as a gift from God to the Jewish nation, and part of a **covenant** with God. Jewish people obey God's law and in return he protects them. The **Torah** (or Pentateuch) is the Old Testament books of Law: Genesis, Exodus, Leviticus, Numbers and Deuteronomy.

In the New Testament, Jesus extended the covenant with God to **Gentiles** as well as Jews. Peter and Paul both taught that Christians could have freedom from the complex restrictions of the law, instead requiring only faith in return for Christ's gift of saving grace.

Most Christians agree that moral behaviour is still important. Even though Jesus' teachings in the New Testament indicate that Christians no longer need to obey each letter of the Jewish law, personal sin can still get in the way of a person's relationship with God.

Differing ways of interpreting biblical writings

Christians describe the Bible as the word of God – his revelation to humanity – but they may have different views about what that means.

- Some think the Bible was dictated by God to humans, who wrote it down word for word. No human writer had any control over the content of the Bible. Every word of the Bible is literally true and inerrant.
- Many believe that God inspired humans with his message, and they wrote it down in a way that was understandable to people at the time. The stories that convey God's message do not all require a literal interpretation. Christians must interpret the message in the cultural context that it was given and apply it to life today. The Church can help Christians to do this.
- A few Liberal Christians believe the Bible is not God's direct revelation. It is a human writing about people's experience of God and their responses to him. The stories it contains are not literally true but have hidden meanings.

How a Christian understands the Bible affects how they use it and whether they also rely on other sources of authority for matters of faith and morality.

- If the Bible is the inerrant and complete word of God, then it is all a Christian needs when making decisions of faith and morality.
- If the Bible must be interpreted according to the time, then Church authority is needed to ensure this is done correctly. The Catechism of the Catholic Church or the 39 Articles of the Church of England offer this kind of help by instructing Christians on matters of doctrine and belief.
- If the Bible is a human response to an experience of God, then it can contain errors or cease to be relevant to people today.

Most Christians describe the Bible as God's word, his revelation to humanity

Useful terms

covenant – an agreement or promise between human beings and God
Torah – the Jewish books of Law; the first five books of the Old Testament in the Bible
Gentiles – non-Jewish people
glossolalia – speaking in 'tongues' (languages unknown to the speaker)

Sin as preventing salvation

Salvation means being saved from the consequences of sin. When Adam and Eve ate the forbidden fruit, they brought sin into the world and it is now part of human nature to make sinful choices. For Christians, sin is something which separates people from God and requires punishment. Through his death on the cross, Jesus saved humanity by taking the punishment for sin and making it possible to be close to God again. Salvation is a free gift, offered unconditionally. However, if a Christian wilfully continues to sin, it is like refusing God's gift. A person must accept the gift of salvation to receive its full value. They can do this by believing in Christ and avoiding sin.

Grace and the Spirit

Grace is the word used for God's unconditional gift of love and forgiveness for everyone through Christ. God's gift of grace is unearned and is offered no matter how imperfect a person is. The new covenant means Christians are saved by the grace of God through Christ's sacrifice.

Christians differ over what this means for their behaviour:

- Most Protestant Christians argue that faith in Christ is all that is now required for salvation. Their behaviour will not affect God's forgiveness.
- Others, such as Catholics, argue that good works are still needed to ensure salvation. For example, a Christian should receive the sacraments of Baptism or the Eucharist to receive God's forgiveness.

Before his ascension, Jesus promised to send the disciples his Holy Spirit. Christians believe that this is God's presence with them here and now in the world. Acts 2:2–4 describes when the disciples first felt the force of the Holy Spirit.

Christians claim that the Holy Spirit is present in the world in different ways. It is what gives the sacraments their power and inspires people to follow Christ's example. Some Christians also claim that it can move them personally through their private prayer and inspire them to work for change in the world.

The Holy Spirit in Evangelical worship

Evangelical worship is usually founded on the understanding that the Bible is God's direct revelation to human beings and is the sole authority. The Holy Spirit inspires people directly to understand and follow God's will.

Evangelical worship makes time for the Holy Spirit in church. It is common for prayer to be noisy as everyone lifts their own prayers to God. They may be inspired by the Holy Spirit to speak in tongues, to give prophesy, to ask for physical or emotional healing and claim to receive it.

> 'Suddenly a sound like the blowing of a violent wind came from heaven and filled the whole house where they were sitting. They saw what seemed to be tongues of fire that separated and came to rest on each of them. **All of them were filled with the Holy Spirit and began to speak in other tongues** as the Spirit enabled them.'
> *Acts 2:2–4*

- The Day of Pentecost is a Jewish festival that the disciples were celebrating.
- The Holy Spirit enabled the disciples to spread the news of Christ's salvation to visitors who did not share their language.
- Some Christians believe they experience this gift of **glossolalia** under the influence of the Holy Spirit today.

The Bible describes how tongues of fire rested on each of the disciples and they were filled with the Holy Spirit

Knowledge recall

1. Define the following concepts: omnibenevolent, sacraments. (You can find these definitions on page 101.)
2. List three different ways of interpreting biblical writings.
3. Suggest two Christian responses to whether good works are needed for salvation.

Evaluation practice

4. Give an argument for and an argument against relying on the Holy Spirit for guidance.
5. Which argument do you think is the strongest and why?

The afterlife

Eschatological beliefs

Biblical writers believed they were living in the end times. Although Jesus had ascended to heaven, they expected him to return at any moment and establish a new world order. This belief is known as the **Parousia**.

> 'My Father's house has many rooms; if that were not so, would I have told you that I am going there to prepare a place for you? And **if I go and prepare a place for you, I will come back and take you to be with me** that you also may be where I am.'
> *John 14:2–7*

- Jesus is comforting his disciples over the news that he will soon be leaving.
- Jesus confirms he will return and that there is an existence beyond this life.

When Christ did not immediately return, Christians had to reinterpret Jesus' teaching about the end times. These **eschatological** concerns are most obvious in John's gospel.

> 'I am the resurrection and the life. **The one who believes in me will live, even though they die**; and whoever lives by believing in me will never die. Do you believe this?'
> *John 11:25–26*

- Jesus was speaking to Martha, whose brother Lazarus had died.
- Four days after Lazarus' death, Jesus raised him back to life.
- Jesus confirms that through faith in him, death is not the end.

Some Christians still await the Parousia as a divine intervention by God. Others do not interpret this teaching literally. Instead they believe it means God's plan is not yet complete, or that the Kingdom of God is something they can be part of now through their spiritual and ethical behaviour.

Judgement

Christianity teaches that when Christ returns and the world ends, humans will be resurrected and judged. People will then be sent to either heaven or hell. On this Day of Judgement, God will judge people for their actions in this life. In the gospel of Matthew, the parable of the sheep and the goats explains this:

- Christ returns and gathers all nations before him.
- He separates people like a shepherd separates sheep from goats.
- He welcomes the sheep on his right, to inherit his kingdom.
- Christ tells the goats on his left to go, cursed into the eternal fire because they did not help those in need.

> 'For **I was hungry and you gave me something to eat**, I was thirsty and you gave me something to drink, I was a stranger and you invited me in, I needed clothes and you clothed me, I was ill and you looked after me, I was in prison and you came to visit me.'
> *Matthew 25:35–36*

Useful terms

Parousia – the second coming of Christ on the Day of Judgement
eschatological – concerned with the end times or 'last things' in the history of the world
soma pneumatikon – a spiritual body
purgatory – the purification of souls still tainted by less serious sins

This parable teaches Christians to invest in their afterlife by acting well in the present. The quality of their lives will be judged by God.

The parable of the rich man and Lazarus in Luke 16:19–31 emphasises that wealth and luxury will be of no help after death. People should be generous and kind now so they will be judged well when their earthly lives are over.

Read about the parable of the rich man and Lazarus on page 92.

Resurrection

Christian ideas about the afterlife are based on the **resurrection** of Jesus. The Bible tells how Jesus' resurrected body was not identical to his earthly body. He could walk through locked doors and was not always recognisable. However, he could touch, eat and speak, suggesting that he was still a physical being.

Christians believe that humans consist of both body and soul. The Apostle Paul says that when a person dies, their soul will be clothed in a new body that resembles the old one but is **soma pneumatikon**. Paul describes how people's resurrected bodies will not be their resuscitated earthly bodies. Instead they will be transformed into a glorified state in preparation for a new life with God.

Christians believe Jesus will return to judge humanity on their behaviour

'So will it be with the resurrection of the dead. The body that is sown is perishable, it is raised imperishable; it is sown in dishonour, it is raised in glory; it is sown in weakness, it is raised in power; **it is sown a natural body, it is raised a spiritual body.**'
1 Corinthians 15:42–44

- Paul emphasises the difference between a material body and a spiritual body.
- The resurrected body is different and superior to the earthly body.
- There is continuity of identity between the earthly life and the resurrected life but, like a caterpillar becoming a butterfly, they are not the same.

Traditional and contemporary beliefs about heaven and hell

Jesus taught that there would be eternal life after death. In Luke's gospel, he tells a criminal who is crucified with him that 'today you will be with me in paradise' as a result of his faith.

Christians believe heaven is the goal of earthly life. It is an existence in the presence of God for eternity. In the Bible, heaven is described as a beautiful place. Some Christians understand this literally, but others consider heaven to be a spiritual state of bliss where suffering no longer exists.

Christianity teaches that the existence of hell allows people to use their free will to reject God. Some still see hell as a literal place of fiery torment, while others think it is just distance from God. Some argue that it is complete annihilation.

Catholicism teaches that some will go to **purgatory**, a temporary place of purification that prepares a person for heaven. This teaching is not accepted by Protestant Churches, but for Catholics it means that if a person dies with lesser unrepented sins but has faith in God, they will not be punished for eternity.

Knowledge recall

1 Define the following concepts: atonement, resurrection. (You can find these definitions on page 101.)
2 List four things that will happen on the Day of Judgement according to Christian teaching.
3 Give one example of how Christians believe people will be judged by God after death.

Evaluation practice

4 Give one reason why some Christians believe heaven and hell are real places, and one reason why others believe they are not.
5 Which do you think is the most reasonable belief? Give two reasons why.

Skills practice

On these exam practice pages you will see example answers for each of the exam question types: **a**, **b**, **c** and **d**. You can find out more about these on pages 5–9.

Question (a)

*Question (a) tests your knowledge and understanding. You will always be asked to **define a key concept** in this question. You can find a list of the concepts at the beginning of the chapter.*

> (a)   What do Christians mean by 'incarnation'?   [2]

Student response

> Incarnation is to do with resurrection or birth.

Improved student response

> Incarnation is to do with God becoming human or being 'made flesh' by being born as Jesus.

🕐 **Over to You!** Have a try at answering this question:

> (a)   What do Christians mean by the 'Trinity'?   [2]

Helpful hints
To help you answer this question effectively, you could use the check list below to make sure you include the most important things:

- **Synonym** – Include a synonym or another way of describing the term 'Trinity'.
- **Example** – Give an example of something that Christians use to try to help people understand the relationship between the three parts of the Trinity.

Now give yourself **two minutes** to answer this question by yourself:

> (a)   What do Christians mean by 'omnipotent'?   [2]

Question (b)

*Question (b) tests your knowledge and understanding. It will always ask you to **describe** a belief, a teaching, a practice or an event that is included on the specification.*

> (b)   Describe the crucifixion of Jesus.   [5]

What went well
The candidate has understood that the incarnation is connected with new life and has hinted towards a link with Christ.

How to improve
You must use a synonym (another word that has the same or similar meaning) for 'incarnation' to show that you understand what it means, e.g. 'made flesh'.

You should learn the exam board's definition of the word at the start of this chapter.

You could develop your answer to demonstrate your understanding, e.g. specifically stating that Jesus was born as a human.

Tip
In this response, the candidate has used the exam board definition by talking about God becoming human, but they have also used the literal term ('made flesh') and demonstrated their understanding of the incarnation by mentioning Jesus.

Student response

Jesus knew he was going to be betrayed so he revealed this at the Last Supper with his followers and he told them he knew that. He broke the bread and shared the wine and told them that this symbolised his body and his blood. He also knew that one of the disciples would betray him and he revealed this to them too. Judas told the Romans where Jesus was, and they found him, and arrested him. He had to carry his cross to the top of the hill. He got nailed to a cross with a crown of thorns put on his head. And to make sure he was dead, they stabbed him in the abdomen.

Improved student response

Jesus was flogged after his trial and mocked by being dressed as a king and having a crown of thorns placed on his head. He should have carried his own cross up the hill to Golgotha, but he was too weak, so Simon of Cyrene was forced to do it for him. He was nailed by his hands or wrists to the crossbeam and hoisted on to the main beam where he was nailed by his feet. A sign was placed over his head that declared him the 'King of the Jews' to mock him. He was offered wine mixed with gall to drink but he refused. At the sixth hour into his crucifixion, the land went dark. It took him nine hours to die and just before he died, he called out 'My God, My God, why have you forsaken me?'

Over to You! Have a try at answering this question:

(b) Describe Christian teaching about the role of humans. [5]

Helpful hints

Use the check list below to make sure you include the most important things:

- **How/Why** – Explain what Christians teach about God's purpose in creating humanity.
- **Example** – Give an example of a teaching or story from the Bible or from Church teaching about the purpose of human life or what God commanded humans to do.
- **Repeat** – Then repeat the above process for two more Christian ideas about the role of human beings in the world.

Study Challenge:

The exam board will only ever ask a question **(b)** that asks you to describe an area from the specification, for example, a belief, teaching, practice or event.

- Look back at the specification focus boxes at the top of each page in this chapter.
- Choose one area from the list that has not yet appeared in the questions above.
- Write your own **(b)** question on this area that begins with the word 'Describe'.
- Now give yourself **five minutes** to answer this question by yourself!

What went well

The candidate has included some description of the crucifixion of Jesus by mentioning that he should have carried his cross, that the crucifixion happened on a hilltop, the crown of thorns and the soldier checking that Jesus was dead.

How to improve

You must focus on the aspect of the question that asks about the crucifixion rather than unnecessary detail of what led up to it.

You should try to go through the sequence of events in chronological order.

You could include evidence of detailed knowledge by quoting the Bible or including names of people or places.

Tip

The best answers will go through as many of the chronological events of the crucifixion as possible. They will include reference to scripture and details such as who was present and the words that were spoken.

Question (c)

Question (c) tests your knowledge and understanding. You need to give detailed evidence and reasoning to support your explanation of the topic. You may need to show how belief influences religious practice. This is not an evaluation question so you don't need to evaluate different viewpoints.

> (c) Explain why Christians believe the Resurrection of Jesus is important. [8]

Student response

It is supposed to show that God can perform miracles. Because bringing someone back to life whose body is almost completely intact somehow shows the power of an omnipotent God and doing this one act somehow gives Christians all the proof they need that God is the most powerful being that is possible to exist. For someone who has infinite power, bringing just one human being back to life doesn't really seem worth it. Obviously bringing someone back to life is a powerful thing and he would have to be powerful to do that, but he is supposed to have infinite power and bringing one human back to life whose body was almost completely intact doesn't seem that impressive really.

Improved student response

The Resurrection of Jesus is important to Christians because it shows that God performs miracles in the world today. The gospels say that Jesus was brought back to life after being dead for three days, and Christians are expected to believe this as it says in the Nicene Creed that Christians recite, 'I believe... he rose again on the third day.' This is the ultimate miracle, showing God's omnipotence. This belief is of central importance in the Christian Church as it shows God's power over death, sin and the devil. Jesus died so that humans can be forgiven for their sin, but then he was raised back to life so that people can have a new start with their relationship with God. It even goes as far as to show that Jesus is part of the Trinity – he is the Son of God if he can even defeat death. It also means that Christians can now expect the same to happen to them, and that they will be resurrected after death. As Paul says in I Corinthians, 'If Christ has not been raised, our preaching is useless.'

🕐 **Over to You!** Have a try at answering this question:

> (c) Explain why Christians believe the Bible is important. [8]

Helpful hints

Include **more than one belief** for why the Bible is important (e.g. it contains examples of Christian moral behaviour; it is the word of God).

- For each belief give an **example** from the Bible to demonstrate it (e.g. Jesus mixed with people who were outcasts; it contains the Ten Commandments).
- Explain **why** Christians might believe this (e.g. they are influenced by other teachings about the nature of Christ as the perfect human, or the nature of God as all powerful).

What went well

This response mentions God's power and uses specialist vocabulary. It also mentions that God is active in the world by saying that God performs miracles.

How to improve

You must stick to the requirement of the question to explain why Christians believe it is important, rather than attempting to evaluate.

You should give at least three specific reasons why Christians value the resurrection.

You could include some short quotes or examples as evidence of the beliefs you are explaining.

Tip

This response is improved because it quotes Christian scripture and creeds; it uses specialist vocabulary; and it gives several reasons why the belief is so important.

Now give yourself **eight minutes** to answer this question by yourself:

> (c) Explain why Christians believe heaven is important. [8]

Question (d)

*Question (d) tests your ability to **evaluate**. This means you need to show you have considered more than one point of view and that you have referred to religion and belief. You will need to be able to make judgements that are supported by detailed reasoning and argument.*

> (d) 'For Christians, the Bible is the most important source of authority.' Discuss this statement showing that you have considered more than one point of view. (You must refer to religion and belief in your answer.) [15] Marks for spelling, punctuation and the accurate use of grammar are allocated to this question. [6]

What went well

There is some awareness of two different points of view, including from within Christianity. There is some accurate use of specialist vocabulary.

How to improve

You must avoid subjective personal statements that are not supported by reasoning or evidence.

You should evaluate the ideas that you raise throughout the whole response, avoiding simple descriptions of different views.

You could refer to or even quote sources of wisdom and authority to support your answers.

Student response

The Bible is the most important book for Christians because it is holy, and it tells them what they want to know about morals and about God. They believe what the Bible says about these things and will always do it. Not everyone agrees with Christians though. Muslims follow the Qur'an and so they would say that the Qur'an is the most important source of authority as it is directly from Allah and the Bible is wrong as it has been changed over the years of being passed down, but the Qur'an hasn't. That means that the Bible is not important and so it is not worth following.

I wouldn't follow what someone wrote thousands of years ago because they were not as well-educated as us. Some Christians take the Bible literally and they say that the Bible is the word of God which means it is inerrant and that every word of it is true. Other Christians say that it is not literally true, but we should understand the stories to be a bit like parables where they have a hidden meaning to them that can teach us something, but they didn't really happen. Like the story of Adam and Eve. There was not really a talking snake. But the story shows us that human beings can easily be tempted to do things that they shouldn't. The Bible has lots of stories like this that are not true but might have a moral to the story. Jesus told lots of stories like that.

This candidate makes regular references to the question throughout the response.

Improved student response

The Bible is the most important book for Christians because it is God's revealed word. It is read aloud in church and Christians turn to it regularly for guidance. The Bible is the most important source of authority because it is divine dictation from God, inerrant and literally God's word. However, Conservative Christians argue that if God revealed his word to humans, they would have then written it down in a way that was meaningful to people at the time. So we must also rely on Church authorities like the Pope or the creeds to help us interpret it correctly. The Bible is important, but so is Church teaching. However, Church teaching could not exist without the scripture to inform it, so the Bible is still the most important book for Christians.

Some Christians argue that the Bible is not the most important source of authority; it is one source as God revealed truth to people back then, but he continues to do so

In each paragraph there is a counter-argument which turns the response into analysis rather than just description.

In every paragraph, the candidate gives a reason why one point of view can be chosen as the best.

now through his Holy Spirit. Therefore, the human conscience (or individual revelation through the Holy Spirit) is just as important as the Bible. For instance, if a Christian were given a prophecy at a church service, this would be just as authoritative as the scripture that is read out. However, this view is worrying to other Christians who say that 'revelation' could be corrupted by human interests. If anything can be revealed as the truth, I could declare something false and mislead people. Therefore, revelation should be consistent with scripture. This means that the Bible is still the most important source of authority.

The Bible does not speak on every subject that humans in the twenty first century want guidance on. It does not teach about abortion and does not answer questions about the Trinity. Its content also cannot be proved using scientific evidence. Therefore, some Christians argue that we need other sources of authority to teach us as well, like the Pope for Catholics, or the Book of Common Prayer for Anglicans. Furthermore, there are different kinds of literature in the Bible, things like songs, poetry, letters and so on. These cannot possibly be literal truth. Liberal Christians argue that the Bible may just be human responses to God, not God's revelation at all. So, while the Bible is important, it is not most important if it contains nothing that can be confirmed as the voice of God.

Examples are given of alternative Christian approaches to the authority of scripture, and they are described using appropriate specialist vocabulary.

The candidate uses evidence of the Christian practice of reading the Bible aloud in church services to demonstrate its importance.

The candidate gives examples of the different types of content in the Bible to support their answer.

🕐 **Over to You!** Have a try at answering this question:

(d) 'Christian beliefs about hell are out of date.'
Discuss this statement showing that you have considered more than one point of view. (You must refer to religion and belief in your answer.) [15]
Marks for spelling, punctuation and the accurate use of grammar are allocated to this question. [6]

Helpful hints

If you find it difficult to answer this question effectively, you could use the A, B, C, D structure or a variation of it to help you set out your paragraphs (see page 32).

In addition, remember that you should be analysing and evaluating throughout your response.

- **Analysis** – studying an idea in detail to gain more understanding of it.
- **Evaluation** – judging or calculating the value of an idea.

This means you need to try to think about the question from more than one angle, see what evidence there is for the statement, and judge which view is the best one. In every paragraph, try to make sure you include more than one point of view.

Now give yourself **fifteen minutes** to answer this question by yourself:

(d) 'Jesus was just an ordinary man.'
Discuss this statement showing that you have considered more than one point of view. (You must refer to religion and belief in your answer.) [15]
Marks for spelling, punctuation and the accurate use of grammar are allocated to this question. [6]

Tip
Remember that in this question there are up to six marks attached for spelling, punctuation and grammar. In particular, make sure you learn how to spell the key words.

Tip
Think of yourself as a detective, looking for clues to see whether the statement in the question is true or false. You will find evidence on both sides but then you need to weigh up that evidence and decide which would be most convincing in court!

Chapter 6:
Christianity: Practices

Introduction

In this chapter, you will consider how Christian beliefs are expressed in practice through the daily lives of Christians in Great Britain and across the world. Christianity is a living, vibrant world faith that is expressed in a wide range of different ways, and there has been disagreement between denominations regarding the correct way to worship or the importance of sacraments and festivals. Christians around the globe must respond to the reality of the modern world and have developed a range of ways to do this. As you learn about the ways that Christians practise their faith, you will see that there are differences based on culture as well as denomination and personal preference.

Things to remember:

- Christianity is still the main religion in Great Britain, although there has been a rise in the number of people who consider themselves Atheist, Buddhist, Hindu, Jewish, Muslim or Sikh. Not all Christians in Britain express their faith in the same way.

- The church a person chooses to attend may be affected by their upbringing and their cultural origin. Pentecostal and free churches are popular amongst Christians who have moved to Britain from West Africa or the Caribbean. These churches often have a different atmosphere to Catholic or Church of England churches.

- Christianity has split into many different denominations since Jesus' time. This process has been bitter at times, and some Christians still reject each other's faith. However, there have been huge efforts made by Churches to bring reconciliation. For example, through the development of the ecumenical movement (see page 138).

- Christianity is an evangelical religion. Christians believe that faith in Jesus can save people from eternal damnation, and they wish to share this belief with as many people as possible so they can be saved too. This is evident in the practice of mission and evangelism. When a Christian shares their faith, they do so because they believe it will help someone.

Concepts

Omnipotent – the all-powerful, almighty and unlimited nature of God

Omnibenevolent – the state of being all-loving and infinitely good – a characteristic often attributed to God

Trinity – the three persons of God; God the Father, Son and Holy Spirit

Incarnation – God becoming human in the form of Jesus

Atonement – the belief that Jesus' death on the cross healed the rift between humans and God

Resurrection – the belief that Jesus rose from the dead on Easter Sunday, conquering death

Sacraments – an outward sign of an invisible and inward blessing by God. For example, Baptism, the Eucharist

Evangelism – preaching the gospel to others with the intention of converting them to the Christian faith

Forms of worship

Christian worship shows devotion to God and the practice varies widely according to denomination, culture and personal preference. The most important weekly worship service occurs on Sunday, reflecting the day that Jesus was raised to life. When this follows a set pattern, it is called liturgical worship.

Liturgical worship

Liturgical worship is when the worship follows a traditional, formal structure to ensure that any beliefs or practices contained within it are consistent with the Bible and do not commit heresy. The **liturgy** used differs between denominations. The Catholic Church structures their **corporate** act of celebrating the Eucharist using the **Missale Romanum**, whereas the main official liturgy of the Anglican Church is the Book of Common Prayer.

Liturgy dictates things like the colour of priests' robes throughout the year, the ritual actions performed, the order of set prayers or readings, the recitation of creeds and the topics for sermons. It sets the order of events for occasions like the Eucharist, Baptism, confirmation, weddings, ordination, funerals and ordinary services.

Informal worship

Informal worship happens in all denominations and is particularly popular among congregations containing young people. Informal worship is also corporate but more spontaneous in style. It may follow a structure of songs, prayers and a sermon, but the service leader chooses any themes, readings and music. Evangelical, Pentecostal and free churches favour this style of worship because of the emphasis placed on biblical teaching and allowing the Holy Spirit to work in the worshippers' lives.

Individual worship

The Bible teaches that both corporate and individual worship are important:

> ❛But when you pray, go into your room, close the door and pray to your Father who is unseen.❜
> *Matthew 6:6*

When worshipping alone, a person may pray, meditate, read the Bible or use a study guide to interpret God's word. Individual worship gives Christians space to hear the Holy Spirit's guidance.

It is possible for one church to participate in all three types of worship. Some churches set aside separate services for liturgical and informal worship to suit the needs of the whole community.

The nature and importance of prayer

The Bible often shows Jesus praying and teaching about the importance of communication with God. The reasons why a person prays can be remembered with the acronym **ACTS**:

Adoration – praising God

Confession – saying sorry and asking for forgiveness

Specification focus

Forms of worship: The nature and significance of liturgical, informal and individual worship: Matthew 18:20; the nature and importance of prayer: The Lord's Prayer; set prayers and informal prayers: different forms of worship across the different Christian traditions with reference of Society of Friends and Evangelical worship.

Liturgy can dictate every detail of the events in a service

> ❛For where two or three gather in my name, there am I with them.❜
> *Matthew 18:20*

Useful terms

liturgy – the prescribed set of words and rituals that take place during a church service

corporate – shared by a whole group, not just an individual

Missale Romanum – Roman Missal. Contains the exact wording and pattern for Catholic worship.

intercession – to ask on behalf of another person

doxology – an expression of praise

charismatic – lively, informal worship that emphasises the Holy Spirit

Thanksgiving – thanking God for what he has done

Supplication – asking for something for oneself or **intercession** for others

In the gospels, Jesus taught his followers how to pray in what is known as the Lord's Prayer, which incorporates three of these reasons for prayer. The prayer as it appears in Matthew's gospel is recited in church services today with the addition of the final sentence below, known as the **doxology**.

> 'Pray continually, give thanks in all circumstances; for this is God's will for you in Christ Jesus.'
> *1 Thessalonians 5:17–18*

Our Father in heaven,
hallowed be your name,
Your kingdom come, your will be done
On earth as it is in heaven. — **Adoration**

Give us today our daily bread. — **Supplication**

And forgive us our debts,
As we also have forgiven our debtors. — **Confession**

And lead us not into temptation,
But deliver us from the evil one. — **Supplication**

For the kingdom, the power,
and the glory are yours
now and for ever.
Amen. — **Adoration**

Prayer is also for thanksgiving. In the Bible, Jesus regularly thanks God and Paul tells the Thessalonians to give constant thanks to God.

Set prayers and informal prayers

Set prayers, like the Lord's Prayer, are recited by the congregation as part of liturgical worship. Alternatively, a priest says part of a prayer and the congregation answers. For example, there is a prayer known as the Intercession in which the congregation prays for the Church and the world. After each prayer, the priest says 'Lord, in your mercy', to which the congregation responds 'Hear our prayer'.

Extemporaneous (informal) prayers are more spontaneous and personal. These may be public or private and use everyday language guided by the Holy Spirit.

Quaker worship is informal with no leader or liturgy, and prayer is extemporaneous. The emphasis in Quaker worship is to listen to God and reflect on his message. Worship takes place in a Meeting House; chairs may be arranged in a circle around a table that only contains a Bible. Services are usually silent until someone feels moved to speak, sing or pray aloud (called 'giving ministry').

Charismatic Evangelicals tend to favour more informal worship, often with modern musical instruments. It is believed to be led by the Holy Spirit and to contain the gifts of the Spirit that were seen by the disciples on the Day of Pentecost. It is lively and relaxed, with clapping, shouting, dancing, glossolalia and raised hands to receive the Holy Spirit. Some services contain a time for people to pray for and receive healing.

Informal evangelical worship can be very noisy and spontaneous

Read about the Day of Pentecost on page 115.

Knowledge recall

1 Define the following concepts: omnipotent, evangelism. (You can find these definitions on page 123.)
2 List and define three different types of worship.
3 State four different purposes of prayer.

Evaluation practice

4 Give one reason why some Christians might prefer liturgical worship and one reason why others might prefer informal worship.
5 Which of these views do you think is most convincing and which is least convincing? Give a reason why for each.

The sacraments: Baptism

Diverse beliefs regarding the sacraments

A **sacrament** is defined as an outward, visible sign of an inward, invisible blessing by God. This means a **rite** is performed that is believed to be linked to a spiritual gift of grace from God.

The Catholic Church teaches that there are seven sacraments, which were all established by Christ through his example in the gospels and are necessary for salvation.

1. Baptism	
2. Confirmation	Sacraments of Initiation
3. Eucharist	
4. Penance	Sacraments of Healing
5. Anointing of the Sick	
6. Ordination	Sacraments of Service
7. Marriage	

The Church of England and many other Protestant denominations only recognise the gospel sacraments. These two sacraments of Baptism and the Eucharist were directly commanded by Christ in the gospels and are necessary for salvation.

Not all Protestants see the sacraments as necessary for salvation or even recognise them at all. The Quakers (the Society of Friends) and the Salvation Army reject all sacraments because they believe:

- Jesus did not intend for Baptism or the Eucharist to become a rigid constraint for people.
- Rituals are a distraction. They become the focus of worship, with the inward grace forgotten.
- There is no need for a ritual to be performed to secure God's grace.
- God can speak directly to an individual's heart. He does not need a mechanism to do it.

The meaning of Baptism

All four gospels tell of Jesus' Baptism in the river Jordan by John the Baptist. As Jesus came out of the water, the heavens opened, the Holy Spirit descended on him like a dove and God's voice was heard. Jesus was baptised as an adult and the event marked the beginning of his **ministry**.

For most Christians, Baptism marks initiation into the Christian Church. It is also a sacrament that is essential to salvation. Jesus made this clear in his teaching:

> ❝Jesus replied, "Very truly I tell you, no one can see the kingdom of God unless they are born again." "How can someone be born when they are old?" Nicodemus asked. "Surely they cannot enter a second time into their mother's womb to be born!" Jesus answered, "Very truly I tell you, **no one can enter the kingdom of God unless they are born of water and the Spirit**. Flesh gives birth to flesh, but the Spirit gives birth to spirit."❞
> *John 3:3–6*

Specification focus

Sacraments: Diverse beliefs regarding Sacraments; the role, meaning and celebration of Baptism: John 3:3–6; diverse interpretations of Baptism with reference to the beliefs of the Catholic and Protestant Churches.

In 2019, actor and hip hop artist Lecrae Moore was baptised in the river Jordan

Useful terms

rite – religious ceremony or practice
ministry – a period of service or work
font – a large container for baptismal water, often made of stone
Believer's Baptism – Baptism as an adult
testimony – the story of someone's personal journey into the Christian faith
penitence – confession and repentance for sin, resulting in forgiveness

The outward sign of Baptism is speaking the words of the **Trinity** and the use of water, signifying the death of the old, sinful life and birth into a new life with God. The inward grace is receiving the Holy Spirit, being cleansed of sin and being welcomed into God's Kingdom.

After his resurrection, Jesus instructed that all Christians should be baptised, and stated the formula to be used, which is described in Matthew 28:19.

In the Catholic tradition, Baptism is the first sacrament. It is required to access all other sacraments and be welcomed into the Church. Baptism is the only way to wash away the stain of Original Sin. The Catholic Church practises Infant Baptism so that anyone, even a baby, can receive God's forgiveness, be saved from sin and access eternal life in heaven. This is vital if a child is sick or dying.

> 'Therefore go and make disciples of all nations, baptising them in the name of the Father and of the Son and of the Holy Spirit.'
> *Matthew 28:19*

The celebration of Baptism

A person can only receive Baptism once in their lifetime. It is performed by a priest or authorised layperson at a Sunday church service. In Infant Baptism:

- Some Christians like to dress the infant in white to symbolise purity.
- The baby's head is anointed with oil in the sign of the cross.
- Water is poured from a **font** over their head three times to represent the three persons of the Trinity.
- Parents and godparents make promises on behalf of the child.
- Promises are made using a question-and-answer liturgy to accept the creed, renounce evil and raise the child as a Christian.
- A lighted candle is given to the child's family as a sign of Christ, the light of the world.

Infant Baptism can also be found in the Anglican and Orthodox Churches as well as a Protestant denomination called Presbyterianism.

Infant Baptism means that even a baby can receive God's forgiveness

While the Church of England sacrament resembles the Catholic tradition, other Protestants such as Baptists or Pentecostals practise **Believer's Baptism**. This is partly because Jesus was an adult when he was baptised, but also because only adults can choose faith in God for themselves. For these Churches, Baptism is a sign a person has been anointed by the Holy Spirit, but it is not needed for salvation.

Believer's Baptism is usually by full immersion where the person's whole body goes into the water. Some churches have a small, deep pool called a baptistry, or a person might travel to a river, the sea or a swimming pool to be baptised.

- Baptists usually give their **testimony**, telling of their conversion or their journey into the Christian faith.
- Those who are to be baptised publicly declare **penitence** for their sins.
- The person's whole body is fully immersed into the water, for some this happens three times. This symbolises death to the old life and rebirth into the new.
- There is no need for parents or godparents to be present because the person can make the decision to turn to Christ themselves.

Knowledge recall

1 Define the following concepts: Trinity, sacraments. (You can find these definitions on page 123.)
2 List the seven sacraments of the Catholic Church.
3 State two different ways in which Baptism is practised by different Christian Churches.

Evaluation practice

4 Give two reasons why some Christians accept Infant Baptism and two reasons why others do not.
5 Which of these views do you think is the most compelling? Give a reason why.

The sacraments: the Eucharist

Specification focus

Sacraments: Diverse beliefs regarding Sacraments; the role, meaning and celebration of the Eucharist; diverse interpretations of the Eucharist with reference to the beliefs of the Catholic and Protestant Churches.

The meaning of the Eucharist

The Eucharist is known by many different names: The Lord's Supper, the Divine Liturgy, the Breaking of Bread and Holy Communion. It is the central act within a worship service for most Christians.

The Eucharist is the re-enactment of the Last Supper that Jesus shared with his disciples at Passover, before his arrest and crucifixion. At this meal, Jesus shared bread and wine with his disciples, and then instructed them to do the same in his memory.

Christians today share bread and wine, remember Christ's death for the forgiveness of sins, and thank God for his gift of grace as part of their worship. In 1 Corinthians, Paul gives liturgical directions to Christians so that they celebrate correctly. These words are repeated during a service containing the Eucharist.

Read more about the Last Supper on page 110.

> 'The Lord Jesus, on the night he was betrayed, took bread, and when he had given thanks, he broke it and said, "This is my body, which is for you; do this in remembrance of me." In the same way, after supper he took the cup, saying, "This cup is the new covenant in my blood; do this, whenever you drink it, in remembrance of me." '
> *1 Corinthians 11:23–25*

This Bible passage refers to the new covenant. In the Old Testament, a covenant was made between God and the Jews which ensured God would take care of them and in return the Jewish people would obey his commands. The new covenant allowed **Gentiles** to participate in God's promise. It gave them forgiveness from sin and the promise of eternal life simply in exchange for faith.

Useful terms

Gentiles – non-Jewish people
consecrated – made sacred
altar – a table at the front and centre of the church from which the Eucharist is celebrated
chalice – a large cup or goblet used for carrying and sharing the wine during the Eucharist
transubstantiation – where there is a complete change in the substance of the bread and wine to become the body and blood of Christ
absolution – forgiveness for sin

Celebration of the Eucharist

Catholics, Orthodox Christians and Anglicans follow a clear Eucharistic liturgy to mark this covenant. There is a fixed order of service that sets out which prayers should be said and how the Eucharist is to be shared.

The Catholic Church states that Christians should celebrate the Eucharist at least once a year at Easter, but preferably they should receive it at least once a week,

The Eucharist is a re-enactment and remembrance of the Last Supper

as it is essential to bring them into union with Christ. To receive the Eucharist in a Catholic Church, a person must:

- be a Catholic.
- be baptised and confirmed.
- have fasted for at least an hour beforehand.
- be in a state of grace. This means they should have confessed their sins. The liturgy includes a prayer of confession before the **sacrament**, but Catholics should also attend confession.

During the service, the Eucharistic prayer is recited as the bread and wine are **consecrated**. This is a prayer of thanksgiving to God for all that he has given the Church through Christ's crucifixion and **resurrection**. During the Mass, members of the congregation approach the **altar** and are given small wafer discs to eat, and wine from a shared cup or **chalice**.

Catholics believe that during the consecration of bread, **transubstantiation** occurs. This is where God causes a complete change in the substance of the bread and the wine so they become the actual body and blood of Christ, while their outward appearance remains the same.

Protestant understandings of the Eucharist

Many Protestants also celebrate the Eucharist but do not accept transubstantiation. There are two main ways in which Protestants have interpreted the Eucharist in the past:

- Consubstantiation – Christ's real presence coexists alongside the bread and the wine after consecration in a real mystical event. The bread and wine do not transform, but they are more than just symbolic.
- Memorialism – there is no real presence of Christ in the bread and wine; they are symbolic representations of Christ.

Today, not all Protestants agree on what happens during the Eucharist. Some take the view that Christ is present spiritually, while others believe that he is not literally present at all.

There are also variations in how the Eucharist is celebrated between different Protestant Churches:

- Some use wafers, others use real bread.
- Some share wine in individual glasses, others from a single cup or chalice.
- Some use wine, others a non-alcoholic substitute like grape juice.
- Some follow a ritual to consecrate the bread and wine, others do not.
- Some pass the wine and bread from person to person; others have it administered by a priest.

Not all Protestant Churches require a person to have been confirmed or even baptised to receive the Eucharist. For some, provided the individual has made a personal commitment to Christ then there is no reason to refuse them. Others, like Baptists, require the person to have been baptised.

Many Protestants do not see the Eucharist as necessary for obtaining God's grace, and not all Protestant Churches require the Eucharist to be celebrated frequently. Baptists usually celebrate once a month, others may celebrate even less often. In addition, some Churches do not require an ordained minister to administer the bread and wine. The difference in practice relates to beliefs about the sacrament. If the bread and wine are considered to be the body and blood of Christ or if the Eucharist ensures **absolution** for sin, then it is treated with more reverence.

Quakers do not celebrate the Eucharist. They do not accept that there needs to be a special ritual to be in communication with God or to receive his grace, and they believe reliance on these rituals is an attempt to constrain the Holy Spirit.

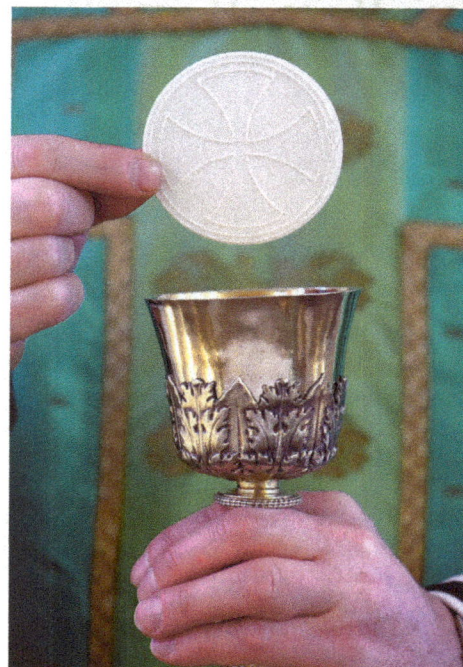

In many traditional churches, the wine is taken from a shared cup called a chalice

Knowledge recall

1 Define the following concepts: resurrection, sacraments. (You can find these definitions on page 123.)
2 List three things that Catholics do as they celebrate the Eucharist.
3 State three different ways that Christians may interpret what happens to the bread and wine in the Eucharist.

Evaluation practice

4 Give two reasons why some Christians celebrate the Eucharist and two reasons why others do not.
5 Which of these reasons is most persuasive? Give a reason why.

Pilgrimage

Specification focus

Pilgrimage and celebrations:
The importance of pilgrimage:
Walsingham, Taizé.

The importance of pilgrimage

Pilgrimage is a journey to a holy place or a sacred site. Christians believe the act of pilgrimage is symbolic of their journey through life as they become closer to God. It can also be an act of **penance**, showing repentance for sin and a desire to change.

In the early days of Christianity, pilgrimages were made to the Holy Land, to places where Jesus had lived and taught, such as Jerusalem, Bethlehem and Nazareth. Such journeys were expensive, dangerous and time-consuming, so it became common for pilgrims to travel to holy places closer to home. For example, Lourdes in France and Fatima in Portugal are the sites of miraculous visions of Mary. Canterbury in the UK was where an archbishop was martyred for his faith.

Some Christians today do not think that pilgrimage is essential to Christian life. They argue that it is religious tourism or that God should be integral to all aspects of a believer's life, not just a specific event. Protestant Christians do not see it as essential to forgiveness since this is already given through Christ's death on the cross. Other Christians, especially Catholics, still perform pilgrimages. They believe that by doing so they can connect with the events of Christ's life or with God's work on earth and be changed spiritually. Some believe God will bless or heal them through their journey.

During the National Pilgrimage, pilgrims process through Walsingham village carrying a statue of Mary

Walsingham

The village of Walsingham in Norfolk has been a popular pilgrimage site for centuries. It is the site of a vision of Mary that took place in 1061:

> Richeldis de Faverches, a Saxon noblewoman, had a recurring vision of Mary, the mother of Jesus. In the vision, Mary took Richeldis to her home in Nazareth where the angel Gabriel had announced Jesus' birth. Richeldis was instructed to make a replica of the house. She was given a sign of two possible sites where it could be built and chose one, but having kept an all-night prayer vigil, she discovered the Holy House had been miraculously built on the second site overnight.

This legend led to Walsingham being called 'England's Nazareth'. Many people in the Middle Ages travelled to visit the Holy House to pray and connect with God. A **priory** was built to house the Holy House, and this became the focus of pilgrimage. Both were destroyed by King Henry VIII after he split from the Catholic Church in 1534. In the 1930s, a new Holy House was set inside the Shrine Church.

Today, Walsingham is a place of pilgrimage for both Catholic and Protestant pilgrims. It is the site of several events that bring thousands of people to Walsingham. Annually, on the last May bank holiday, the National Pilgrimage begins on Sunday night with an all-night prayer vigil in the Shrine Church. On Monday there are two outdoor services and then pilgrims process through the village. At the end of the day a quiet service is held in the Shrine Church.

Useful terms

penance – demonstration of remorse for sin through the performance of prayer, good works or sacrifice

priory – a building where monks or nuns live, work and pray

ecumenical – encouraging the different Christian churches to unite

commune – a group of people living and working together who share all possessions

monastic – monks or nuns who live simply under a vow of chastity with few possessions so they can dedicate themselves to worship

The Youth Pilgrimage attracts hundreds of young people to camp outdoors for a week, meet other young Christians and learn more about their faith. They attend daily services and join in prayer, workshops and worship as well as barbeques, music and celebrations. It is popular to walk the Holy Mile from the Slipper Chapel to the Shrine Church. This may be done barefoot as an act of penance.

Christians of all denominations who attend these events are looking to find a way out of the distractions of ordinary life and to connect with the spiritual. By visiting Walsingham, they can look at what it means to be a Christian in today's world and refocus when they go back to their everyday lives.

Taizé

Taizé in France is the site of an **ecumenical** Christian **commune**, founded by Roger Schütz before the Second World War. It now houses over 100 **monastic** residents from various denominational backgrounds. These 'brothers' have taken vows of poverty, chastity and obedience and aim to live simple lives.

> In 1940, Brother Roger moved to the French town of Taizé from Switzerland. He wanted to live a simple life, devoted to God and guided by the scriptures. At the start of World War II, Roger and his sister hid refugees and vulnerable people fleeing from the Nazis. They were discovered and had to flee, but returned when the war ended. Together, they sheltered children orphaned by the war and former German prisoners of war.

The commune expanded as more brothers joined and took their monastic vows. The emphasis is on simple living. The brothers do not accept donations or inheritance, and instead give all money to the poor. They live self-sufficiently and spend their lives in prayer. Some brothers have been sent to very poor places around the world to live alongside those who suffer, as a presence of peace and love.

Taizé is well known for its music. Simple, quiet, chant-like song based on scripture is used as a focus for prayer and meditation. Brothers wear ordinary clothes but use white robes during worship. Pilgrims to Taizé are expected to participate in daily prayers three times a day, attend workshops and Bible study groups, and participate in the work of running the commune. They camp in nearby fields and attend candle-lit, silent services in which they meditate on God's presence.

Taizé is a popular destination for young pilgrims, but they have also welcomed Popes, Archbishops and Patriarchs. Pilgrims travel to Taizé to help manage a life change, to search for a deeper spirituality or to set aside time to listen to God without the distractions of everyday life.

Visitors to Taizé take part in candlelit, silent worship three times a day

Knowledge recall

1. Define the following concepts: evangelism, omnibenevolent. (You can find these definitions on page 123.)
2. List four reasons why a Christian might make a pilgrimage.
3. State three actions that a Christian might perform while on a pilgrimage.

Evaluation practice

4. Give two reasons why some Christians think a pilgrimage is essential to faith and two reasons why other Christians might disagree.
5. Which of these views do you find most convincing? Give a reason why.

Celebrations

Christian celebrations

Religious festivals or holy days are a time when religious communities come together to mark special events that play an important part in their faith. For Christians, the Liturgical Year determines the celebrations of Christ's **incarnation** and **resurrection**, providing focus for their central beliefs. Christians gain a sense of community from celebrating these events together, and it reinforces their faith and commitment.

Christmas

Christmas celebrates the incarnation of Jesus. Christ is unlikely to have been born on 25th December, but the celebrations traditionally occur at this time every year. This date is likely to have been chosen to Christianise the meaning of an existing Pagan festival. The Orthodox Church calendar leads Orthodox Christians to celebrate Christmas on or around the 6th or 7th January.

Read about the incarnation on pages 108–109.

Advent

'Advent' means the arrival of something that has been anticipated. During Advent, Christians await and prepare for the coming Christ Child. Preparations begin four Sundays before Christmas Day. Each Sunday, a candle is lit on an advent wreath. Advent calendars are used to count down the days, and many arrange nativity scenes in their homes or churches. Orthodox Christians observe a nativity fast that lasts for 40 days by avoiding animal products.

During the Advent period, Christians may attend several different services:

- Christingle services come from a German tradition where children are given an orange wrapped in a red ribbon. A candle and four cocktail sticks laden with dried fruit or sweets are placed in the orange. The items represent God's gifts to the world, his blood that was shed and the light of Christ.
- In a nativity service, there are readings from the gospel stories of Christ's birth and the events are re-enacted.
- In a carol service, traditional Christmas carols are sung alongside the readings about Christ's birth.

Christingle services occur during Advent

Christmas Eve

Midnight Mass is a service celebrated on the night of Christmas Eve. A final candle, called the Christ Candle, is lit on the Advent wreath. Carols are sung, readings and a sermon are heard, and the Eucharist is shared at midnight, often by candlelight. Orthodox Christians observe a full fast, abstaining from all food as they prepare for Christ's birth.

Christmas Day

The main Christmas Day service is held mid-morning and the Eucharist is celebrated together as a church community. It is a joyful time and ministers from robed traditions wear gold or white. In the Orthodox Church, all-night services are held that end with a proclamation on Christmas morning that Christ is born.

The Salvation Army uses Christmas as a time of work to ensure the homeless are provided for during the winter, as they remember that Jesus' family was poor and

Useful terms

Vatican – term used to describe the chief residence of the Pope and his authority and government
Paschal – relating to Easter or Passover

without shelter before his birth. They form bands to play carols in towns to raise awareness and funds to provide for the poor.

Christmas celebrations in the Western world are more commercialised than in the East, with the buying and receiving of gifts and cards. In the UK, many people celebrate the holiday and its traditions even if they are not Christians.

Easter

Easter is the most important celebration in the Christian calendar, commemorating the death of Jesus and celebrating his resurrection. This celebration marks the central belief of Christianity: Jesus' death for humanity's salvation from sin and his rising to new life and a new covenant.

Easter is a moveable feast so the date on which it is celebrated varies from year to year. In Western Churches it is celebrated on the first Sunday after the full moon, on or after 21st March. The Orthodox Church times it differently so that it always occurs after the Jewish Passover.

Ash Wednesday

The preparation for Easter begins with Lent. This starts on Ash Wednesday and lasts for 40 days. This period recalls Jesus fasting in the desert after his Baptism. During Lent it is traditional to give up a luxury or to fast as an act of penance. Ash Wednesday includes a church service where worshippers receive a cross of ash on their foreheads.

Palm Sunday

The week leading up to Easter is called Holy Week and begins on Palm Sunday. The services remember Jesus' triumphal entry into Jerusalem on a donkey, when the crowds laid palm branches before him. Services may take place outside and can involve a circuit of the church or a walk through the town waving crosses made of palm leaves.

Maundy Thursday

This day marks the Last Supper, Jesus' betrayal and his arrest with an evening Eucharist. Christians remember Jesus' commandment to love each other. Catholic priests may wash the feet of twelve churchgoers as an act of service, just as Jesus washed the feet of his disciples. The Pope holds celebrations in the **Vatican** and washes the feet of those often shunned in Christian society.

Good Friday

This is a day of quiet reflection and mourning. Jesus is believed to have died at 3pm, so services take place in the afternoon around this time. No **sacraments** are shared on this day and Catholics may hold a fast. Some churches hold a parade in the streets carrying a cross. Others hold Passion Plays that re-enact the story of Jesus' death.

Easter Sunday

On Saturday night, some churches hold an all-night or early-morning vigil around a fire outside the church until sunrise. Easter morning is welcomed with joyful celebrations. The **Paschal** candle is lit and Catholics place five pieces of incense in it to represent the five wounds of Christ. The Eucharist is shared and the service is celebratory. Robed ministers will wear white or gold on this day, and flowers fill the church.

The sharing of chocolate Easter eggs is a popular custom. It represents the new life offered by Jesus' resurrection, and is shared by many non-Christians as well. It has become part of UK culture and marks the beginning of spring.

Read about Jesus' resurrection on pages 112–113.

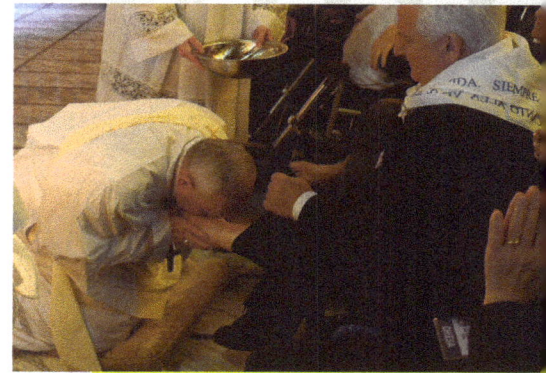

Pope Francis washes the feet of prisoners or people of other faiths as a gesture of servitude and brotherhood on Maundy Thursday

Knowledge recall

1 Define the following concepts: incarnation, resurrection. (You can find these definitions on page 123.)
2 List four ways that a Christian might prepare for Christmas during Advent.
3 State five different ways that Christians celebrate Easter.

Evaluation practice

4 Give one reason why some people might celebrate Christmas by giving lots of gifts and one reason why some Christians might not.
5 Which seems to be the most reasonable view and why?

Christianity in Britain

Specification focus

Christianity in Britain: Results of the 2011 census compared to the 2001 census; UK laws, festivals and traditions are rooted in the Christian traditions whilst also celebrating the festivals, beliefs and cultures of other religious and non-religious traditions; the role of the Church in the local community: a place of worship, social and community functions.

The 2001 and 2011 censuses

Every 10 years a census collects and presents a complete picture of the UK. It is a survey that gathers information about the UK population by asking everyone the same set of questions. It helps the government to plan and run public services.

In 2001 and 2011, the census for England and Wales asked 'What is your religion?' It gave seven options to choose from: Buddhist, Christian, Hindu, Jewish, Muslim, Sikh and none. It was a voluntary question and if people chose not to answer, they were recorded as 'religion not stated'.

Religious affiliation	2001	2011
Christian	71.7%	59.3%
Non-Christian religions	5.7%	8.4%
…of which Muslim	2.9%	4.8%
No religion	14.8%	25.1%
Did not state	7.7%	7.2%

The statistics show that Christianity remains the main religion in Great Britain, but in the ten years between censuses, the number of Christians reduced significantly from 41 million people to 33.2 million.

The data also show a rise in members of non-Christian religious faiths – especially for Islam, which in 2011 was the second largest group with 2.7 million people in England and Wales. Closer analysis shows a rise in the proportion of Christians who have minority ethnic backgrounds. This suggests that increases in the popularity of religion may come from more recent migration.

Another change is the significant rise in the number of people who stated 'no religion' on their census form. This suggests a significant rise in the number of people who are Atheist or Agnostic, from 8.6 million people in 2001 to 14.1 million in 2011.

All this presents Great Britain as an increasingly **pluralist** society, with people from a diverse range of backgrounds living alongside each other. The censuses also show that Britain is increasingly secular with many more people claiming to have 'no religion'.

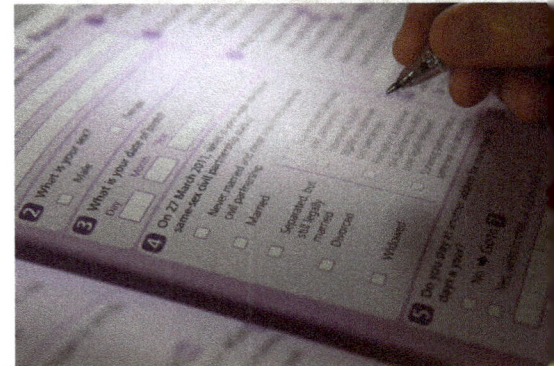
There is a census in the UK every ten years

UK laws

The Church of England is the Anglican Church, which is a Protestant denomination and is the official religion of the UK. It is similar in character to the Catholic Church but, among other differences, it does not recognise the Pope as a source of authority. The Queen is the official head of the Church of England, and she is also the head of state. This means that while she does not make laws, she opens Parliament, agrees to legislation and officially appoints the prime minister.

This means the Church is still influential in UK law. There are two levels of administration of law in the UK. The House of Commons contains elected people known as **MPs**. The House of Lords contains unelected people, including 26 Church of England bishops. For a law to be approved, it must be passed by both

Useful terms

pluralist – distinct cultural, ethnic and religious groups existing together in the same society
MP – Members of Parliament; elected politicians who represent people from a fixed area when the government make laws

houses. So the Church has a role in shaping laws that affect everyone, whether they are Christian or not.

Laws in the UK generally reflect a Western understanding of Christian ethics. Witnesses in court are asked to swear an oath to tell the truth while placing their hand on a Bible or other sacred text.

Christianity's influence on UK festivals

Christian festivals in the UK are part of cultural tradition. This means that the major religious festivals such as Christmas and Easter are observed nationally, with bank holidays on Christmas Day, Boxing Day, Good Friday and Easter Monday. People of other faiths or none in the UK may also observe these holidays simply because they structure the calendar in the UK. Saints days are also enshrined in UK tradition as they represent the nation as well as the Christian faith, for example, St George's Day in England or St David's Day in Wales.

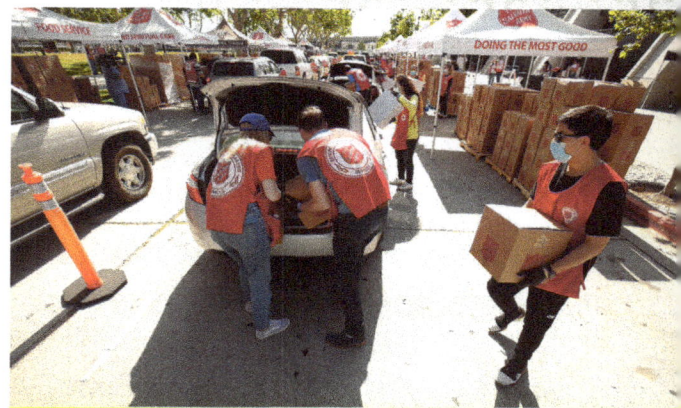

The Salvation Army is a Christian Church that offers support to homeless people in the community

Remembrance Day is another national event that has a strong Christian undertone. It is observed across the UK with silence, hymns and prayers and occurs on a Sunday: the Christian day of worship. While Sunday is no longer observed nationally as a day of rest, opening hours in shops are still reduced.

While festivals from other faiths are becoming increasingly familiar in the UK, they are not currently enshrined in UK culture. Therefore, while Shabbat is the Jewish day of rest, activity in the UK is not restricted to reflect this. The Muslim festivals of Id-ul-Fitr and Id-ul-Adha are celebrated but are not bank holidays.

The church in the local community

Churches are primarily places of worship. They are used to hold religious services and to mark key life events in the community, such as births, weddings and deaths. The UK is arranged into parishes; each church is responsible for a small geographical area (their parish) and will provide for the local community's spiritual and often practical needs.

Most churches have community halls that are used for social events and special occasions. For example, prayer breakfasts, Bible study groups, coffee mornings, youth clubs and nurseries might all operate from a church community.

Churches often work with the local council to provide food banks, and work with charities to collect money or goods. Churches may support faith schools and community hubs for those who live in poorer areas and need support. Churches in areas with a high proportion of immigrants can help to provide translators or offer support with accessing facilities.

Some churches work with the Ascension Trust to provide Street Pastors. These are Christians who have undergone training to go out onto city streets on Friday and Saturday nights when many people like to visit pubs and clubs. They work in cooperation with the police and the local councils to provide support to those who have drunk heavily and are in difficulty.

Churches like the Salvation Army help to provide funds and facilities to support homeless and poorer members of their community. They set up soup kitchens, food banks and youth groups. They support those involved in substance abuse and arrange events for the elderly to avoid isolation. During the COVID-19 pandemic in 2020, churches such as the Salvation Army helped to provide shelter and basic necessities for the homeless so they could isolate safely.

Knowledge recall

1 Define the following concepts: Trinity, omnipotent. (You can find these definitions on page 123.)
2 List three changes that the 2001 and 2011 censuses showed.
3 State three ways in which UK law and culture is affected by Christian tradition.

Evaluation practice

4 Give one reason why the Church might be seen as a valuable part of UK society and one reason why people might think it is not.
5 Do you agree with either of these reasons? Why or why not?

Mission and persecution

Specification focus

The worldwide Church:
The importance of mission, evangelism and church growth; the work of Tearfund: Christian beliefs in action; persecution of Christians past and present.

The importance of mission and evangelism

The gospel of Matthew finishes with the last words that Jesus spoke to his disciples before his ascension, known as the Great Commission.

Christians believe that Jesus' final command to them was to spread the word of Christianity and **convert** others to the faith. This is called **evangelism**. It is the duty of every Christian to share their faith with all people, whether this is through their daily life, or through huge evangelical rallies or 'crusades' like those of the late American preacher, Billy Graham.

Christianity began as a small movement within the Jewish faith, but grew into the world's largest religion. It was easier to join than Judaism, and with support from Rome after Emperor Constantine converted, it spread quickly. The colonisation of countries in Asia, Africa and Latin America by Western Europe helped Christianity to spread across the globe.

A **mission** is a special assignment or purpose. Christian mission involves spreading the gospel story to everyone, especially overseas. Historically, this has been controversial as some consider it disrespectful to the culture and faith of places visited by missionaries. Non-Christians may feel that mission interferes with a person's choice to believe what they want. Therefore, many missions today place more emphasis on providing help for people in need and putting Christ's love (agape) into action.

> ‘Therefore go and make disciples of all nations, baptising them in the name of the Father and of the Son and of the Holy Spirit, and teaching them to obey everything I have commanded you. And surely, I am with you always, to the very end of the age.’
> *Matthew 28:19–20*

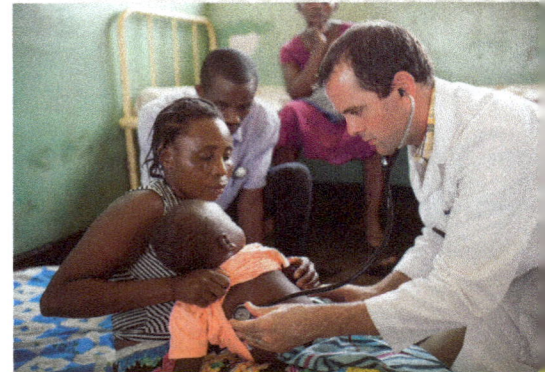
Missionaries today are often involved in offering practical help to those in need

Church growth in the UK

The UK is an increasingly secular country as Christianity is on the decline. Consequently, there is a rise in what has become known as 'reverse mission', where missionaries from Africa, Asia and Latin America now come to the West to spread the gospel. Missionaries to the UK have been involved in **church planting**, evangelism and supporting those in poverty.

While mainstream Christian denominations are declining, Pentecostal churches, free churches and church plants are on the rise, as young people and those who migrate to the UK are attracted to livelier or more familiar worship styles. The Ichthus Christian Fellowship and Vineyard Churches are organisations involved in church planting across the UK. Their aim is to start new, fully functioning churches that expand and send out new church plants elsewhere.

Modern churches must also think creatively to attract interest in an age of church decline. Projects like Messy Church give young families a chance to meet monthly for craft activities, food and a short celebration. These projects enable Christians to reach out to people who do not normally attend church.

The work of Tearfund

Tearfund is an example of Christian mission. It is a Christian charity that aspires to place agape – Christ's unconditional love – as central to their work by bringing practical help to vulnerable people.

Useful terms

convert – to change to a new religion or belief

mission – spreading the message of Christianity, often overseas, and offering practical help to those in need

church planting – starting a completely new church where one did not exist before

martyred – being killed for refusing to reject one's religious faith

Tearfund has been operating for over 50 years and works in over 50 different countries in Latin America, the Caribbean, Asia and Africa as well as the UK. They provide emergency disaster relief and long-term projects such as building toilets in poor communities, linking churches with partners overseas, and running education and youth volunteer schemes.

Tearfund's recent work has included medical assistance in Rohingya refugee camps in Bangladesh. They work to provide child-friendly spaces for orphans and traumatized children, as well as education, water and hygiene provisions.

Persecution of Christians

Jesus warned his followers to expect persecution for their faith.

Early Christians, like Jesus, were persecuted and even **martyred** for their faith by the Pharisees and the Romans. Stephen was stoned to death, and Peter was imprisoned and eventually crucified. Saul, later called Paul, persecuted Christians before his own conversion. He was imprisoned and eventually beheaded. Christians in the second century were thrown to wild animals for refusing to give up their faith, and church leaders were put to death.

The persecution of Christians has continued up to the present day; in 2010, Pope Benedict XVI called Christians the most persecuted group in the modern world. The World Evangelical Alliance reports that over 100,000 Christians are violently killed every year and millions are denied their fundamental human rights because of their faith.

During the 1990s, the Cultural Revolution in China saw Christian buildings closed, destroyed or converted as the government tried to control religion. Church leaders in China today are arrested and Christians imprisoned for attending unregistered churches or refusing to renounce their faith. North Korea is reported to be imprisoning Christians in detention camps and torturing and starving them.

Christian Freedom International and Open Doors are organisations based in the UK who help persecuted Christians. Christian Freedom International is a human rights organisation that advocates for persecuted and oppressed Christians. They provide spiritual support through prayer, and physical help by distributing food, water, medicine, clothing and Bibles. They also build hospitals and schools in refugee camps. They look to scripture for their inspiration.

Open Doors works in over 60 countries, supplying Bibles, training leaders how to resist persecution, and providing practical support and emergency relief for Christians who suffer for their faith. Founded by Brother Andrew from the Netherlands, the charity began its work in Eastern Europe and expanded to work in Africa, Asia, Latin America, China and the Muslim world.

Tearfund is an example of a Christian mission that brings practical help to vulnerable people

> 'You will be hated by everyone because of me, but the one who stands firm to the end will be saved.'
> *Matthew 10:22*

> 'Remember those in prison as if you were together with them in prison, and those who are ill-treated as if you yourselves were suffering.'
> *Hebrews 13:3*

Knowledge recall

1 Define the following concepts: evangelism, atonement. (You can find definitions for these terms on page 123.)
2 Give two reasons why Christians choose to evangelise.
3 State four examples of projects or work done by Tearfund.

Evaluation practice

4 Give one reason why a Christian should keep firm to their faith in God and one reason why they should be prepared to set it to one side.
5 Which reason do you find most persuasive and why?

The Ecumenical Movement

Specification focus

The worldwide Church: Working for Reconciliation: World Council of Churches, the Ecumenical Movement.

The need for reconciliation

Christians believe the purpose of Christ's death on the cross was to reconcile humanity with God and heal the rift caused by sin. When Christ ascended to heaven, he left one 'church': a small group of followers who were united in their worship of God and their resolve to follow Christ's commands.

As time progressed, the Church encountered differences of opinion over doctrine and practice. At first, early Churches discussed and resolved some of these difficulties. However, as time progressed, the differences became too great.

A significant rift occurred in 1054 with an event known as the Great **Schism**. The Eastern and Western Churches disagreed over which **Patriarch** had the greatest authority, resulting in a permanent divide between the Catholic and Orthodox Churches.

In the sixteenth century, the Reformation saw the formation of Protestant Churches. Reformers like Martin Luther and John Calvin objected to corruption and doctrinal issues in the Catholic Church, such as the sale of **indulgences** or the teaching of salvation through good deeds. In England, Henry VIII split from Rome and formed the Anglican Church when the Pope refused to allow his divorce.

As missionaries from these denominations were sent out to **evangelise**, the Churches fought for converts. In some places, the rifts between Catholic and Protestant Churches have become violent. Therefore, there has been a great need for reconciliation.

The Ecumenical Movement

In the Gospel of John, Jesus offers prayers for unity between his followers:

The same desire for unity inspired the Edinburgh World Missionary Conference in 1910, which marked the start of the Ecumenical Movement. The aim of this movement is to coordinate the efforts of missionaries and promote unity between Christian denominations and organisations.

Working separately had caused disagreements and hostility, even where missionaries had worked alongside each other. New converts were confused and frustrated by Western denominational differences, so it was seen as time to begin to heal the divisions.

The conference received delegates from 176 Protestant missionary societies. They met with the common goal to work together in their missionary and evangelising activities. There was no discussion of doctrine or **sacraments** to avoid conflict, but instead they prayed and worshipped together and discussed Christian unity.

The Catholic and Orthodox Churches were not invited to this event. However, several organisations were created to continue the dialogue and cooperation that the conference had begun, and the Orthodox and Catholic Churches were welcomed as observers to later assemblies.

In 2010, a 'centenary conference' was held in Edinburgh to celebrate the centenary of the Edinburgh Conference and to explore new forms of mission in the modern world. Both the Orthodox and Catholic Churches attended.

> 'My prayer is not for them alone. I pray also for those who will believe in me through their message, that all of them may be one, Father, just as you are in me and I am in you… May they be one as we are one – I in them and you in me – so that they may be brought to complete unity. Then the world will know that you have sent me and loved them even as you have loved me.'
>
> *John 17:20–23*

Useful terms

schism – division or separation
Patriarch – the highest-ranking authority in the Orthodox and Catholic Churches (the Pope is the Patriarch of Rome)
indulgences – pardon for sin, granted by a senior priest through good works or, in medieval times, through payment
excommunication – to exclude or expel people from membership within the church

World Council of Churches

In 1948, the different organisations that had emerged from the Edinburgh Conference united to become the World Council of Churches (WCC). Today there are 350 member Churches, including most of the Orthodox Churches. The Catholic Church is not a member but since 1965 has participated in joint working groups with the WCC, and some projects include Catholic members.

The rationale of the WCC is not to form a 'super Church', but to recognise the common faith each Church shares in Christ. Therefore, in accordance with Christ's prayer in John 17, they work together to fulfil God's calling and evangelise to the world together.

There are three main areas of work for the WCC:

- Making Christian unity visible.
- Working together to serve others.
- Encouraging other groups to join.

The World Council of Churches encourages unity and cooperation between all Christian denominations

Churches must agree to the following statement if they wish to apply to be members of the WCC: "a fellowship of churches which confess the Lord Jesus Christ as God and Saviour according to the scriptures, and therefore seek to fulfil together their common calling to the glory of the one God, Father, Son and Holy Spirit."

One of the WCC's projects is the Commission on Faith and Order. This brings together representatives from different Churches (including the Catholic Church) to consider questions of doctrine and structure that will help Churches to work together as one Christian Church.

The continuing Ecumenical Movement

There is increased recognition of the importance of unity between Churches, and other events, organisations and communities have arisen to support Christian cooperation.

In 1965, Pope Paul VI and the Patriarch of Constantinople – the leaders of the Catholic and Orthodox Churches – retracted their mutual **excommunications** that dated from the Great Schism. Since then, there have been continued attempts from the two denominations to create bonds and recognise common ground.

The Anglican-Roman Catholic International Commission was established in 1967. This commission works with representatives from the Anglican and Catholic Churches to identify common ground between the two denominations.

Churches Together in England formed in 1990. It has 50 member Churches and coordinates opportunities for English Churches to work together, such as by organising ecumenical prayer events.

The Global Christian Forum has met since the late 1990s to promote positive relationships across denominations, especially between Churches that have not had the opportunity to work together in the past. They aim to foster mutual respect, work towards common goals and deal with common challenges.

Ecumenical communities such as Taizé have also arisen, welcoming people from all denominations across the world to praise God, to unite and to learn together.

Knowledge recall

1 Define the following concepts: evangelism, omnibenevolent. (You can find these definitions on page 123.)
2 Suggest two reasons why there is need for reconciliation in the Christian Church.
3 Give three goals of the World Council of Churches.

Evaluation practice

4 Give one argument to show that the ecumenical movement is successful and one argument to show that it is not.
5 Which do you think is the most persuasive argument? Why?

Read about Taizé on page 131.

Skills practice

On these exam practice pages you will see example answers for each of the exam question types: **a**, **b**, **c** and **d**. You can find out more about these on pages 6–21.

Question (a)

*Question (a) tests your knowledge and understanding. You will always be asked to **define a key concept** in this question. You can find a list of the concepts at the beginning of the chapter.*

> (a)   What do Christians mean by 'sacraments'?   [2]

Student response

> A sacrament is like a wedding or a christening.

Improved student response

> A sacrament is an outward, physical sign or symbol of an invisible and inward grace from God. For example, the ritual of Baptism.

🕐 **Over to You!** Have a try at answering this question:

> (a)   What do Christians mean by 'atonement'?   [2]

Helpful hints

To help you answer this question effectively, you could use the check list below to make sure you include the most important things:

- **Synonym** – Include a synonym for the word 'atonement'.
- **Example** – Give an example of the key event in which atonement is achieved.

Study Challenge:

The exam board will only ever ask a question **(a)** that asks for concepts listed in the specification.

- Look back at the list of concepts at the beginning of the chapter
- Choose one from the list that has not yet appeared in the questions above
- Write your own **(a)** question using the concept you have chosen
- Now give yourself **two minutes** to answer this question by yourself!

What went well

The candidate has given two examples of events that are related to sacraments.

How to improve

You must use vocabulary that demonstrates the meaning of the word sacrament (e.g. grace, symbol).

You should learn the exam board's definition of the word at the start of this chapter.

You could give examples that all Christians agree are sacraments, such as the Eucharist or Baptism.

Tip

The candidate's use of the words 'grace' and 'symbol', coupled with the example of Baptism, show a successful use of specialist vocabulary to demonstrate knowledge.

Question (b)

*Question **(b)** tests your knowledge and understanding. It will always ask you to **describe** a belief, a teaching, a practice or an event that is included in the specification.*

> (b)   Describe a celebration of Baptism.   [5]

Student response

> Baptism happens to a baby in a church. It is when a mum and dad are Christians and they want the baby to be a Christian too. It is a kind of naming ceremony, so once the baby has been christened, they are going to be called that name. Everyone dresses up and people go to church who don't usually go. The vicar makes you sing songs and say prayers, the family stand up at the front and the vicar takes the baby and pours water on their head. They usually cry. Afterwards there is often a party with cake, cards and gifts.

Improved student response

> Infant Baptism involves dressing the baby in white to symbolise purity and anointing the child's head with oil in the sign of the cross on which Christ died. Parents and Godparents make vows to renounce evil, follow Christ and raise the child as a Christian. Water must be poured on the child's head three times to represent the Trinity and it is done in the name of the Father, Son and Holy Spirit. The family is given a candle, lit from the Pascal candle to show Jesus is the light to the world. Believer's Baptism involves the full immersion of an adult. The priest and person go into a small pool, called a baptistery, and the person is lowered under the water three times in the name of the Trinity.

Over to You! Have a try at answering this question:

> (b)   Describe Evangelical worship.   [5]

Helpful hints

Use the check list below to make sure you include the most important things:

- **How/Why** – Use specialist vocabulary to state a feature of evangelical worship (e.g. it is led by the Holy Spirit).
- **Example** – Describe how this feature takes place during worship (e.g. people call out in praise using languages they have never learned).
- **Repeat** – Then repeat the above process for other features of the worship.

Now give yourself **five minutes** to answer this question by yourself:

> (b)   Describe how Tearfund helps those in need.   [5]

What went well

The mention of church, water and Infant Baptism is relevant to this question. There is mention of the content of the service, a minister, and that it is a welcoming into the faith.

How to improve

You must use vocabulary that is subject-specific, such as vows, anointing and Trinity.

You should include specific examples from the Baptism ceremony itself.

You could refer to adult baptism as well.

Tip

This question is asking for a description of the important religious events that happen during the Baptism ceremony (like making vows) rather than secular ones (such as having parties or eating cake).

Question (c)

Question (c) tests your knowledge and understanding. You need to give detailed evidence and reasoning to support your explanation of the topic. You may need to show how belief influences religious practice. This is not an evaluation question so you don't need to evaluate different viewpoints.

> (c) Explain the social role of the Church in the local community. [8]

Student response

A church is usually in the middle of a village or town. Lots of people go to church for special events like weddings, funerals or sometimes at Christmas. People from churches that are quite lively sometimes come out and talk in the streets, trying to convert you to their religion. They usually have a hall that you can book if you want to have a party. Sometimes they come into school and give you talks about Jesus and God. They do come around to people's houses sometimes with leaflets about raising money for charity or for the church.

Improved student response

Churches are situated in parishes; this is a geographical area that the church is responsible for. Since many people do not regularly attend church, Christians often go out into their parish to provide for those in need. They may deliver supplies to people who are stranded in their homes due to sickness or disability. They run coffee mornings for families or older people. This is because they are a community of believers who were commanded by Christ to share their faith and care for others.

Many churches reach out into the community by working with councils to run food banks, soup kitchens or to open their churches to the homeless. They believe that doing this mirrors the way Christ acted on earth as the perfect man. Churches also provide outreach to people who would not otherwise have contact with the church. Activities like Messy Church welcome young families through craft activities and food. Other churches offer youth programmes and sport or music opportunities. This is because they believe that Christ commanded that they spread their faith through evangelism, and this is a way to connect with non-Christians.

🕐 **Over to You!** Have a try at answering this question:

> (c) Explain why pilgrimage to Taizé is important to Christians. [8]

Helpful hints

- Include **more than one belief** for why pilgrimage is important (e.g. it is an act of penance; it gives a believer time to connect with God).
- For each belief give an **example** of what a pilgrim may do to demonstrate it (e.g. they pray in silence or attend candlelit services).
- Explain **why** Christians might believe this (e.g. they are influenced by Christ's example or gospel values).
- Suggest **how** pilgrimage to Taizé might affect a Christian (e.g. what their lives may be like as a result or what they hope to achieve).

What went well

The candidate has understood the question correctly and has tried to give examples of times when church members may try to reach out to people who do not usually come to church.

How to improve

You must use specific examples of organisations, events or work that churches do to support people in their area.

You should use specialist vocabulary to describe the examples that are being used (e.g. Street Pastors, parishes, Messy Church).

You could explain the context of these activities to show why churches need to work in this way.

Tip

If you can show specific knowledge of key events or features in your answer, you will find it easier to access more marks than if you write very generally or vaguely. Learning key words or useful terms will help you to achieve this.

Now give yourself **eight minutes** to answer this question by yourself:

> (c)   Explain why Baptism is important for many Christians.   [8]

Question (d)

Question **(d)** tests your ability to **evaluate**. This means you need to show you have considered more than one point of view and that you have referred to religion and belief. You will need to be able to make judgements that are supported by detailed reasoning and argument.

> (d)   'Pilgrimage is the most important Christian practice.'
>   Discuss this statement showing that you have considered more than
>   one point of view. (You must refer to religion and belief in your answer.)   [15]

Student response

Pilgrimage is important to Christians because they want to perform penance so they can be forgiven for their sins. When a Christian goes on a pilgrimage to somewhere like Walsingham, they might walk the last mile to the Shrine barefoot. This is painful and so is a penance to God that shows their devotion and their desire to be forgiven by God. Other Christians might argue that you don't need to go on a pilgrimage to show penance to God. It is more important to confess your sins all the time and he will forgive you if you are sorry as he knows what is in your heart. This is more consistent with what Christians believe about God being omniscient.

Pilgrimage is important to Christians because they want to get away from the pressures of daily life and make time for God. Therefore, when a Christian goes on a pilgrimage to somewhere like Taizé, they like the simplicity of the life lived by the monks, and go to the candlelit prayer vigils because it gives them time to think about God and meditate about what he wants from them in their lives. Other Christians say that you should change the way you live your everyday life so that God is a part of it, rather than taking a holiday from life. This is consistent with what Christians believe about God being omnipresent.

Pilgrimage is important to Christians because it helps them to feel part of a community of like-minded people, all working to achieve something for their faith. They can come away enriched by the experience and more in tune with their faith. Other Christians might argue that God is not a magician and that the Church is required to help a person develop in their faith where they are. There is no need to perform a pilgrimage to do these things. Overall, it seems that pilgrimage is not important to every Christian, only to some.

Improved student response

Pilgrimage is important to Christians because they want to perform penance so they can be forgiven for their sins. When a Christian goes on a pilgrimage to Walsingham, they may walk the last mile to the shrine barefoot to show their devotion and desire for forgiveness. However, the Protestant Churches do not see penance as a sacrament like Catholics do. This means that sacraments such as Baptism or the Eucharist are far more important than making a pilgrimage. It seems more likely that an omniscient God would not set pilgrimage as the most vital duty for Christians if he knows the

---

What went well

Specialist vocabulary is used appropriately and in context. Relevant examples are used to illustrate ideas, and the answer is well-organised with different points of view.

How to improve

You must answer the full question. The question asks whether pilgrimage is the 'most important' Christian practice. This candidate argues about whether pilgrimage is important at all.

You should make decisions about how successful one argument is against another and give reasons to support your claim.

You could show understanding of different Christian practices that might be important.

This statement begins to address the question of whether pilgrimage is the 'most' important practice.

Some examples are given of other Christian practices that could be deemed more important.

repentance that is in their hearts because not everyone can perform this kind of action, but many more people can participate in Baptism or the Eucharist.

Pilgrimage is vital to allow Christians to escape the distractions of daily living and make time for God. When a Christian goes on a pilgrimage to somewhere like Taizé, attends the silent prayer vigils and lives the simple life, they have the time and space to meditate on God's will and reconnect with him. However, others argue that a Christian priority is to work for the benefit of those in need and that this is more important than taking a religious holiday. Jesus commanded his followers to love other people and to serve them. It seems more likely that an omnibenevolent God would rather that Christians worked to serve those in need rather than focusing on themselves.

Pilgrimage is the most important practice for Christians because they can connect with other like-minded people and significant spiritual events that have occurred in history. This allows them to come away enriched and strengthened by the experience. In some cases, they may even be healed. Others point out that this kind of 'religious tourism' is a distraction from true faith. God is not a magician who does tricks on command – it is more important to build links with a home church and to participate in its practices regularly to develop faith and receive comfort. Overall, while it seems that pilgrimage is important to some Christians, it is not the most important Christian practice, because it is a single event in time, whereas other practices such as daily prayer, charity work and the sacraments are ongoing and more vital.

> The conclusion to the paragraph has been supported with a reasoned argument.

> The examples work well to show why pilgrimage may be important.

> The mini conclusion has been developed to address the question more fully.

> The final decision is well-reasoned and uses appropriate vocabulary to directly address the full question.

🕐 **Over to You!** Have a try at answering this question:

(d) 'Christianity in Britain is on the decline.'
Discuss this statement showing that you have considered more than one point of view. (You must refer to religion and belief in your answer.) [15]

Helpful hints

If you find it difficult to answer this question effectively, you could try using the A, B, C, D structure or a variation of it to help you set out your paragraphs (see page 32).

In addition, consider trying to make use of some of the following important vocabulary:

- Census
- Atheist
- Agnostic
- Pluralist
- Denominations
- Pentecostal
- Free Churches

- Festivals
- Culture
- Tradition
- Community
- Secular
- Diverse
- Worship

Tip

This question has the most marks available and should take the most time. Use this as your chance to show off how well you can argue both sides, and to make use of the specialist terms you have learned.

Tip

It is important to use specialist vocabulary correctly in your sentences. This will help the examiner to see that you know the meaning of the words.

Now give yourself **fifteen minutes** to answer this question by yourself:

(d) 'Great Britain is a Christian country.'
Discuss this statement showing that you have considered more than one point of view. (You must refer to religion and belief in your answer.) [15]

Chapter 7:
Islam: Beliefs and teachings

Introduction

In this chapter, you will study the beliefs and teachings of Islam. The main source of these teachings is the Qur'an, which Muslims believe is the word of Allah. Another important source of teaching is the Sunnah (the example, practices and teaching of Muhammad) as recorded in the hadiths. Islamic belief and teaching has been formulated in a different way to the beliefs of Christianity; a lot of the work of early Islamic scholars was taken up with tracing the chains of transmission of the hadiths so that trustworthy teachings could be found. Understanding the way in which Islam developed through the life of Muhammad and the appointment of the Caliphs and Imams is helpful for understanding the Islamic faith.

Things to remember:

- Different branches of Islam have evolved since Muhammad's time. The two main groups are Sunni and Shi'a Muslims. The differences between them mostly stem from beliefs about leadership. For example, Sunni and Shi'a Muslims accept different people as successors to Muhammad. This influences which hadiths and therefore which teachings they accept.

- Islam accepts the prophets from Judaism and Christianity. They revere figures like Isa (Jesus) and Ibrahim (Abraham) as prophets who recited Allah's word. However, they reject the idea that Jesus can ever been viewed as the Son of God or in any way equal in authority to God. Even Muhammad is not to be worshipped or viewed as having any divine status.

- The Qur'an is the final source of revelation for Muslims and is the word of Allah, so it is vital that it is kept in exactly the form in which it was revealed to Muhammad. Muslims learn Arabic so they can read and hear the Qur'an in Allah's original words. Translations may be misinterpreted.

- Scriptures from Judaism and Christianity are not completely rejected. They were Allah's original revelation but have been corrupted or lost. Therefore they are not as authoritative as the Qur'an because only the Qur'an is Allah's pure revelation untainted by humanity.

Concepts

Tawhid – 'oneness' in reference to God and is the basic Muslim belief in the oneness of Allah

Prophethood – ('risalah' in Arabic) is the term used of the messengers of Allah, beginning with Adam and ending with the Prophet Muhammad

Halal – actions or things which are permitted within Islam, such as eating permitted foods

Haram – any actions or things which are forbidden within Islam, such as eating forbidden foods

Greater/Lesser jihad – the word jihad means 'to strive' and there are two forms of jihad:

- Greater jihad is the daily struggle and inner spiritual striving to live as a Muslim

- Lesser jihad is a physical struggle or 'holy war' in defence of Islam

Mosque – ('Masjid' in Arabic) a 'place of prostration' for Muslims; it is a communal place of worship for a Muslim community

Shariah (straight path) – a way of life; Muslims believe Allah has set out a clear path for how Muslims should live. Shariah Law is the set of moral and religious rules that put the principles set out by the Qur'an and the hadiths into practice

Ummah – means 'community' and refers to the worldwide community of Muslims who share a common religious identity

The nature of Allah

Specification focus

The nature of Allah: The teaching about the nature of Allah: the belief in the oneness of Allah (Tawhid): Qur'an 3:18; nature of Allah: immanence, transcendence, omnipotence, beneficence, mercy, fairness and justice: Qur'an 46:33; Adalat in Shi'a Islam.

Read about the Six Articles of Faith and Five Roots of Usul ad-Din on pages 168–169.

Tawhid

The most fundamental belief in Islam is **tawhid**. From an Arabic word meaning unification or oneness, this is the belief that there is only one indivisible God. This monotheistic belief is held by all Muslims. Tawhid is the first of the **Six Articles of Faith** in Sunni Islam and the first of the **Five Roots of Usul ad-Din** in the Shi'a tradition.

> 'God bears witness that there is no god but Him, as do the angels and those who have knowledge. He upholds justice. **There is no god but Him with the power to decide.**'
> *Qur'an 3:18*

For Muslims, anyone who rejects tawhid commits the sin of **shirk**. Shirk is the only unforgivable sin and is committed by anyone who places another being as equal to Allah. So **polytheists** commit shirk by worshipping other gods and Christians commit shirk through belief in the Trinity and the divinity of Christ.

Muslims avoid creating artwork that depicts Allah or any prophet in case it leads to shirk through people worshipping them in error. Placing work, money, status or fame as a greater goal than Allah is shirk and a denial of tawhid. The first pillar of Sunni Islam is the **Shahadah**: a creed proclaiming the oneness of Allah.

The Shahadah states: There is no God but Allah, and Muhammad is the messenger of Allah

Allah's characteristics

Ninety-nine of Allah's names can be found in the Qur'an and the hadiths. These, in a limited way, describe Allah's nature. It is believed that by meditating on the divine names, Muslims can grow closer to Allah; memorising the names enables them to go to paradise. No single name of Allah should ever be worshipped as separate from him or most vital. This would be shirk. Some of Allah's characteristics are as follows:

The Immanent (Al-Baatin) – Allah is very close to humans. No being can live without him and he is present in all things. He is present in human activity, including prayer and religious observances. Muslims believe that science and learning are the processes of discovering more about him. A Muslim can communicate directly with Allah – there is no need for a go-between.

> 'We created man – We know what his soul whispers to him: We are closer to him than his jugular vein.'
> *Qur'an 50:16*

The Transcendent (Al-Muta'ali) – Allah is above and beyond the material universe. He is responsible for the creation of all things, with no helpers or associates. He is outside all space and time, separate from the universe that he has made. Allah is therefore unlimited and worthy of human worship.

Useful terms

Six Articles of Faith – the fundamental beliefs accepted by all Sunni Muslims

Five Roots of Usul ad-Din – the fundamental beliefs accepted by all Shi'a Muslims

shirk – an unforgiveable sin of associating other beings with Allah (idolatry or polytheism)

polytheists – those who believe in or worship more than one god

Shahadah – the declaration of faith: 'There is no God but Allah, and Muhammad is the messenger of Allah'

Bismillah – the words that preface all but one of the chapters of the Qur'an: 'In the name of Allah, the beneficent, the merciful.' Used in prayer and as a blessing

predestination – the belief that all actions are willed by Allah in advance and that he has already chosen some for Jannah and some for Jahannam

The Omnipotent (Al-Jabbar) – Allah has absolute power over all things. He is in complete control over everything that happens with no dependence upon anyone or anything else. This also implies his omniscience (complete knowledge of all things) and his infinite, limitless existence. Allah's power ensures that the only things that happen are according to his will.

Read more about the Shahadah on page 169.

> ❝Do the disbelievers not understand that God, who created the heavens and earth and did not tire in doing so, has the power to bring the dead back to life? Yes indeed! **He has power over everything.**❞
>
> *Qur'an 46:33*

The Beneficent (Ar-Rahman) – this name appears in a blessing known as the **Bismillah**, which begins almost every Qur'anic chapter. Allah acts for the benefit of humanity. When he appointed people as khalifahs of his creation, he gave them everything they needed (including the prophets and the laws in the Qur'an) to support and help them in their role.

The Merciful (Ar-Rahim) – Allah is compassionate. He forgives those who make mistakes as they try their best to do his will. He could punish people who get things wrong, but he accepts repentance. This name also forms part of the Bismillah.

The Just (Al-Adl) – Allah sent the message of Islam to everyone so all can have the chance to enter paradise. He treats all people equally and will punish or reward them justly for their behaviour. He is consistent and fair in his actions.

Adalat in Shi'a Islam

All Muslims believe that Allah is infinitely just. 'Adalat' means justice, and Muslims must accept Allah's justice even if they cannot understand his infinite wisdom. Shi'a Muslims believe Allah's justice is absolute and that on the Day of Judgement, he will judge all people according to his objective moral framework. This is the second of the Five Roots of Usul ad-Din.

For Allah to judge people justly for their behaviour, they must have free will to perform morally good or bad actions. Therefore, Shi'a Muslims do not accept **predestination**. They believe it would not be just for Allah to send someone to Jannah or Jahannam for something they could not control. Humans can understand correct behaviour by reading the Qur'an, listening to the prophets and following **Shariah** Law. If they choose to act correctly through their free will, they will be rewarded justly.

Sunni Muslims agree that Allah is just, but they accept predestination. They argue that while Allah judges people on their moral choices, he has complete power over all human action.

Read more about predestination on page 154.

Knowledge recall

1. Define the following concepts: tawhid, Shariah. (You can find these definitions on page 145.)
2. List three sources of authority that tell Muslims there is only one God.
3. State four other characteristics of Allah and what they mean about his nature.

Evaluation practice

4. Give one reason why Muslims argue that shirk is the worst sin and one reason why non-Muslims might argue there are worse sins than shirk.
5. Which of these views do you think is most convincing? Give two reasons why.

Prophethood (risalah)

The nature of prophethood

Risalah (or Al-Nubuwah) means 'divine message' and is used to refer to **prophethood** or the channel of communication between Allah and humanity. Belief in the prophets is one of the Six Articles of Faith and one of the Five Roots of Usul ad-Din.

Islam teaches that since the creation of the world, every generation has been sent a prophet, finishing with Muhammad. Tradition says there have been 124,000 prophets, but the Qur'an mentions 25 names, 21 of which also appear in Jewish or Christian scriptures.

Adam, Ibrahim (Abraham), Isa (Jesus) and Muhammad are examples of the greatest of Allah's messengers. They were all sent by Allah to carry his **infallible** guidance to humanity. They:

- are human, not divine
- all confirm each other's revelation
- are recognised by their great wisdom and moral excellence
- performed or received miracles through Allah's power.

The prophets act as a perfect example of how to live according to Allah's will and none of them take credit for his message or miracles. They bring the message about Allah's nature, the nature of the unseen world (such as angels or life after death), and of Allah's will for humanity.

Adam, the first prophet

Islam teaches that Adam was the first man, first prophet and first Muslim: the ancestor of the whole human race. The Qur'an says that Allah formed Adam from a handful of clay and breathed his spirit into him. Adam and Hawwa (Eve) were formed from the same soul and they were married. Adam was created as Allah's representative on earth and Allah commanded all his angels to bow down before Adam.

Adam fell from grace when he disobeyed Allah and was tempted by **Shaytan** to eat the fruit from the tree of knowledge. He was banished from Eden and confessed his sin to Allah on Mount Arafat, where he was forgiven and appointed as the first prophet. Adam accepted **tawhid** and built the first **Ka'ba**, which was later destroyed in the Flood.

Ibrahim (Abraham)

There were other great prophets after Adam, but Islam records Ibrahim as being a particularly significant prophet who challenged polytheism. Ibrahim was a **hanif**. He had an instinctive knowledge of tawhid even though he lived in a polytheistic society.

Ibrahim had two sons: Ishma'il and Ishaq (Isaac). Ishma'il was the firstborn child of Hagar, a slave to Ibrahim's wife Sarah. Ishaq was the second son, born from Sarah.

Specification focus

Prophethood: The nature of prophethood; why are prophets important? Qur'an 2:136; the importance of Adam as the first prophet; Ibrahim as father of Isaac and Ishma'il and his significance for the Muslim religion; Isa as a prophet for Muslims: Qur'an 2:87.

> So [you believers], say, "We believe in God and in what was sent down to us and what was sent down to Abraham, Ishmael, Isaac, Jacob, and the Tribes, and what was given to Moses, Jesus, and all the prophets by their Lord. **We make no distinction between any of them,** and we devote ourselves to Him."
> *Qur'an 2:136*

Useful terms

risalah – divine message or prophethood
infallible – incapable of being wrong
Shaytan – (Iblis) the devil/Satan
Ka'ba – a cube-shaped shrine at the centre of the Great Mosque in Makkah
hanif – a true monotheist who is not Christian, Jewish nor an idol worshipper

Ishma'il became prophet to the Arabs and ancestor to Muhammad. Ishaq became prophet to the Jews.

The hadiths tells how Ibrahim, Ishma'il and Hagar travelled to Makkah. Ibrahim left them there and while he was gone Ishma'il became thirsty. Hagar searched for water, and in a panic ran back and forth between the hills of Al-Safa and Al-Marwah. When she returned, Allah had caused a spring, the Zamzam, to rise up from the ground.

Ibrahim was later commanded by Allah to sacrifice Ishma'il as a test. Shaytan tempted Ibrahim to disobey, but Ibrahim was faithful and threw stones to chase Shaytan away. Ishma'il willingly agreed to be sacrificed, but Allah protected him from harm and provided a ram for the sacrifice instead. These two stories are reflected in practices at Hajj.

The Qur'an says that Ibrahim and Ishma'il rebuilt the Ka'ba, having first ploughed the land to reveal Adam's original foundations. Allah revealed a holy book to Ibrahim called the Scrolls of Ibrahim. The Qur'an refers to this book, but there is no trace of it today.

Read about Hajj on pages 174–175.

Ibrahim rebuilt the Ka'ba that had originally been built by Adam

Isa (Jesus)

The Qur'an recognises Isa as one of the great prophets of Islam, but it clearly rejects his divinity. Like Adam, Isa was created by Allah without a biological father, but this does not make him divine.

During his lifetime, Isa confirmed and was faithful to the message of tawhid brought by all other prophets. Unlike the other prophets, he remained unmarried, but like all the others he was sinless after he was called by Allah to be his prophet. He performed miracles of healing that surpassed anything physicians could do, and was given the holy book, the Injil (Gospels). Isa made clear that everything he did was from Allah.

Muslims do not believe that Isa was crucified, but they believe he was taken up to Allah. Many await the Parousia when Isa will return to earth on the Day of Judgement.

The Qur'an tells how each prophet brought Allah's word – the message of Islam – for their generation. But, except for Muhammad, their words were ignored, forgotten or corrupted, so a new prophet was always required. Isa's message was distorted because the Injil was lost and not re-recorded by his followers until long after his life on earth had ended, making it unreliable. Muslims accept all the prophets, but believe that only the Qur'anic account of their lives and teachings has not been corrupted over time.

> ❛We gave Moses the Scripture and We sent messengers after him in succession. **We gave Jesus, son of Mary, clear signs and strengthened him with the holy spirit.** So how is it that, whenever a messenger brings you something you do not like, you become arrogant, calling some impostors and killing others?❜
>
> *Qur'an 2:87*

Knowledge recall

1 Define the following concepts: tawhid, prophethood. (You can find these definitions on page 145.)
2 List four features of a prophet in Islam.
3 State three ways that Ibrahim showed his faithfulness to Allah.

Evaluation practice

4 Give two reasons why Muslims might reject Isa as the Son of God.
5 Give one reason why some people might accept these arguments and one reason why others might reject them.

The Prophet Muhammad

Who is Muhammad?

Islam teaches that Muhammad was a prophet, not a deity or divine being. Muslims do not worship Muhammad – to do so would be to commit shirk. However, Muhammad is regarded as the seal of the prophets. This means that he is the final prophet of Islam, sent to confirm the monotheistic teaching of the other prophets and to convey Allah's **revelation**.

The prophecies revealed to Muhammad by Allah are recorded in the Qur'an. This is believed to be the final and complete revelation of Allah to humanity. It is the word of Allah, dictated without human editing. Muhammad was Allah's mouthpiece.

The hadiths are also held in high authority in Islam as they are accounts of the sayings and life of Muhammad. These come from writers who knew Muhammad or lived close to the time he was alive. They collected the oral traditions of his sayings together into books.

Muhammad's early life

Muhammad was born in Makkah in the sixth century CE into the ruling Quraysh tribe. Makkan society was polytheistic, but Muhammad had contact with Jews, Christians and hanifs as well. He is believed to have been a direct descendant of the prophet Ibrahim, through his son Ishma'il.

Makkah was a wealthy trading post and important Arabic shrine. The Ka'ba had been built by Adam, and then rebuilt by Ibrahim and Ishma'il. While it was originally dedicated to Allah, at this time it was used to house idols of hundreds of other deities.

Muhammad was orphaned by the age of six, so was raised by his grandfather and later his uncle. He built a reputation for himself as a person of excellent character and a capable diplomat. People called him Al-Ameen (the trustworthy). In his twenties, Muhammad was employed by a wealthy, widowed businesswoman called Khadijah. They were later married and had children.

Muhammad retreated to a cave on Mount Nour for meditation

The Night of Power

Muhammad became increasingly frustrated by the practices of the polytheists in Makkah. In 610 CE, Muhammad was meditating in a cave called Hira on Mount Nour (Jabal al-Nour or the Mount of Light) near Makkah when the angel Jibril suddenly appeared to him. Jibril showed Muhammad some words and ordered him to recite them.

Muhammad protested that he could not read, but the angel ordered him to 'recite' Allah's message, and suddenly Muhammad was given understanding of what the words said. He was ordered by Jibril to learn them and recite them to others. The first revelation from Allah was:

> ' Read! In the name of your Lord who created: He created man from a clinging form. Read! Your Lord is the Most Bountiful One who taught by the pen, who taught man what he did not know. '
> *Qur'an 96:1–5*

Useful terms

revelation – God's direct communication to humanity

revert – when a non-Muslim becomes a Muslim: they 'revert' because they return to the state that Allah created them in

Hijrah – migration; Muhammad's journey to Medina that marks the beginning of the Muslim calendar

polygamy – the practice of a man marrying more than one wife at a time

This event became known as Laylat al-Qadr (The Night of Power) and it is celebrated by Sunni Muslims on the 27th day of Ramadan, or the 23rd day of Ramadan for Shi'a Muslims.

It was some time before Muhammad received another revelation. During that time, he prayed, meditated and devoted himself to Allah. The revelations then continued for 23 years. The words he received at each revelation were recorded and now form the text of the Qur'an.

Persecution of the first Muslims

The revelations to Muhammad contain the following themes:

- Tawhid – Polytheism is wrong. There is only one God.
- Risalah – Muhammad was a prophet, bringing the message of Islam to the world.
- Akhirah – People will be judged by Allah for how they live their lives, so they should repent and change.

Makkah was a centre for trade and brought many visitors to the Ka'ba to worship the idols. When Muhammad began preaching and won **reverts**, he was viewed as a threat to business because the polytheistic visitors did not like his preaching against idol worship. He was only safe from persecution because he was protected by the support of his uncle and influential wife.

Muhammad's followers were not protected in the same way and were harassed, tortured or killed. He sent many away to seek refuge outside of Makkah. To make matters worse, in 619 CE Khadijah and his uncle both died and with them his protection.

The Hijrah

After Khadijah's death, Muhammad seemed to have no future in Makkah. He was forced to emigrate to Yathrib (now called Medina), where he was welcomed for his diplomatic skills by the warring tribes who were situated there. This event is known as the **Hijrah** and marks the beginning of the Muslim calendar.

In Medina, Muhammad's charter for peace enabled the warring tribes to practise their own faith freely, while cooperating if under attack from external forces. He encouraged them to join together as one **ummah**.

Muhammad lived in a simple home even though he was a ruler. He encouraged his followers to treat people kindly, releasing slaves and showing charity. He married again, this time practising **polygamy**, as was the custom to enable vulnerable women to be financially provided for and protected.

Eventually, Muhammad's work in Medina made him the political leader, with Islam as the main religion. While there were many battles between Medina and Makkah, Muhammad was in a strong political position.

Muhammad's return to Makkah

In 628 CE, Muhammad had a vision of himself on a pilgrimage to Makkah for Allah, so he marched with his army toward Makkah in preparation. He did not want to fight and so made a treaty with the Makkans. However, the Makkans broke the treaty and in 630 CE Muhammad led his army against them, taking over the city with few casualties. Muhammad entered the Ka'ba and destroyed all the idols. Most of the population reverted to Islam.

In 632 CE, Muhammad made his last pilgrimage to Makkah. The practice of Hajj was revealed to him and he gave the example for all future Hajj. He gave his last sermon on Mount Arafat and died shortly after at the age of 63.

Read more about the Night of Power on page 183.

Read about Hajj on pages 174–175.

The city of Medina is the second holiest city in Islam after Makkah

Knowledge recall

1 Define the following concepts: tawhid, ummah. (You can find these definitions on page 145.)
2 List two reasons why Muhammad is so important in Islam.
3 State three events of importance in the Night of Power.

Evaluation practice

4 Give one reason why Muhammad is viewed as the most important prophet, and one reason why some might say he is not.
5 Which of these views do you think is the most persuasive? Give a reason why.

Angels (malaikah)

The significance of angels in Islam

Teachings about angels (**malaikah**) can be found in the Qur'an and the hadiths. According to the Qur'an, Allah created angels before human beings. They are immortal and sinless, made from light and created with no free will.

According to tradition, angels do not require food, shelter or sleep. They cannot be tempted away from Allah, whom they never tire of praising. The Qur'an describes angels as genderless, but they are often reported as taking human form and then they appear as males.

Angels are not divine beings, so are not to be worshipped or prayed to. Their purpose is primarily to worship Allah. However, their role also includes communicating messages from Allah to humanity through the prophets. As they are sinless, they can be in Allah's presence, and since they are not divine, they can appear to humans.

> ❝The Messenger believes in what has been sent down to him from his Lord, as do the faithful. **They all believe in God, His angels, His scriptures, and His messengers.** "We make no distinction between any of His messengers," they say, "We hear and obey. Grant us Your forgiveness, our Lord. To You we all return!"❞
> *Qur'an 2:285*

As angels have no free will, they cannot sin and they cannot fall. Therefore, Shaytan (Iblis) is not a fallen angel. Shaytan and his evil spirits are **jinn**. A jinn has free will and is mortal, so it can sin and can be judged and punished.

In the Qur'an, Shaytan refused Allah's instruction to bow down to Adam and so was thrown out of heaven. Allah agreed to delay his punishment until the Day of Judgement, when he will be thrown into hell to be tormented by his own demons. In the meantime, Shaytan can tempt humans away from Allah.

There is scholarly disagreement over whether humans or angels are the superior beings:

Humans are superior beings	Angels are superior beings
Allah asked his angels to bow before Adam.	Angels are inerrant; they cannot make mistakes.
Angels have no free will. Humans have a greater challenge to be obedient to Allah.	Angels cannot sin as they experience no temptation.

But generally, it is regarded that humans are superior as they have both physical form and intellect, whereas angels only have intellect.

Angels and free will

Belief in angels is one of the Six Articles of Faith in Sunni Islam. They are not mentioned in the Five Roots of Usul ad-Din for Shi'a Muslims.

Generally, Sunni and Shi'a Muslims believe the same things about angels. One difference is regarding the issue of free will. While Sunni Muslims believe that

Specification focus

Angels: The significance of angels in Islam: Qur'an 2:97–98, Qur'an 2:285; diversity in beliefs between Shi'a and Sunni Muslims regarding angels and free will; the significance of Jibril's revelation of the Qur'an to Muhammad: Qur'an 2:97–98; the significance of Mika'il placed in charge of plants and rain; the significance of Israfil to announce the Day of Resurrection.

Vector - ISRS 10   Allah and His angels send blessings on the Prophet, O ye who believe they arrived and handed him recognition

Angels are not physical beings. Their representation in art as people is controversial since many Muslims wish to avoid the risk of shirk

Useful term

malaikah – the Arabic word used for angels

angels have no free will, Shi'a Muslims argue that while they cannot act against Allah's will, they have some limited free will, with no desire to sin.

An important difference between Sunni and Shi'a Muslims concerns Muhammad's successor. Sunni Muslims recognise Abu Bak'r who was elected as successor to Muhammad, but Shi'a Muslims believe that Muhammad appointed Ali, his cousin and son-in-law, to be his successor, whereas Sunni Muslims reject this.

Shi'a Muslims believe that on his final hajj, Muhammad received an angelic visitation in which he received a verse of the Qur'an, instructing him to announce Ali as his successor. Shi'a Muslims then believe that Muhammad did this at Ghadir Khum (a pond on the road between Makkah and Medina).

Read more about Muhammad's successor on page 169.

Jibril

Jibril (Gabriel) is described in some hadiths as the most important archangel. He is mentioned by name in the Qur'an, where he is also referred to as the Holy Spirit. Jibril is the angel of revelation. The message of Allah that he brings is the path to Jannah and a good life.

Jibril appeared in various forms to Muhammad and revealed each verse of the Qur'an to him. Sometimes he appeared as a handsome disciple, sometimes a desert traveller. At other times, only his voice was heard.

Jibril also appeared to Maryam and foretold the birth of Isa. He is also said to have appeared to Adam and to Musa.

> ‘Say [Prophet], "If anyone is an enemy of **Gabriel – who by God's leave brought down the Qur'an to your heart,** confirming previous scriptures, as a guide and good news for the faithful – if anyone is an enemy of God, His angels and His messengers, of Gabriel and Michael, then God is certainly the enemy of such disbelievers."’
> Qur'an 2:97–98

Mika'il

Mika'il (Michael) is an archangel who provides everything needed for life on earth. He brings the seasons, rain, wind and thunder to earth. He sustains life in troubled times and oversees the angels responsible for the laws of nature. Mika'il is known as the Angel of Mercy. He protects the souls of the faithful, keeping Shaytan out of heaven and asking Allah to forgive people's sin.

Mika'il is mentioned once in the Qur'an and is spoken of in the hadiths. Some believe he was one of three angels who visited Ibrahim to announce that his wife, Sarah, would give birth to Ishaq.

Israfil

Israfil (Raphael/Uriel) is the archangel commissioned to blow the trumpet that will announce the end of time when everyone will die. He will sound it again on the Day of Judgement, to announce people's resurrection. Israfil means 'burning one'. He is mentioned in several hadiths and it is said that he is always ready, with a trumpet at his lips, waiting for Allah's command.

Mika'il is an archangel who brings rain to the earth

Knowledge recall

1 Define the following concepts: prophethood, ummah. (You can find these definitions on page 145.)
2 List two purposes of angels in general.
3 State two differences between Sunni and Shi'a beliefs about angels.

Evaluation practice

4 Give one reason why a Muslim might believe angels are superior to humans and one reason why other Muslims might believe humans are superior.
5 Which of these views do you think is most consistent with what you have learned about Islam? Give a reason why.

Predestination and human responsibility

Specification focus

Akhirah: Al-Qadr (predestination): implications for human freedom; Akhirah: human responsibility and accountability; Muslim beliefs and teachings about the afterlife; human freedom and its relationship to the Day of Judgement.

Al-Qadr

For Muslims, the fundamental belief in **tawhid** means that every event in the universe happens according to the will of the omnipotent Allah.

> ‘[Prophet], glorify the name of your Lord the Most High, who created [all things] in due proportion; who determined their destinies and guided them.’
> *Qur'an 87:1–3*

This means that events only occur if Allah has willed them and implies that human beings have no free will to do as they please. However, this has implications for the punishment of wrong behaviour. Allah is just and merciful, so surely he would not punish humans for acts beyond their control.

Either:

Allah controls everything and humans are not free. (This means punishment is unjust, but Allah is still omnipotent.)

Or:

Allah does not control everything, and humans are free. (This means punishment is just, but Allah is not omnipotent.)

Neither of these solutions are acceptable for Muslims.

Sunni Muslims believe in **Al-Qadr**. This is one of the Six Articles of Faith. Allah is the omnipotent creator, and nothing happens unless he wills it. He has set a course for the universe and knows everything that will happen, including the free choices that humans will make. He exists outside of time and foreknows what is in the future for humans. Therefore, humans are both free and predestined and they deserve judgement.

Shi'a Muslims believe that humans have genuine free choice. They agree that events only occur according to Allah's will, but since he is just, he has willed that humanity is free to choose. He guides humans through the Qur'an, the prophets and the Imams, but people can reject his help. So while Allah foreknows what choices people will make and allows them to happen, humans are responsible for them. Shi'a Muslims believe in Adalat, or divine justice, which is one of the Five Roots of Usul ad-Din, meaning that Allah only punishes or rewards those who deserve it.

A common Arabic phrase used in Islam is 'Insha'Allah' (meaning 'God willing'). This is frequently used by most Muslims to express the belief that events only happen if Allah wills them. This does not mean a person's actions do not matter. It means if a person works hard, but there is an unexpected outcome to their actions, then they did not fail. It is simply that the outcome they hoped for was not according to Allah's will.

The whole of a Muslim's life should be lived in submission to Allah

Useful terms

Al-Qadr – predestination; one of the six articles of faith in Sunni Islam
akhirah – life after death
barzakh – a state of waiting for the soul
Yawm ad-Din – the Day of Judgement
Al-Ma'ad – (resurrection) restoring a dead person back to earthly life

Akhirah

Akhirah is one of the Six Articles of Faith for Sunni Muslims and one of the Five Roots of Usul ad-Din for Shi'a Muslims. It is a fundamental belief of Islam that this life is a preparation or a test for the next life.

For Muslims, the purpose of human life in the present is to be Allah's khalifahs on earth. If a person does this well, they can expect to be rewarded in the next life. If they do not perform this role then there will be punishment. Therefore, the whole of a Muslim's life is lived in the constant awareness of submission to Allah's will. Following the law and observing all religious practices is an act of worship in preparation for the afterlife.

There are different understandings of what happens to a person between their death and the Day of Judgement. Some say that when a person dies, their ruh (soul) is separated from the body in a state of **barzakh** until the Day of Judgement. At death, Izra'il (the angel of death) takes the ruh for questioning. If the ruh answers correctly with the Shahadah, then it will be shown its place in heaven. If the ruh answers wrongly, it will be tortured until the Day of Judgement. Others argue that the ruh simply resides with the body in a sleeping state, or hovers over the grave until the Day of Judgement.

Read more about akhirah on page 156.

The Day of Judgement

Islam teaches that on **Yawm ad-Din**, there will be the sound of a trumpet blown by Israfil and everything will cease. At the sound of a second trumpet, the soul will rejoin the body in **Al-Ma'ad** or **resurrection**. People will be standing naked and whole, ready for judgment. No one knows when this day will be.

Decisions made during a person's life will be recorded by two angels who serve as Al-Kiram and Al-Katibun (noble writers). These angels are responsible for keeping a record of all the good and bad deeds people do. At the resurrection, everyone will be brought to stand before Allah and read out the book of their life.

Allah will judge people based on a mixture of both their faith and their actions during their earthly life. Those who have rejected the Shahadah will be punished and even the smallest act will not be ignored. However, Allah is merciful, so anyone who has tried their best but sinned can be forgiven if Allah wills it or if they have repented.

> ❛On that Day, people will come forward in separate groups to be shown their deeds: whoever does an atom's-weight of good will see it, but whoever does an atom's-weight of evil will see that.❜
> Qur'an 99:6–8

During Hajj, pilgrims pray to Allah on Mount Arafat, and ask for His forgiveness in preparation for the Day of Judgement

Knowledge recall

1 Define the following concepts: tawhid, mosque. (You can find these definitions on page 145.)
2 List three things that will happen on Yawm ad-Din.
3 State one way in which Sunni and Shi'a Muslims differ over Al-Qadr.

Evaluation practice

4 Give one reason why some Muslims believe that humans are predestined and one reason why other Muslims argue they have genuine freedom to choose.
5 Does it make sense to accept both free will and predestination? Give one reason for your answer.

Heaven and hell

Specification focus

Akhirah: Muslim beliefs about the nature, stages and purpose of heaven; Muslim beliefs about the nature and purpose of hell.

Heaven

Islam uses several different words to talk about the afterlife. 'Paradise' (Jannah) contrasts with hell. Jannah literally means paradise garden, and Muslims hope to be sent there once they have been through judgement on the Last Day as a reward for their faithfulness to Allah.

The 'heavens' are contrasted with earth. Heaven is beyond the earth and will also be transformed on the Last Day when Israfil will sound his trumpet and the world will come to an end. The Qur'an describes the heavens as having seven layers or degrees. In each of the heavens, one of the prophets is said to dwell and each level of heaven is closer to Allah than the last.

Jannah is found beyond the heavens where Allah's footstool and His throne can be found. Allah is seated on his throne in the highest position possible.

When he was about 40 years old, Muhammad had a vision known as the Night Journey. He was visited by Jibril who transported him on a heavenly, winged beast to the furthest mosque in Jerusalem and then through the seven tiers of heaven, where he spoke with each of the prophets. Muhammad then journeyed to Allah in Jannah and was given the instructions for **salah**.

Jannah is described in detail in the Qur'an as a place where every physical desire is met, but most importantly where inhabitants will be near to Allah. This is the greatest reward.

> 'Did We not build seven strong [heavens] above you?'
> *Qur'an 78:12*

Read about salah on pages 170–171.

> 'For these will be the ones brought nearest to God in Gardens of Bliss: many from the past and a few from later generations. On couches of well-woven cloth they will sit facing each other; everlasting youths will go round among them with glasses, flagons, and cups of a pure drink that causes no headache or intoxication; [there will be] any fruit they choose; the meat of any bird they like; and the beautiful-eyed maidens like hidden pearls: a reward for what they used to do.'
> *Qur'an 56:11–24*

The Al-Aqsa Mosque in Jerusalem, where Muhammad was taken first on the Night Journey

The basic criterion for entry to Jannah is belief in **tawhid**, but belief in the Six Articles of Faith for Sunni Muslims or the Five Roots of Usul ad-Din for Shi'a Muslims is important too.

Islam teaches that not everyone will qualify to go to Jannah. Prophets and the righteous will live at the highest levels. Those who die in defence of Allah (such as martyrs) or those who die while on Hajj go straight to Jannah without passing through judgement because their exceptional deaths purify their sins.

Some Muslim scholars argue that Christians and Jews could be eligible for Jannah since they have faith in Allah and the Day of Judgement. They also understand the importance of righteous behaviour. However, others argue that the Qur'an is clear that Islam alone is the path to paradise.

Useful term

salah – ritual prayers

> ❝If anyone seeks a religion other than [Islam] complete devotion to God, it will not be accepted from him: he will be one of the losers in the Hereafter.❞
> *Qur'an 3:85*

Hell

Jahannam means the depths. It is the place of punishment that sinners can expect to be sent to if they are judged to have rejected Allah, worshipped other gods, or committed grave sins.

Islam teaches that after the Day of Judgement, everyone will walk over the bridge of Sirat that stretches over the fires of hell. If they have not obeyed Allah's will, the bridge will be thinner than a hair and sharper than a sword and they will fall in. The hadiths state that the drop is so deep that a stone, if thrown in, would fall for 70 years before reaching the bottom.

The suffering in Jahannam is physical, mental and spiritual. It is described in detail in several places in the Qur'an:

> ❝They will dwell amid scorching wind and scalding water in the shadow of black smoke, neither cool nor refreshing. Before, they overindulged in luxury and persisted in great sin…. you who have gone astray and denied the truth will eat from the bitter tree of Zaqqum, filling your bellies with it, and drink scalding water, lapping it like thirsty camels.❞
> *Quran 56:42–55*

Shaytan will also be punished along with any jinn who joined him. There is disagreement over whether Jahannam is eternal or not. Some Modernist Muslims argue that since Allah is merciful, he may allow most people to go to Jannah once they have been purified. Others argue that purification is only possible for sinful Muslims, not non-believers.

Hell has seven gates that are monitored by angels. There are seven levels of hell that increase in terrible punishment, in accordance with the sins that people have committed.

According to Sunni hadiths, the traditional layers for hell are:

1 A fire for Muslims who have sinned
2 A fire for Jewish sinners
3 A fire for Christian sinners
4 A burning fire for one who deserts Islam
5 A place for witches and fortune tellers
6 A furnace for the disbelievers
7 A bottomless abyss for hypocrites who pretend to be faithful.

Most Muslims accept the teachings of the Qur'an as literally true. A small number of scholars see these descriptions as metaphorical because the pleasures described in Jannah and the punishment described in Jahannam sound like earthly experiences rather than spiritual ones.

There is disagreement in Islam over whether Christians and Jews can enter Jannah

> ❝The one whose good deeds are heavy on the scales will have a pleasing life, but the one whose good deeds are light will have the Bottomless Pit for his home – what will explain to you what that is? – a blazing fire.❞
> *Qur'an 101:6–11*

Knowledge recall

1 Define the following concepts: halal, greater/lesser jihad. (You can find these definitions on page 145.)
2 List four features of Jannah.
3 State the main criteria required for entry into Jannah.

Evaluation practice

4 Give one argument for and one argument against Christians and Jews being allowed to enter Jannah.
5 Which argument do you think is most consistent with teaching in the Qur'an and why?

Foundations of faith

Specification focus

Foundations of faith: The Six Articles of Faith in Sunni Islam; the Five Roots in Usul ad-Din in Shi'a Islam.

Sunni and Shi'a beginnings

All Muslims are expected to have faith in certain foundational beliefs that make Islam different from all other world faiths. These foundations provide the basis for worship and moral behaviour. While Sunni and Shi'a Muslims all have faith in Allah and Muhammad as his prophet, there are some significant differences between them.

Both Sunni and Shi'a Muslims share belief in Allah and his prophets. They also agree that Ali ibn Abi Talib (Muhammad's cousin and son-in-law) was Muhammad's constant companion and the first to accept Islam.

Shi'a Muslims believe that Ali was the first Imam and that only Muhammad's descendants could be his successor. These successors are the twelve Imams. Sunni Muslims disagree with this. They believe that Muhammad appointed no successor, so after Muhammad's death, the ==ummah== prioritised political concerns and chose Abu Bak'r (Muhammad's father-in-law) as **Caliph** because he was popular among the tribes in both Makkah and Medina.

The next Caliphs were Umar (Muhammad's father-in-law) followed by Uthman (Muhammad's son-in-law). After the assassination of these Caliphs, Ali was left as the only possible successor. In Sunni Islam, these four men are known as the rightly guided Caliphs, who model righteous leadership.

However, Shi'a Muslims do not recognise the first three, arguing that they should never have been appointed. Shi'a Muslims believe that Ali was the first **Imam** and the only successors to Muhammad should be his descendants.

The hadiths

All Muslims accept the Qur'an as the word of Allah, recited by Muhammad. When he died, Muhammad left the example of his life that is preserved in the hadiths. These are the stories of Muhammad's teaching and behaviour that can be used to help Muslims make decisions on matters not mentioned in the Qur'an.

The collections of hadiths quickly became huge and scholars needed to develop a method of working out which hadiths were reliable, and which were not. They did this by examining the chains of transmission. This means they traced who the hadith had been passed to and from. The more reliable the people, and the more unbroken the chain, the more reliable the hadith. Shi'a Muslims accept different chains of transmission than Sunni Muslims because of the disagreement over leadership. Therefore, they will only accept hadiths from Shi'a chains of transmission.

The Six Articles of Faith

Sunni Muslims are expected to accept certain fundamental beliefs known as the Six Articles of Faith. These are derived from the Qur'an:

1 ==Tawhid== – belief in one God (see page 146)
2 Malaikah – belief in angels (see page 152)
3 Kutub – belief in the scriptures (see page 160)
4 Risalah – belief in the prophets (see pages 148–151)

Belief in Kutub (the scriptures) is one of the Six Articles of Faith in Sunni Islam

> ❛You who believe, believe in God and His Messenger and in the Scripture He sent down to His Messenger, as well as what He sent down before. Anyone who does not believe in God, His angels, His Scriptures, His messengers, and the Last Day has gone far, far astray.❜
> *Qur'an 4:136*

Useful terms

Caliph – the deputy or successor of Muhammad in Sunni Islam
Imam – for Sunni Muslims: a Muslim prayer leader. For Shi'a Muslims: one of the twelve infallible successors to Muhammad chosen by Allah to guide humans towards Him

5 Akhirah – belief in the afterlife and Day of Resurrection (see pages 154–157)

6 Al-Qadr – belief in predestination (see page 154)

The Six Articles of Faith are the fundamental beliefs of Sunni Islam that are expressed through the practice of the Five Pillars of Islam.

The Five Roots of Usul ad-Din

The Five Roots of Usul ad-Din are the fundamental beliefs of Shi'a Islam. There are some similarities with the Six Articles of Faith:

1 Tawhid – belief in one God (see page 146)

2 Adalat – belief in God's justice (see page 154)

3 Al-Nubuwah – belief in the prophets (see pages 148–151)

4 Imamah – belief in the Imams (see page 176)

5 Al-Ma'ad – belief in the afterlife and Day of Resurrection (see page 154)

The Five Roots of Islam underpin the Ten Obligatory Acts (Furu al-Din). For Shi'a Muslims, they are essential beliefs in accordance with the Qur'an and the teachings of Muhammad and the twelve Imams. The Ten Obligatory Acts are the outward expression of this inward faith.

Read about the Five Pillars and Ten Obligatory Acts on pages 168–169.

There are shared beliefs between the two groups of Muslims, but over time, diversity has developed. Some of the key differences between the fundamental beliefs are as follows:

Read more about Al-Qadr on page 154.

● **Al-Qadr** – Shi'a Muslims reject the idea that humans are predestined. Allah cannot be responsible for evil in the world as he infinitely good. Therefore, humans must have free will and be responsible for sin in the world. Allah foreknows what humans will choose and so when he punishes or rewards humanity on the Last Day, he does so justly. According to Sunni Islam, nothing takes place without the will of Allah and whatever he wills takes place.

● **Kutub** – While both groups of Muslims accept the Qur'an as the unaltered word of Allah, Sunni Muslims believe it is the perfect copy of the eternal Qur'an that has always existed in paradise, whereas Shi'a Muslims believe it was created by Allah. For Shi'a Muslims, the message in the Qur'an must be interpreted by Muhammad and his family – the twelve Imams and his daughter Fatima.

● **Imamah** – For Sunni Muslims, an Imam is a man who leads Friday prayers. For Shi'a Muslims, an Imam is Muhammad's legitimate successor. He is infallible, has divine wisdom and is a descendant of Muhammad. The Twelver Shi'as believe there have been twelve Imams who were given the divine light by Allah. The twelfth, Imam Mahdi, went into hiding and will return to bring in the end of the world. Other Shi'a groups disagree, believing there were either five or seven Imams. But they all agree that Ali was appointed by Muhammad as his successor.

An Imam in Sunni Islam is someone who leads the salah (daily) prayers

Knowledge recall

1 Define the following concepts: Shariah, ummah. (You can find these definitions on page 145.)

2 List three beliefs that Sunni and Shi'a Muslims have in common.

3 Suggest one example of a key difference in belief between Sunni and Shi'a Muslims.

Evaluation practice

4 Give one reason why Sunni Muslims accept predestination and one reason why Shi'a Muslims do not.

5 Which do you think is the most convincing belief? Give two reasons why.

Islamic attitudes towards other scriptures

Specification focus

Foundations of faith: Islamic attitudes towards Kutub (books), Sahifah (Scrolls), Injil (Gospel), Tawrat (Torah), Zabur (Psalms).

Islamic attitudes towards Kutub

All Muslims accept that faith in the Kutub or scriptures is important. For Sunni Muslims it is the fourth of the Six Articles of Faith. Kutub are the revelations of Allah to his messengers. They are the direct word of Allah, written into the language of the prophet and their community.

Muslims believe the Qur'an was not the first revelation of Allah. There were other books revealed by Allah to his prophets and four of these are mentioned in the Qur'an (along with confirmation that the Qur'an itself is also Allah's revelation):

- Sahifah – the Scrolls of Ibrahim
- Tawrat – the Torah of Musa
- Zabur – the Psalms of Dawud
- Injil – the Gospel of Isa

The Qur'an is the final revelation given by Allah to all people. The preceding four books were given by Allah to the Jewish nation and then to Christians. While they are respected, they are believed to have undergone **tahrif**. This means that although they were pure when they were revealed by Allah and contained the same message, they have since been lost or distorted and can no longer be trusted.

The Qur'an is the final revelation of Allah to his prophet Muhammad

Sahifah

The Sahifah are the word of Allah revealed to the prophet Ibrahim. They are mentioned in the Qur'an.

The exact content of these scrolls is not clear since they are lost scripture. They were written in Hebrew and seemingly contained some teaching regarding judgement and the afterlife.

> ❛All this is in the earlier scriptures, the scriptures of Abraham and Moses.❜
> *Qur'an 87:18–19*

Tawrat

The Tawrat is Allah's revelation given to the prophet Musa. It contains the Ten Commandments and the law. Whereas other prophets were given revelation through the angel Jibril, Musa was given the Tawrat directly from Allah.

The Qur'an mentions the Tawrat in chapters that focus on law and social custom. Muhammad speaks of it in the hadith. However, Muslims consider the Tawrat that Jewish people use today (the Torah) as inauthentic, having undergone tahrif and no longer giving Allah's pure word. For example, it mentions the sins of prophets like Lut, but Muslims believe prophets do not sin once they are appointed.

> ❛We gave Moses the scripture and We sent messengers after him in succession.❜
> *Qur'an 2:87*

Useful terms

tahrif – the change or corruption of an original text
kalam – the word of Allah in scripture
abrogates – cancels or revokes
tafsir – commenting about the meaning

Zabur

The Arabic word Zabur is said to come from a Hebrew word that means 'song'. The Zabur was revealed to Dawud and is the psalms of the Hebrew Bible. These psalms are poems or prayers to praise and worship Allah.

In the Qur'an, Dawud is presented as a model Muslim, praising, fasting, prostrating and fighting for the honour of Allah.

Injil

The Injil is the gospel revealed to Isa. It literally means 'good news'. It is not considered to be the same as the four gospel books found in the New Testament today. It was originally given by Allah, not written by humans, and it was written in Aramaic. But the Injil was lost and so followers of Isa wrote their own accounts, which Christians follow today. These accounts in the New Testament preserve fragments of the original but are not the authentic **kalam**. For instance, they claim that Isa was the son of God, which is shirk.

Qur'an

Muslims believe the Qur'an is the final revelation of Allah to all humanity and is the only authoritative book that contains the kalam in its original, pure form.

> 'We sent to you [Muhammad] the Scripture with the truth, confirming [all] the Scripture that came before and protecting it...'
> *Qur'an 5:48*

The Qur'an confirms all previous revelation from Allah but **abrogates** any text where there appears to be contradiction. It was revealed by Allah to Muhammad over the course of 23 years, beginning on the Night of Power in 610 CE.

The Qur'an forms the basis of **Shariah** Law. It is arranged into chapters (surah) and verses (ayahs). Those revealed to Muhammad in Makkah are most concerned with beliefs such as tawhid, risalah and akhirah. The revelations received in Medina are more concerned with political and social issues.

Muhammad could not write, so he did not record Allah's revelations by himself. He passed each revelation to scribes who carefully recorded it on any available material. They were then cared for by one of Muhammad's wives.

When Muhammad died, the Qur'an was finished but not yet set into a particular order. Caliph Abu Bak'r instructed Muhammad's scribe to organise the revelations so they were arranged in order of length from longest to shortest. The third Caliph, Uthman, declared that all Qur'ans must be written in the original Arabic as an exact copy of the original to prevent tahrif.

Shi'a Muslims use this Qur'an but argue that Muhammad gave Ali the first Qur'an to care for. It was arranged chronologically, so that the first revelation was at the beginning, and it contains the **tafsir** of Muhammad. Ali shared it with the other Imams, and it is now with the last Imam.

> 'Your Lord knows best about everyone in the heavens and the earth. We gave some prophets more than others: We gave David a book [of Psalms].'
> *Qur'an 17:55*

> 'We sent Jesus, son of Mary, in their footsteps, to confirm the Torah that had been sent before him: We gave him the Gospel with guidance, light, and confirmation of the Torah already revealed – a guide and lesson for those who take heed of God.'
> *Qur'an 5:46*

Read about the Night of Power on page 183.

Knowledge recall

1 Define the following concepts: Shariah, mosque. (You can find these definitions on page 145.)
2 List the five Kutub mentioned in the Qur'an.
3 Suggest one example of tahrif that Muslims believe has occurred to other scriptures.

Evaluation practice

4 Give one reason why some Muslims argue that only the Qur'an should be trusted as authoritative. Give one reason why Christians or Jews may disagree.
5 Which do you think is the most compelling argument? Give two reasons why.

Skills practice

On these exam practice pages you will see example answers for each of the exam questions types: **a**, **b**, **c** and **d**. You can find out more about these on pages 5–9.

Question (a)

*Question **(a)** tests your knowledge and understanding. You will always be asked to **define a key concept** in this question. You can find a list of the concepts at the beginning of the chapter.*

> (a)   What do Muslims mean by 'tawhid'?   [2]

Student response

> Tawhid means the oneness of Allah. This is expressed in the Shahadah which is a creed or statement of faith and it is a basic belief of Islam. It is the sin of shirk to worship any other God.

Improved student response

> Tawhid means the basic Muslim belief in the oneness of Allah.

🕐 **Over to You!** Have a try at answering this question:

> (a)   What do Muslims mean by 'prophethood'?   [2]

Helpful hints

To help you answer this question effectively, you could use the check list below to make sure you include the most important things:

- **Synonym** – Include a synonym or another way of describing the term 'prophethood'.
- **Example** – Give an example of a prophet that is important in Islam.

Now give yourself **two minutes** to answer this question by yourself:

> (a)   What do Muslims mean by 'mosque' (masjid)?   [2]

What went well

The candidate understands the meaning of the word 'tawhid' accurately and shows this in the first sentence.

How to improve

You must remember that there are only two marks for this question, so there is no need to give lengthy responses or multiple examples.

You should learn the exam board's definition of the word at the start of this chapter.

You could practise responding within the two minutes you would have in a real examination.

Tip

In this response, the candidate has used the exam board definition of tawhid and has not included unnecessary details or explanations of other terms.

Question (b)

*Question (b) tests your knowledge and understanding. It will always ask you to **describe** a belief, a teaching, a practice or an event that is included on the specification.*

> (b)   Describe Muslim beliefs about Adam. [5]

Student response

Muslims believe that Adam was a prophet. He was the first prophet of Islam who was married to Eve. He sinned by eating an apple on a tree that Allah had told him not to, so he was thrown out of the Garden of Eden and made to work the land. He was responsible for the sins of the whole world.

Improved student response

Muslims believe that Adam was the first prophet of Islam and the first human being. He was made by Allah from clay and Allah breathed life into him. He was married to Eve and they lived in the Garden of Eden. He sinned by eating fruit from a tree that Allah had forbidden, so he was thrown out of the Garden of Eden. He repented on Mount Arafat and was forgiven and appointed prophet. He built the first Ka'ba.

🕐 **Over to You!** Have a try at answering this question:

> (b)   Describe the significance of Mika'il to Muslims. [5]

Helpful hints

Use the check list below to make sure you include the most important things:

- **How/Why** – Explain one Muslim belief about who Mika'il is or what he does and why this is important.
- **Example** – Give an example from scripture or a story about Mika'il that can show his importance.
- **Repeat** – Repeat this for two or more beliefs about Mika'il.

Now give yourself **five minutes** to answer this question by yourself:

> (b)   Describe Muslim beliefs about the tawhid (oneness) of Allah. [5]

What went well

The candidate knows who Adam is and can recall some accurate facts about him.

How to improve

You must make sure that you do not mix up Christian beliefs about Adam with Muslim beliefs.

You should consider the creation of Adam by Allah as well as Adam's sin.

You could refer to Adam's repentance and appointment as prophet.

Tip

When you are revising, try making numbered lists of as many beliefs about each prophet as you can. This will help when you must recall them under pressure.

Question (c)

Question (c) tests your knowledge and understanding. You need to give detailed evidence and reasoning to support your explanation of the topic. You may need to show how belief influences religious practice. This is not an evaluation question so you don't need to evaluate different viewpoints.

> (c) Explain why prophethood is important in Islam. [8]

Student response

Prophethood is known as risalah. It is one of the Six Articles of Faith for Muslims. Prophets are treated with respect. There are 25 prophets mentioned in the Qur'an. They all teach the same thing, but not all their writings have survived so only the Qur'an is treated as authoritative. Muhammad is the seal of the prophets. He had the Qur'an revealed to him by the angel Jibril. There are other prophets that are important too. E.g. Isa (Jesus) and Ibrahim (Abraham). Christians and Jews believe in those ones too, but Muslims believe in all the prophets.

Improved student response

Prophethood or risalah is important because prophets are messengers that Allah used to guide humans. For example, Muhammad was given the Qur'an from Allah so that people could understand his will. Prophethood is one of the Six Articles of Faith for Sunni Muslims and one of the Five Roots for Shi'a Muslims. Prophets are human but sinless after their appointment and so are examples of how to live. Although Adam sinned before he was prophet, his repentance gives an example for everyone. All 25 prophets named in the Qur'an teach the same about Tawhid and are all important. The Qur'an says, 'We make no distinction between any of them.' Muhammad is the seal of the prophets, the final one. The prophets brought knowledge of the unseen world that humanity has no other way of knowing about. For example, understanding about the afterlife and Allah's will for humanity that cannot be learned through science or reasoning. Therefore, prophets such as Muhammad are considered wise, and his own teaching and example are authoritative.

🕐 **Over to You!** Have a try at answering this question:

> (c) Explain why the revelation of the Qur'an to Muhammad is important in Islam. [8]

Helpful hints

- Include **more than one belief** for why revelation of the Qur'an is important (e.g. it is the only uncorrupted book; it contains the word of Allah).
- For each belief try to give an **example** from the content of the Qur'an or stories connected with its revelation to demonstrate the belief (e.g. stories about the Night of Power).
- Explain **why** Muslims might believe this (e.g. they are influenced by other teachings about Allah, prophethood or angels).

What went well

There is a significant amount of correct information included in this response and it is all relevant to the question.

How to improve

You must notice the word 'why' in the question and concentrate on this more than 'what' a prophet is.

You should include some reasoning that shows why a Muslim would consider the prophets important, rather than just listing information about them.

You could select three beliefs about the importance of the prophets and try to give evidence to back up why Muslims would believe this.

Tip

This response is improved because it does more than just list information about the prophets. It gives reasoning to support why the prophets are important by emphasising their role as messengers and guides for humanity, as well as their contact with Allah.

Study Challenge:

The exam board will only ever ask a question **(c)** in the religion papers, that asks you to explain. For example, 'Explain how...' or 'Explain why...'

- Look back at the specification focus boxes at the top of each page in this chapter.
- Choose one area from the list that has not yet appeared in the questions above.
- Write your own **(c)** question on this area that begins with the word 'Explain' and asks for the area you have chosen.
- Now give yourself **eight minutes** to answer this question by yourself!

Question (d)

*Question **(d)** tests your ability to **evaluate**. This means you need to show you have considered more than one point of view and that you have referred to religion and belief. You will need to be able to make judgements that are supported by detailed reasoning and argument.*

> (d) 'Belief in angels is no longer important for Muslims.'
> Discuss this statement showing that you have considered more than one point of view. (You must refer to religion and belief in your answer.) [15]

Student response

Belief in angels is one of the Six Articles of Faith in Sunni Islam and so belief in them is important for Muslims. However, belief in angels is not consistent with a modern scientific understanding of the world. It is far more important that a Muslim accepts Tawhid than worries about angels. The first argument is the strongest. Islam requires lots of different beliefs that are outlined in the Six Articles and belief in angels is one of them.

Belief in angels is fundamental to all the Islamic accounts of the prophets and to beliefs regarding the afterlife. For example, Jibril is in the story of the revelation of the Qur'an and Israfil is required for the Day of Judgement. However, belief in angels is not one of the Five Roots of Usul ad-Din. This suggests that it is not as important as previously suggested. I think the first argument is the strongest. The second argument is weak and does not give a reason why Muslims should not believe in angels.

Modernisers in Islam may argue that belief in angels is unnecessary. These people may argue that angels are a myth. However, Muslims believe in the authority of the Qur'an as it is the word of Allah. If it says that angels exist, then it is essential for Muslims to believe this, even in the modern age. So, the first argument is weak and belief in angels is important for Muslims.

Improved student response

Belief in angels is important in Islam because it is an Article of Faith in Sunni Islam and forms part of a list of beliefs that cannot be rejected. Angels are frequently mentioned in the Qur'an and they appeared at significant moments in the lives of the prophets. However, belief in angels is not consistent with modern scientific understanding of the world, and there is no reason why modern Muslims should reject what reason tells us. It is far more important that a Muslim accepts Tawhid and avoids shirk, than believes in angels. However, Islam has many complex beliefs; the Six Articles outline the basics and they do not restrict a Muslim to Tawhid alone. Therefore, it is clearly part of the Muslim faith to believe in angels.

The candidate includes reasoning that shows why they are arguing that belief in angels is important.

Key specialist vocabulary is used appropriately and in context.

Throughout the response, reasoning is given to support a view. Here, there is a reason why the counter-argument in this paragraph has been rejected.

Belief in Malaikah is vital to the accounts of the prophets and their beliefs about the afterlife. Jibril is central when the Qur'an was revealed and Israfil is needed on the Day of Judgement. Islam requires belief in angels and Muslims must accept Allah's word in the Qur'an which says 'If anyone is an enemy of God, His angels and His messengers... God is certainly the enemy of such disbelievers.' However, belief in angels is not one of the Five Roots of Usul ad-Din. It is possible to believe in Allah's justice and the afterlife without accepting that angels exist. The Imamate is of more significance in Shi'a Islam. However, angels played a key role in the appointment of Ali as Imam and rejection of them seems to send human beings away from Allah's will. If a Muslim accepts that there is one God and an afterlife, there is no reason why belief in angels is less reasonable.

Modernisers may choose to argue that belief in angels is unnecessary because they are just symbolic beings in stories that are trying to help humans understand a deeper teaching. They may argue that angels are myths within accounts of the prophets or what happens after death. However, it is hard to see how a faithful Muslim might justify rejecting belief in angels without rejecting other parts of the Qur'an or the hadith. Muslims do not doubt the authority of the Qur'an as it is the word of Allah. If it says that angels exist, then Muslims must believe this, even in the modern age.

> Appropriate examples regarding angels and their roles in Islamic belief are given to support a reasoned argument.

> The candidate does not just state which argument is stronger from the paragraph, they support it with reasoning.

> Space is given to consider counter-arguments fully so that the response is balanced, not one-sided.

🕐 **Over to You!** Have a try at answering this question:

(d) 'Ibrahim is the most important prophet in Islam.'
Discuss this statement showing that you have considered more than one point of view. (You must refer to religion and belief in your answer.) [15]

Helpful hints

If you find it difficult to answer this question effectively, you could try using the A, B, C, D structure or a variation of it to help you set out your paragraphs (see page 32).

In addition, remember that analysis and evaluation require **reasoning** to support them. This means using evidence or arguments to support your ideas, or drawing conclusions based on evidence.

You should always consider why a view is a successful one, or why a view is weak or ineffective. It is always important to give reasoning to support every conclusion and every argument that you present.

Now give yourself **fifteen minutes** to answer this question by yourself:

(d) 'Belief in Allah is the most important Muslim belief.'
Discuss this statement showing that you have considered more than one point of view. (You must refer to religion and belief in your answer.) [15]

Tip

When you make an argument in question (d), it is important to give reasoning to support your point. This is true in arguments for and against the question. It is also true when you are suggesting which argument is stronger.

Tip

When presented with a question that seems like it has only one answer, try to imagine that you are someone else. For example: what kind of life would a Muslim be living to prioritise something else over belief in Allah? (Living among people who suffer and need help? Hoping that they will be judged for their good deeds after death?) It is then perfectly acceptable to demonstrate all the problems with this position.

Chapter 8:
Islam: Practices

Introduction

In this chapter, you will consider how the beliefs of Muslims are expressed in practice through their daily lives in Great Britain and across the world. There are some differences between Sunni and Shi'a practices based on the differences in their beliefs, but broadly, most Muslims share in the same or very similar practices. It is important to remember that Muslim practice has been set out by a mixture of directions from the Qur'an, the hadiths and Shariah Law. This means that practices should be very similar no matter where a Muslim lives in the world. However, Muslims from different countries experience different challenges and may also be influenced by their home cultures. This means that some things practised by some Muslims are not always directly taught in Islam.

Things to remember:

- Muslims believe the Qur'an is the revealed word of Allah that has not been altered since it was revealed to Muhammad. This means that when the Qur'an sets out how a practice is to be performed, Muslims will make every effort to make sure they follow those instructions exactly as Allah wills, even to the tiniest detail. For example, the exact details of how to perform salah or hajj.
- The Qur'an does not give instructions for every detail of practice, so when Muslims need more information, they look to the hadiths. The hadiths are not the word of Allah but a collection of writings that record the Sunnah (examples, practices and teachings of Muhammad). The authority of each hadith depends on who recorded and passed it on. The more authoritative the chain of transmission, the more authoritative the hadith.
- Shi'a and Sunni Muslims do not always accept the same hadiths because of their disagreement over the succession of leadership after Muhammad's death. Their practices may therefore sometimes differ because they accept different hadiths. For example, Shi'a Muslims will not accept hadiths from those who were appointed Caliph before Ali.
- Another source of authority and guidance for Muslim practice is Shariah Law. Shariah Law is based on the Qur'an, the Sunnah as revealed in the hadiths, ijma (the agreement of scholars), and qiyas (analogy and logical reasoning from scholars). There are different schools of law in Islam who interpret Shariah Law in different ways. While most practices appear the same or very similar across the world, there may be some differences based on the different interpretations of Shariah Law.

Concepts

Tawhid – 'oneness' in reference to God and is the basic Muslim belief in the oneness of Allah

Prophethood – ('risalah' in Arabic) is the term used of the messengers of Allah, beginning with Adam and ending with the Prophet Muhammad

Halal – actions or things which are permitted within Islam, such as eating permitted foods

Haram – any actions or things which are forbidden within Islam, such as eating forbidden foods

Greater/Lesser jihad – the word jihad means 'to strive' and there are two forms of jihad:

- Greater jihad is the daily struggle and inner spiritual striving to live as a Muslim
- Lesser jihad is a physical struggle or 'holy war' in defence of Islam

Mosque – ('Masjid' in Arabic), a 'place of prostration' for Muslims; it is a communal place of worship for a Muslim community

Shariah (straight path) – a way of life; Muslims believe Allah has set out a clear path for how Muslims should live. Shariah Law is the set of moral and religious rules that put the principles set out by the Qur'an and the hadiths into practice

Ummah – means 'community' and refers to the worldwide community of Muslims who share a common religious identity

The Five Pillars, the Ten Obligatory Acts and the Shahadah

Specification focus

The Five Pillars of Sunni Islam:
Shahadah: The Muslim statement of faith: Qur'an 3:18
Ten Obligatory Acts of Shi'a Islam.

The Five Pillars of Sunni Islam

While Islam began in Arabia, it has since spread across the globe and absorbed many cultures as it expanded. There are many practices observed by Muslims today that reflect their native customs rather than the Islamic faith.

Yet the Five Pillars of Sunni Islam bring uniformity to Muslim practice. Sunni Muslims are expected to fulfil their duty by performing the Five Pillars wherever they are in the world. The pillars were established from the Qur'an and the hadiths as basic, fundamental elements of Islam and a foundation of worship.

The Five Pillars must be performed with **niyyah** to show devotion and submission to Allah. They must also be performed in the right way, according to the customs laid out in the Qur'an and the hadiths.

The Five Pillars of Sunni Islam are:

1. Shahadah – the confession of faith
2. Salah – prayer
3. Sawm – fasting
4. Zakah – charitable giving
5. Hajj – pilgrimage

The Ten Obligatory Acts of Shi'a Islam

For Shi'a Muslims, it is impossible to be a Muslim unless one has faith in the Usul ad-Din. These are the roots of faith – the fundamental beliefs required for Islam. The **Furu ad-Din** or Ten Obligatory Acts are practices that act as 'branches': they grow from the roots of faith and demonstrate faith in Allah.

The Ten Obligatory Acts are:

1. Salah – prayer
2. Sawm – fasting
3. Hajj – pilgrimage
4. Zakah – charitable giving
5. Khums – giving alms
6. Jihad – the struggle for Islam
7. Amr-bil-Maroof – encouraging the good
8. Nahil Anril Munkar – discouraging evil
9. Tawalia – love and respect for the **Ahl al-Bayt**
10. Tabarra – turning away from those who are unjust towards the Ahl al-Bayt

These ten practices are given great importance in the Qur'an and the hadith, but living life as a faithful Shi'a Muslim is not limited to only following these practices. Other practices and laws are also important for a Shi'a Muslim with the niyyah to develop a closer awareness of Allah and unity among the **ummah**.

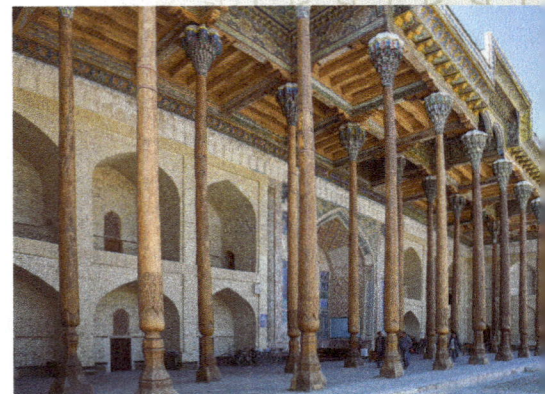

An Arabic building requires pillars for support

Read about the **Five Roots of Usul ad-Din** on page 159.

Useful terms

niyyah – the right intention
Furu ad-Din – branches or ancillaries of faith; also called the Ten Obligatory Acts. The rules and laws that organise life for a Shi'a Muslim
Ahl al-Bayt – the family of Muhammad. For Shi'a Muslims this consists of the twelve Imams and Fatima, his daughter. Sunni Muslims include Muhammad's wider family

There is significant overlap between the practices of Sunni and Shi'a Muslims. They are all Muslims from one faith, and while Sunni Muslims no longer observe khums, all other elements are important to all Muslims, even if there is a divergence in the meaning.

The Shahadah

'There is no god but Allah and Muhammad is the messenger of Allah.'

The phrase above is the Shahadah: a creed, or confession of faith in Allah. It is a basic declaration of the fundamental beliefs of Islam and has to be declared publicly if a person is to be considered a Muslim.

The Shahadah is the first and most vital pillar of Islam. It is a duty and a commitment.

The first part of the Shahadah is the acceptance of **tawhid**. In Muhammad's day it was vital to separate the monotheistic Muslims from the polytheists of the time that Muhammad challenged. This first half of the Shahadah is a rejection of the sin of shirk and is laid out clearly in the Qur'an.

> **God bears witness that there is no god but Him,** as do the angels and those who have knowledge. He upholds justice. There is no god but Him with the power to decide.
> *Qur'an 3:18*

The second part of the Shahadah is the acceptance of risalah. It is also stated clearly in the Qur'an. In Muhammad's time, it is what marked out Muslims as distinct from other monotheists. Jews and Christians believed in God but did not accept Muhammad as prophet.

When a person reverts to Islam, the only ritual that is required is to recite the Shahadah before two witnesses. For a person who was born into Islam, they must do this when they reach puberty. The Shahadah is whispered in the ear of a newborn baby and the ear of a person who is dying, so that it is the first and last thing that a Muslim hears.

The Shahadah is announced five times each day during the call to prayer. It is repeated in daily prayers as a reminder to Muslims that they must submit to Allah and be continually aware of him in their lives.

Shi'a Muslims also observe the Shahadah, but it does not appear as one of the Ten Obligatory Acts. However, they add to the Shahadah that Ali is the vice regent of Allah. Shi'a Muslims believe that Muhammad's son-in-law, Ali, was Muhammad's successor and that he was the true deputy of Allah after Muhammad.

Usul ad-Din and Furu ad-Din are the roots and branches of the Shi'a faith

Knowledge recall

1. Define the following concepts: haram, ummah. (You can find these definitions on page 167.)
2. List the two things that the Shahadah declares faith in and state the addition made to the Shahadah in Shi'a Islam.
3. State two reasons why observance of the five pillars or Furu ad-Din is important in Islam.

Evaluation practice

4. Give one reason why some Muslims may argue that faith is more important than action and one reason why other Muslims may argue that actions are more important.
5. Which of these views do you find most persuasive? Give two reasons why.

Salah

The importance of salah

Salah (or salat) is the second pillar of Sunni Islam and the first of the Ten Obligatory Acts in Shi'a Islam. It is the duty of prayer for all Muslims. Salah can be used for praise, petition and intercession (praying for others), and ensures constant awareness of Allah. While some Muslims ask for forgiveness during salah, the practice of regular prayer is considered enough to cleanse a Muslim of sin.

Timings of salah

Muslims follow the practice of Muhammad as recorded in the hadiths to tell them when to pray. Sunni and Shi'a Muslims practise salah in slightly different ways. One of the first significant differences is the times of prayer.

Sunni Islam	Shi'a Islam
1. Fajr (between dawn and sunrise)	1. Fajr
2. Zuhr (after midday until afternoon)	2. Zuhr and As'r
3. As'r (between late afternoon and sunset)	
4. Maghrib (after sunset until dusk)	3. Maghrib and Isha
5. Isha (between dusk and dawn)	

Sunni Muslims pray five times a day. During Muhammad's vision (the Night Journey), Allah revealed the prayers that he required. Muhammad appealed to Allah's mercy because there were so many, and the number was reduced to five. Shi'a Muslims believe that Muhammad made it acceptable to combine some of these prayers, so they pray three times daily.

The practice of salah

The call to prayer is announced by a **muezzin** from the **mosque** tower (minaret) at each prayer time. In Muslim countries this call goes out over a loudspeaker system so that everyone can hear, at which point all other activity stops.

Before prayer, worshippers perform **wudu** to prepare them to stand before Allah. This includes washing hands, arms, face, feet and ankles, nostrils, ears and the head before each prayer. Mosques have an ablution area where wudu can take place.

When praying in the mosque, worshippers remove their shoes before entering. If they are praying elsewhere, they use a prayer mat that has never been trodden on by anything unclean. They should also ensure that their clothing is clean.

During prayer, Muslims face the Ka'ba in Makkah. If praying outside the mosque, Muslims can use a **qibla** compass in their prayer mat to work out the direction of prayer. Shi'a Muslims keep a stone or small piece of clay in front of them while they pray, called the **turbah**. It represents the earth and may be made of clay from Karbala in Iraq, where the third Imam was martyred.

During prayer, there is a prescribed pattern of movements and recitations that a Muslim must follow called a **rakah**. At each prayer time, a worshipper completes

Read about the Night Journey on page 156.

Specification focus

The Five Pillars of Sunni Islam: Salah: the practices of prayer in Islam in the mosque and at home, including Jummah prayer: Qur'an 15:98–99, Qur'an 29:45.

Ten Obligatory Acts of Shi'a Islam: Salat: how Shi'a Muslims perform salat.

> 'Celebrate the glory of your Lord and **be among those who bow down to Him:** worship your Lord until what is certain comes to you.'
> *Qur'an 15:98–99*

Useful terms

muezzin – the person appointed to recite and lead the call to prayer at a mosque

wudu – ablution; ritual cleaning performed to purify a worshipper before salah

qibla – the direction of the Ka'ba building in Makkah

turbah – a small piece of moulded clay on which Shi'a Muslims place their forehead during salah

rakah – the procedure for salah. A unit or cycle of prayer movements that is repeated between two, three and four rakahs. With each movement in the rakah, set verses of praise are recited.

1   Facing the qibla, a worshipper makes their niyyah, focusing their minds on prayer.
2   The worshipper raises their hands to their ears, showing they are ready to listen to Allah.
3   Still standing, Sunni Muslims place their hands on their chest and look to the ground. Shi'a Muslims place arms by their sides.
4   The worshipper bows and places their hands on their knees.
5   They stand upright to say more verses of praise.
6   They prostrate, kneeling on the floor with their toes, knees, forehead and nose touching the ground, their hands either side of their head.
7   They sit up on their knees, and then prostrate a second time. This completes one rakah. The cycle is then repeated.
8   On the final rakah, Sunni Muslims turn their face to the right and then left, saying 'peace be upon you' to the angels who accompany them and fellow worshippers on either side.

If a Muslim cannot say their prayers because of travel or work, they can join prayers together at the next prayer time so they have performed their full quota.

Read about the death of the third Imam on page 182.

One movement in a rakah involves prostrating with the forehead touching the ground

> ‘[Prophet], recite what has been revealed to you of the Scripture; keep up the prayer: **prayer restrains outrageous and unacceptable behaviour.** Remembering God is greater: God knows everything you are doing.’
> Qur'an 29:45

Jummah

Jummah prayers involve Muslims gathering at the mosque on Friday afternoon for a sermon followed by two rakahs of the zuhr prayers. It is considered the duty of all Sunni Muslim men to attend Jummah prayer, but Muhammad encouraged husbands to allow their wives to attend prayers too. In the Shi'a tradition, Jummah prayers are highly recommended but not compulsory.

This practice reminds Muslims of the importance of being united with the ummah in praise of Allah. Everyone in the mosque faces the Ka'ba, indicated by a niche in the mosque wall. They pray in lines behind the Imam, making the same movements and saying the same words. Women may pray behind men, beside them on the other side of a screen or in a different room. There is no day of rest in Islam, so Muslims should return to work after Jummah is observed.

Muslim students or workers in non-Muslim countries face challenges when break times do not coincide with salah and Jummah. Some ask employers or teachers if they can take short breaks within the set times. Others make up prayers later and ask Allah to forgive them. Some schools and employers set aside rooms to help Muslims complete their prayers properly.

Women may pray behind men, beside them on the other side of a screen or in a different room

Knowledge recall

1   Define the following concepts: halal, mosque. (You can find these definitions on page 167.)
2   List the five times of prayer for Sunni Muslims.
3   State two reasons why salah is important.

Evaluation practice

4   Give one reason why it might be difficult for Muslims to observe salah in the UK and one reason why it might not be.
5   Which of these arguments is the most persuasive? Give a reason why.

Sawm, zakat and khums

Specification focus

The Five Pillars of Sunni Islam:
Zakah: how Sunni Muslims make payment of charity tax, alms and how zakat money may be spent; Sawm: how Sunni Muslims fast during Ramadan: Qur'an 2:184; issues relating to Muslims fasting in Britain.

Ten Obligatory Acts of Shi'a Islam: How Shi'a Muslims observe sawm, pay zakat; Khums: how Shi'a Muslims pay savings tax.

Sawm

Sawm is the fourth pillar of Sunni Islam and the second of the Ten Obligatory Acts of Shi'a Islam. It is a month-long fast performed during Ramadan. Ramadan is the ninth month of the Islamic calendar. There is a special night during Ramadan called the Night of Power when, for Sunni Muslims, Muhammad received his first revelation from Allah. For Shi'a Muslims, this was when he received the whole of the Qur'an in his heart.

The strict fast during Ramadan means no food, drink (even water), smoking or sex during daylight hours. Muslims should also work extra hard to avoid sinful actions. When Ramadan occurs during the summer, this means fasting over long, hot days. This can be very challenging, especially in a non-Muslim country if others are not fasting.

Not everyone is expected to fast during Ramadan. Children below the age of puberty, the elderly, sick, and travellers are all exempt. Pregnant, breastfeeding or menstruating women are too. Anyone who cannot fast should make up their fast later, or compensate by giving to charity or feeding the poor. Some Muslims believe young people completing exams should be excused, but many feel they should still fast at this time.

> 'Fast for a specific number of days, but if one of you is ill, or on a journey, then on other days later. **For those who can fast only with extreme difficulty, there is a way to compensate – feed a needy person.** But if anyone does good of his own accord, it is better for him, and fasting is better for you, if only you knew.'
> *Qur'an 2:184*

During Ramadan, a Muslim will wake before fajr prayers to have a **suhur** meal. The fast then begins at dawn. In Muslim countries, businesses may adjust their opening times during Ramadan, but in the UK Muslims will have to attend work and school as usual.

Sunni Muslims break their fast at sunset, but Shi'a Muslims wait until sunset has ended. The fast is broken with an **iftar** meal of water and dates, just before the Maghrib prayer, and is followed by a communal meal in the evening.

The purpose of sawm is to develop self-discipline and compassion for the poor members of the **ummah**. In addition, it shows devotion to Allah and enables each fasting Muslim to grow closer to him.

Zakah

Zakah (or zakat) is the giving of **alms**. As the fourth pillar of Islam, it sets out the duty of all Muslims to provide for those in need. Islam teaches that all people are equal before Allah, so Islamic law includes the duty to pay zakah, where a proportion of a person's wealth is given for the benefit of the poor.

Many people like to attend iftar meals as a large communal event

Useful terms

suhur – a pre-dawn meal consumed before fasting
iftar – breaking fast with a meal at sunset
alms – money or goods, given to the poor
nisab – the threshold of wealth that a person can have before they must pay zakat

A Muslim is only required to pay zakah once their earnings have passed the **nisab**. Islam sees no value to living in voluntary poverty, so it is important for families to have enough to support themselves before they give zakah.

Muslims have a duty to calculate the proportion of their wealth required for zakah at the end of each lunar year. Most Muslims in the UK calculate it as 2.5% of their income above the nisab. In some Muslim countries it is taken as an official tax, but mostly it is up to the individual to pay voluntarily.

Muslims can give their zakah directly to the **mosque** to manage, or they can use charities like Islamic Relief, Penny Appeal or Muslim Hands, who collect zakah and distribute it to those who are eligible. It is used to provide for orphans, widows, the poor and the homeless.

On Id-ul-Fitr, additional zakah payments should be made to the poor or the starving. On Id-ul-Adha, additional charity is given in the form of fresh meat to share with the poor. It is also possible for Muslims to give voluntarily as sadaqah. This is not compulsory giving, but it will bring a Muslim even closer to Allah.

Read about Id-al-Fitr and Id-al-Adha on pages 180–181.

Khums

Khums is one of the Ten Obligatory Acts in Shi'a Islam. It means 'fifth' and is a tax of 20% of a person's yearly profit (any earnings left over after paying for living expenses).

Khums is said to have begun with Muhammad's grandfather, who discovered buried treasure and donated a fifth of it to the poor. This practice was then confirmed in the Qur'an, so it became a duty for Muslims to donate a fifth of any spoils of war or buried treasure.

> ❛Know that one-fifth of your battle gains belongs to God and the Messenger, to close relatives and orphans, to the needy and travellers...❜
> *Qur'an 8:41*

Khums is collected at the end of each financial year and is divided up for different purposes. A portion was once given to Muhammad and any of his descendants who were in need, but Sunni Muslims ceased this practice with the death of Muhammad and the Caliphs.

Today it is divided among Shi'a religious scholars, who may take a portion if they have no other income to enable them to live a basic lifestyle. Other portions are allocated to work for Allah, orphans, poor descendants of the prophet and needy travellers.

Muslims can perform charity directly, or donate their zakah online

Knowledge recall

1 Define the following concepts: prophethood, mosque. (You can find these definitions on page 167.)
2 List three things that a Muslim must avoid during sawm.
3 State the proportion of wealth that is to be given for zakah and for khums.

Evaluation practice

4 Give two reasons why every Muslim should give to charity and two reasons why this might not be true.
5 Which of these views do you think is the most persuasive? Give a reason why.

Hajj

Pilgrimage to Makkah

Hajj is the fifth pillar of Islam for Sunni Muslims and the third obligatory act for Shi'a Muslims. It is a duty commanded by Allah and its practice is set out in the Qur'an and the hadiths.

Adult Muslims should try to perform Hajj at least once in a lifetime if their health and wealth allow it. It takes place over five or six days in the month of Dhu al-Hajja (the twelfth month of the Islamic calendar), and finishes after the festival of Id-ul-Adha. Hajj attracts over 2 million pilgrims from around the world each year.

The destination for Hajj is **Masjid al-Haram** in Saudi Arabia. It is the centre of an area covering several miles that is forbidden to non-Muslims. At the centre of Masjid al-Haram is the Ka'ba: a cube-shaped building covered by the **kiswa**, in which is set a black stone.

Date	Ritual	Meaning
7th	• Perform **ghusl** and dress in **ihram**. • Enter the Masjid al-Haram; express niyyah to perform Hajj.	Ihram helps Muslims to present themselves before Allah in a state of purity.
8th (first day of Hajj)	• Perform **tawaf**. On each rotation, try to touch or kiss the black stone or the Ka'ba wall. • Perform **sa'i** between the two hills of Al-Safa and Al-Marwah. • Travel to Mina for prayers.	Tawaf connects Muslims with the ummah and the prophets. It also shows Allah's central place in life. Sa'i remembers Hagar's search for water.
9th (second day of Hajj)	• Walk to Arafat and stand upright on the plain to confess sins to Allah. • At sunset, walk to Muzdalifa to camp overnight. • Collect 49 small stones (Shi'a collect 70).	Adam repented at Arafat after being evicted from Eden and was made prophet. It is where people will stand before Allah on the Day of Judgement.
10th (third day of Hajj)	• Walk to Mina for 'the stoning of the devil'. • Celebrate Id-ul-Adha: sacrifice an animal to Allah. Eat some – the rest is sent to the poor on refrigerated ships. • Ihram is removed. Men shave their heads, women cut a lock of hair. • Repeat tawaf and sa'i at Makkah. • Drink from the well of Zamzam. • Return to Mina.	Stones are thrown at three walls in Mina to represent Ibrahim's stoning of Shaytan. The sacrifice at Mina commemorates Ibrahim's willingness to offer his son as a sacrifice and Allah's protection. Zamzam is believed to be the spring that Allah made flow as Hagar searched for water.
11th – 13th (fourth to sixth day of Hajj)	• Remain in Mina for two or three days. • Offer the sacrifice if not yet completed. • Throw more pebbles at the three pillars. • Return to Makkah. • Perform a final tawaf and salah.	

Specification focus

The Five Pillars of Sunni Islam: Hajj: how Sunni Muslims undertake pilgrimage to the Ka'ba in Makkah; Qur'an 2:125. Issues relating to Muslims in Britain undertaking Hajj.

Ten Obligatory Acts of Shi'a Islam: Hajj: pilgrimage to Makkah: Qur'an 2:125 and pilgrimage to Shi'a shrines.

> 'We made the House a resort and a sanctuary for people, saying, "Take the spot where Abraham stood as your place of prayer." We commanded Abraham and Ishmael: **"Purify My House for those who walk round it, those who stay there, and those who bow and prostrate themselves in worship."**'
> *Qur'an 2:125*

Read about Id-ul-Adha on page 180.

Useful terms

Masjid al-Haram – the Great Mosque of Makkah

kiswa – black cloth with gold Arabic writing that covers the Ka'ba

ghusl – a ritual wash of the whole body

ihram – clothing of seamless white cloth for men, or plain, modest veil for the head and body, with uncovered face and hands for women

tawaf – walking around the Ka'ba seven times in an anticlockwise direction

sa'i – the act of walking seven times between the hills of Safa and Marwah

ziyarah – visiting places connected with Muhammad or other important figures

Muslims perform Hajj out of obedience to Allah and because Muhammad did so. They can connect more deeply with their faith and with the worldwide Ummah. They walk in the footsteps of the prophets and if they die during Hajj, they will bypass judgement and go straight to Jannah.

Muslims in Britain Undertaking Hajj

Up to 25,000 Muslims travel from Britain to Makkah each year for Hajj. It is easier for Muslims in Britain to participate in Hajj than ever before. While some find it difficult to take 2–4 weeks of holiday from work, it used to take months to make the journey whereas now it takes hours.

Hajj used to be extremely dangerous but British Muslims now experience much safer conditions. It is still costly, but the trip is managed by UK tour operators and UK-based organisations such as the Association of British Hajj and the British Hajj Delegation, who provide doctors and fraud protection.

British Muslims can easily prepare for Hajj by reading guidebooks, watching live satellite broadcasts from Makkah, and attending seminars before they go so they know what to do and how to pray. UK airports provide prayer and dressing rooms for pilgrims to prepare for Hajj before the flight.

Read more about the Arba'een pilgrimage on page 182.

British pilgrims report a sense of unity with the ummah at Hajj and are stirred by the size of the gatherings. Everyone is dressed equally regardless of gender, race or social class. On their return, salah can trigger powerful memories when they face the qibla and remember their own experience.

Pilgrimage to Shi'a shrines

As well as performing Hajj, Shi'a Muslims also perform **ziyarah**. This pilgrimage involves visiting the shrines of Imams in places like Iraq, Iran and Syria. Visiting these shrines involves ritual and prayer but tends to be less expensive and time-consuming than Hajj.

The shrine of Imam Husayn in Karbala, is considered particularly important in Shi'a Islam. It is the third most holy place after Makkah and Medina. During the Arba'een pilgrimage that occurs forty days after the festival of Ashura, millions of pilgrims visit the shrine, often travelling on foot. Visitors wear black clothing of mourning. They recite prayers to Allah and behave in a peaceful and reverent manner.

Some authorities view pilgrimage to Shi'a shrines as shirk so some have been destroyed or left unmarked to prevent visitors from identifying them.

Over 2 million pilgrims visit the Ka'ba during Hajj

Knowledge recall

1 Define the following concepts: haram, greater/lesser jihad. (You can find these definitions on page 167.)
2 List four reasons why a Muslim may make the pilgrimage to Makkah.
3 State three actions that a pilgrim may perform while on Hajj.

Evaluation practice

4 Give two reasons why some Muslims think a pilgrimage is essential to faith and two reasons why other Muslims might disagree.
5 Which of these views do you think is the most reasonable? Give a reason why.

Encouraging good and duty to the Friends of Allah

Specification focus

Ten Obligatory Acts of Shi'a Islam: Amr-bil-Maroof: how Muslims encourage others to do good; Nahil Anril Munkar: how Muslims discourage bad actions; Tawalia: the duty to love the friends of Allah; Tabarra: the duty to express disapproval of evil doers.

Of the Ten Obligatory Acts of Shi'a Islam, the last four are not included in the Five Pillars of Sunni Islam. These four acts are best considered in pairs as they deal with related issues.

Amr-bil-Maroof and Nahil Anril Munkar

Amr-bil-Maroof is the seventh obligation. It means to promote good. A good Shi'a Muslim should lead a life of virtue by performing all the obligatory acts and obeying **Shariah** Law. They should do so with the right niyyah and should support others to do the same.

Nahil Anril Munkar is the eighth obligation. It means to prevent evil. A good Shi'a Muslim should avoid performing any **haram** act, and should also do what they can do prevent others from doing anything haram that is not approved of by Shariah Law.

The idea of doing good and avoiding evil is often spoken of in the Qur'an:

> ❝Be a community that calls for what is good, urges what is right, and forbids what is wrong: those who do this are the successful ones.❞
> *Qur'an 3:104*

Religious life for a Shi'a Muslim involves trying to do as much good as possible to avoid being judged harshly on the Day of Judgement. Those who do good hope to go to Jannah after they have been judged. But promoting good and preventing evil are actions that affect all aspects of a Muslim's life on earth, not just their hopes for the afterlife.

To do good, a Muslim must perform actions that are considered **halal**. These can be obligatory acts such as salah or sawm, or desirable actions such as ziyarah. Desirable actions are voluntary, so a Muslim can choose whether to perform them.

The actions that a Muslim must avoid or prevent are those that are undesirable or haram. For example, adultery is haram and so should always be avoided. Divorce is undesirable so it is best avoided, but it is not forbidden.

Shariah Law is present to help organise and support the ummah as they try to fulfil the two obligations to do good and avoid evil. If there are matters of behaviour that an individual is unsure about then they can consult a Muslim leader (Mullah) for help. They can also follow the example of virtuous people such as Muhammad or the **Imamate**.

Promoting good and forbidding evil can be carried out at different levels. Shi'a Muslims can use their:

- Heart – knowing that evil is wrong and disapproving of it. This is the role of the individual.
- Speech – advising or guiding others. This is primarily the role of religious leadership.
- Action – physically enforcing law. This is the role of those in authority over others.

For Sunni Muslims, an Imam is someone who leads worship. For Shi'a Muslims, the Imam is the successor to Muhammad

Useful terms

Imamate – the religious and political leadership of the Shi'a Muslim community, consisting of twelve Imams
Ahl Al-Bayt – the family of Muhammad. For Shi'a Muslims this consists of the twelve Imams and Fatima, his daughter. Sunni Muslims include Muhammad's wider family
Twelver – the largest sect of Shi'a Islam that recognises twelve Imams
occultation – the belief that the twelfth Imam did not die but will be hidden by Allah until the Day of Judgement is close

Some argue that if someone insists on performing wrong actions and will not listen to reason then it is the responsibility of the individual Muslim not to associate with that person.

Tawalia and tabarra

Tawalia means the duty to love and respect the friends of Allah. For Shi'a Muslims this means the **Ahl al-Bayt**. In particular, for **Twelver** Shi'a Muslims, this includes the twelve Imams, Muhammad and Fatima (Muhammad's daughter).

Tabarra means the duty to express disapproval of evil-doers and so distance oneself from the enemies of the Ahl al-Bayt.

Shi'a Muslims believe that Muhammad passed on his authority to his cousin and son-in-law, Ali, who was appointed Imam. In turn, each Imam passed their authority on to the next. Each is believed to be a descendent of Muhammad and a protector of Islam, chosen by Allah.

The Imamate are considered to be infallible, sinless and wise as they have been appointed by Allah. An Imam is a religious and political leader who guides human beings and explains the Qur'an and divine law. They have the ultimate spiritual authority.

Obedience is required by Shi'a Muslims to the Imam of the age. The Imam of this age is the twelfth and final Imam, Muhammad ibn Hasan, whose life was miraculously extended by Allah and who has been in **occultation** since 941 CE. Shi'a Muslims show respect to the Ahl al-Bayt by:

- Observing Ashura (see page 182) – remembering the events of the Imam's lives and deaths.
- Performing ziyarah (see page 174) – pilgrimage to the Imam's shrines.
- Paying khums (see page 172) – a tax which supports the Imams.
- Performing salah (see page 170) – remembering the Imams in prayers.

Tawalia and Tabarra are inseparable from each other. The word Tawalia derives from the Arabic word 'wali' or guardian, so to gain salvation in the afterlife, it is necessary to accept the guardianship and the authority of the Imams. This requires Muslims to disassociate themselves from those who have fought against or showed disrespect to the Ahl al-Bayt.

Sunni and Shi'a Muslims both agree that Tabarra and Tawalia are important but disagree over who is the 'enemy' of the Ahl al-Bayt because they accept different hadiths as authoritative. For some Muslims, the enemies of the Ahl al-Bayt may be those who have opposed Muhammad and his successors, even if they were later appointed Caliph after his death. Tabarra may involve asking Allah to withdraw his protection from the enemies of the Ahl al-Bayt.

> 'You who believe, do not take as allies those with whom God is angry: they despair of the life to come as the disbelievers despair of those buried in their graves.'
> Qur'an 60:13

Performing ziyarah to a Shi'a shrine is a way of showing respect to the Ahl al-Bayt and performing Amr-Bil-Maroof

Knowledge recall

1 Define the following concepts: haram, Shariah. (You can find these definitions on page 167.)
2 List four ways that a Shi'a Muslim may encourage the good.
3 State four ways that Shi'a Muslims may perform Tawalia.

Evaluation practice

4 Give three reasons why Shi'a Muslims may consider Amr-bil-Maroof to be important.
5 Think of one reason why you might agree and one reason why you might disagree that Muslims should observe this practice.

Jihad

What is jihad?

Jihad is the sixth of the Ten Obligatory Acts in Shi'a Islam. While it is not one of the Five Pillars of Sunni Islam, some argue that it should be considered a sixth pillar, or that it describes the whole practice of the Five Pillars.

The word 'jihad' simply means struggle. It is one of the most controversial concepts within Islam, even for practicing Muslims, and non-Muslims today tend to associate it with violence or fundamentalism.

Greater jihad

Greater jihad refers to the inner struggle of a Muslim to uphold their faith and its practice. This is the duty of all Muslims to do what is good and struggle against what is evil. It requires a pure niyyah, observance of the Five Pillars or Ten Obligatory Acts, and compliance with **Shariah** Law.

Greater jihad helps a Muslim to avoid hypocrisy. It is important that a Muslim does not just say that Islam is the correct way to live, but that they show it through their behaviour by removing **haram** from their lives and performing **halal** actions. This involves effort, especially in Britain for Muslims whose practice of their faith may contrast with the lives of other British people. For example, a Muslim observes greater jihad when they get up before dawn to pray, refuse alcohol or dress modestly, but British society sometimes finds actions like these to be difficult to accommodate.

Greater jihad is performed by a Muslim working hard to know what is good in their heart, speaking only good with their tongue and doing only good deeds. It is the responsibility of every individual Muslim for the good of others and Allah.

Lesser jihad

While greater jihad is a struggle of the individual, **lesser jihad** is a struggle of the community. It refers to the outward struggle to remove evil from the world. Lesser jihad is referred to as 'Holy War' by many, especially in the media, and it is referred to as a military struggle in Islamic writings.

When Muhammad became a prophet, he spread the religion of Islam through his teaching, preaching and arguments. He did not need to use force and his role was a peaceful one. His work in Medina was diplomatic as he worked to cooperate with the Jews rather than attempt to force them to revert. This form of lesser jihad is active but peaceful.

Today, lesser jihad can similarly involve participation in protests, campaigning for equality or a peaceful struggle for justice. This is an active, outward struggle and need not involve warfare.

Later on, Muhammad was involved in many military campaigns and the Qur'an contains many passages that encourage the use of the sword to defend and promote Islam as a form of lesser jihad. The revelations of the Qur'an from this time declare fighting in self-defence (or the defence of others) as a duty, but forbid Muslims from starting wars.

Specification focus

Ten Obligatory Acts of Shi'a Islam: Jihad: the struggle to live as a Muslim.

Jihad: Greater jihad: the daily struggle to live as a good Muslim. Issues regarding living as a Muslim in Britain today and maintaining a Muslim lifestyle; origins, influence, and conditions for declaration of Lesser jihad in the Qur'an and Hadith: Qur'an 2:190, 22:39.

Greater jihad is a personal struggle to do good and avoid evil

Useful term

jihad – to struggle or strive for Allah. The lesser jihad is the outward struggle to remove evil from the world and has been used to justify some military or even terrorist activity

In the early days of Islam, the faith was spread through the practice of lesser jihad. The Qur'an tells Muslims that those who die fighting for the faith will bypass judgement and go straight to Jannah. It is the duty of all Muslims to work to establish good and fight against evil, so fighting for the faith is necessary if Islam is under threat.

> ❝**Those who have been attacked are permitted to take up arms** because they have been wronged – God has the power to help them.❞
> *Qur'an 22:39*

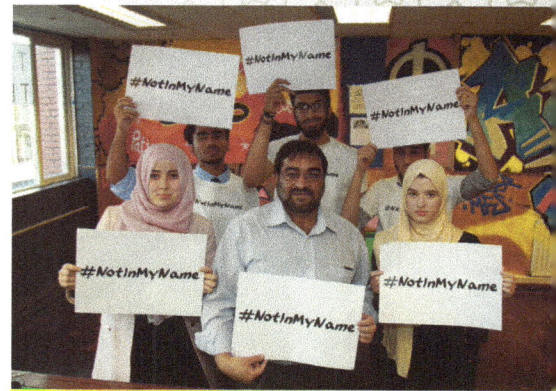

The 'Not In My Name' campaign focuses on the Shariah rules that forbid the use of unnecessary violence and harming innocent people in lesser jihad

Rules of lesser jihad

There is some debate among Muslims about whether lesser jihad can only be in self-defence or whether it can be aggressive. Some Muslims argue that the Qur'an instructs Muslims to fight against unbelievers. However, strict Shariah rules, based on the Qur'an and hadiths, have evolved that govern when lesser jihad is just and acceptable. An armed lesser jihad should only be called:

- in self-defence – if the **ummah** were attacked first
- as a last resort – if everything else has been tried to resolve the problem
- to preserve Islam – to enable Muslims to freely practise their faith when it is under threat
- to protect the oppressed – if the ruler of a country is harming its people
- to punish an enemy who breaks a promise – at a political level when contracts are broken.

There are also strict laws about how soldiers should behave during lesser jihad. It is not acceptable to use unnecessary violence, such as damaging food or water supplies or harming innocent people such as the elderly, women or children. It is not acceptable to force people to revert to Islam, and fighting should cease the moment that the enemy asks for peace. It is also vital that jihad is only declared by a legitimate leader.

> ❝Fight in God's cause against those who fight you, but do not overstep the limits: **God does not love those who overstep the limits.**❞
> *Qur'an 2:190*

There is a difference of opinion among Muslim scholars over whether greater or lesser jihad is more important. Some consider it a duty that a Muslim should at least have intended to involve themselves in the outward struggle for Islam at some stage in their lives. Other Muslim thinkers argue that it is more of a duty to struggle against immorality within the Muslim community rather than against the outside world.

There have been times throughout history when political wars were declared jihad to make them seem noble or legitimate. Yet these wars were not always acceptable according to Shariah Law. Islamic extremists have also made use of the term jihad to justify violence against other people. Yet their acts are not wars declared by a legitimate ruler, nor are they fought according to Shariah principles.

Knowledge recall

1 Define the following concepts: halal, greater/lesser jihad. (You can find these definitions on page 167.)
2 List three ways in which a Muslim can practise greater jihad.
3 State the difference between greater and lesser jihad.

Evaluation practice

4 Give one reason why a Muslim might argue that greater jihad is more important than lesser jihad and one reason why others could say it is not.
5 Do you agree with either of these reasons? Why or why not?

Id-ul-Adha and Id-ul-Fitr

Specification focus

Festivals and commemorations: Id-ul-Adha: the festival of sacrifice. How Muslims celebrate Id-ul-Adha in Britain and worldwide; Id-ul-Fitr: the festival of fast-breaking following Ramadan. How Muslims celebrate Id-ul-Fitr in Britain and worldwide.

Muslims celebrate two major festivals each year that, in both cases, mark the end of a significant period of religious effort.

The importance of Id-ul-Adha

Id-ul-Adha is known as the 'Feast of the Sacrifice' or the 'Great Feast'. It is a four-day event that occurs from the 10th to 13th of the month of Dhu al'hijja. This is the climax of the Hajj ritual to Makkah, but it is celebrated throughout the Islamic world, even by those not on the pilgrimage.

The festival remembers the story where Ibrahim was told by Allah in a dream to sacrifice his son Ishma'il at Mina. Ibrahim shared the dream with his son, who consented to the sacrifice as an act of faith in Allah. Ibrahim was tempted by Shaytan to disobey Allah, but he drove Shaytan away by pelting him with stones. As Ibrahim prepared to kill his son, Allah stopped him and gave him a ram to sacrifice instead.

Read about Hajj on pages 174–175.

> ❛Abraham said, "My son, I have seen myself sacrificing you in a dream. What do you think?" He said, "Father, do as you are commanded and, God willing, you will find me steadfast."❜
> Qur'an 37:102

How Id-ul-Adha is celebrated

Celebrations for Id-ul-Adha begin on the third day of Hajj (the 10th Dhu al-Hijjah). For those on the pilgrimage, this festival marks the end of a time of intense prayer and effort in observing the rites of Hajj correctly.

In the morning, before the fajr prayers, worshippers around the world perform ghusl rather than wudu and put on new or smart clothing. When the sun is clearly visible on the horizon, additional communal prayers (known as Id-salah) are offered at the **mosque** or in the open air, and everyone listens to a sermon. Shi'a Muslims may offer the du'a nudba, a prayer asking for help during the occultation of the twelfth Imam.

Feasts are shared with family and friends during Id-ul-Adha

Following this is the act of **qurbani**. An animal is slaughtered as a sacrifice to Allah, to mark the story of Ibrahim's willingness to sacrifice his son. The animal should be a sheep, goat, cow or camel in good health and must be killed according to the rules of **halal slaughter**.

In the past, qurbani was performed outside in the open. Now it is conducted in hygienic abattoirs and those on Hajj can buy special certificates for their meat, at least a third of which will then be frozen and distributed to the poor. In the UK, the law requires animals to be killed in approved slaughterhouses.

The festival is spent celebrating with family and friends and giving gifts. It is traditional to have a celebration meal that includes qurbani meat. Muslims will wish each other '**Id Mubarak**'. In Muslim countries, this festival is a four-day public holiday, but Muslims celebrating in the UK may have to ask to be allowed to take time off work or school for the celebrations.

Useful terms

qurbani – (slaughter) the sacrifice of an animal to Allah during the festival of Id-ul-Adha

halal slaughter – 'permitted' slaughter that requires the recitation of the Shahadah, with rules over how the animal is to be killed and the meat managed afterwards

Id Mubarak – 'Blessed festival'; a greeting used by Muslims during Id-ul-Adha and Id-ul-Fitr

The importance of Id-ul-Fitr

Id-ul-Fitr is known as the 'Feast of Fast Breaking' or the 'Small Feast'. It is a two or three-day event that occurs on the 1st to 3rd of the month of Shawwal. It marks the end of a long period of fasting through the month of Ramadan.

Muslims are both celebrating the end of the fast and thanking Allah for giving them strength to complete it. Celebrations begin at the sighting of the new moon and so will vary from country to country, but the joy at seeing the new moon is compared to the even greater joy at seeing Jannah after the Day of Judgement.

> 'It was in the month of Ramadan that the Qur'an was revealed as guidance for mankind, clear messages giving guidance and distinguishing between right and wrong.... He wants you to complete the prescribed period and to glorify Him for having guided you, so that you may be thankful.'
> Qur'an 2:185

How Id-ul-Fitr is celebrated

Before Id-ul-Fitr begins, Muslims should give a special donation to the poor, known as Zakah ul-Fitr. The amount is usually about the price of one meal (around £5) for each member of the household. This donation is made even more meaningful after the long fast, since believers have been reminded of the hardship that some people endure and the duty to share what they have with those in need.

After the fajr prayers, Muslims perform ghusl, then put on their best or new clothes and eat a small breakfast with sweet foods.

Additional Id-salah prayers are performed, either at the mosque or in the open air. There is also a sermon. Shi'a Muslims may say the du'a nudba and many visit the graves of loved ones who have died.

Muslims are encouraged to ask Allah for forgiveness and to forgive each other for wrongs. Gifts may be exchanged, homes are decorated, and a feast is shared with family and friends. Sometimes there are processions through the streets. Muslims will greet each other with 'Id Mubarak'.

In Muslim countries, this is a public holiday, so shops are closed. In the UK, this is not the case, so Muslims may have to ask their schools or employers for a day off to celebrate with their families.

Around Id day Shi'a Muslims may visit the graves of loved ones to remind them of the afterlife

Knowledge recall

1 Define the following concepts: halal, prophethood. (You can find these definitions on page 167.)
2 List two differences and two similarities between the celebrations of Id-ul-Adha and Id-ul-Fitr.
3 State the 'effort' that is made before each festival of Id.

Evaluation practice

4 Give one reason why a Muslim might find it more difficult to celebrate Id in Great Britain and one reason why they would not.
5 Which reason is more convincing to you and why?

Ashura and the Night of Power

The importance of Ashura

Ashura means 'tenth' because the festival takes place over the first ten days of the Islamic year, finishing on the 10th of Muharram (the first month in the Islamic calendar). It is celebrated in different ways and for different reasons by Sunni and Shi'a Muslims. In some countries, such as Iran, it is a public holiday.

For Sunni Muslims, Ashura marks the flight of Musa (Moses) and the Israelites from Egypt and their rescue by Allah when he parted the sea for them to escape Pharaoh. They also remember the end of the Great Flood during the time of Nuh.

For Shi'a Muslims, the festival is linked to the martyrdom of Husayn, the third Imam and Muhammad's grandson.

In 680 CE, the people of Kufah in Iraq objected to their ruler, Yazid, who disobeyed Islamic law. They called Husayn to come and assume leadership as successor to the Imams Hasan and Ali. He set off for Kufah with about 50 armed men and the women and children of his family. A 4000-strong army from Yazid intercepted them, headed them off to the plain of Karbala and cut them off from all food and water. When Husayn refused to pledge allegiance to Yazid, he and all his men were killed. The women and children were taken captive.

Husayn's grave became a pilgrimage site shortly after his death and a shrine was built. The festival of Ashura has now become a significant holiday for Shi'a Muslims in which pilgrimage, processions, services and plays take place.

How Ashura is commemorated

Ashura is not a festival of celebration. It is a time of mourning and sorrow. Shi'a Muslims avoid listening to or playing music and will often dress in black. Customs and rituals focus on Husayn's death and the struggle of Muslims against injustice.

- A common practice is the recital of the story of Husayn's martyrdom, called majlis. This can take place in a mosque or in the home. Listeners will often cry in grief and beat their chests, calling out 'Ya Husayn'.
- Some make a pilgrimage to the shrines of the Imams, especially Imam Husayn's shrine in Karbala. This is called the Arba'een pilgrimage and occurs on the fortieth day of mourning after Ashura. Here they perform salah to Allah and may ask the Imam to intercede for them with Allah. This practice is discouraged in Sunni areas where the authorities view it as a form of shirk.
- Mourning processions may be held, where a replica of the shrine of Husayn is carried on shoulders through the streets. There may be rhythmical chanting, crying and beating of chests. In cities like London, Birmingham and Bradford, Shi'a Muslims gather in the streets for mourning processions and speeches.
- In some parts of the world, men perform a controversial practice known as **self-flagellation**. This practice is banned in most countries, but a small minority of Shi'a Muslims beat themselves with knives, whips or chains on their heads and backs to show that they would fight alongside Husayn if he had asked them. This happens in public during the street processions or

Ashura is a festival of mourning for Husayn in Shi'a Islam

Useful term

self-flagellation – a disciplinary practice of punishing oneself as an expression of faith

at re-enactments. Many Shi'a leaders encourage Muslims to donate blood instead, as a more positive and peaceful commemoration.

- In Iran, theatrical plays or Shabih are held on the 10th of Muharram that re-enact the events of Husayn's martyrdom, although many Shi'a scholars have now rejected this practice..

The Night of Power

The Night of Power (Laylat al-Qadr) is usually celebrated on the 27th of Ramadan by Sunni Muslims or the 23rd by Shi'a Muslims, although no one knows its exact date. It remembers the event of Muhammad's first revelation of the Qur'an from Allah via the angel Jibril.

In 610 CE, Muhammad was 40 years old. He was praying in a cave on Mount Hira when Jibril visited him and, although he was illiterate, commanded him to read:

> ❝Read! In the name of your Lord who created: He created man from a clinging form. Read! Your Lord is the Most Bountiful One who taught by the pen, who taught man what he did not know.❞
> *Qur'an 96:1–5*

Sunni Muslims believe that this day marks Allah's revelation of these first verses of the Qur'an to Muhammad. Shi'a Muslims believe that Jibril revealed the whole contents of the Qur'an to Muhammad's heart at this time.

Laylat al-Qadr is a good time for Muslims to take a break from work to focus on Allah and his revelation. Therefore, the last ten days of Ramadan are marked by many Muslim men retreating from daily life, as Muhammad retreated to the cave, and spending more time at the **mosque** in prayer. During this time, many Muslims will attempt to recite the Qur'an from beginning to end as Muhammad did.

On the Night of Power, many adult Muslims choose to stay awake to pray all night. This is the holiest night of the year when angels are sent by Allah to bring forgiveness to the faithful. Muslims may study or recite the Qur'an, make extra rakahs of prayer, perform good works to show their devotion to Allah, and ensure they have given their zakah ul-fitr.

Children who have been attending Qur'an class may visit the mosque to demonstrate their learning, hoping that Allah will see their devotion and forgive their sins.

The Qur'an is believed to be the eternal, uncreated word of Allah that has been accurately preserved since its revelation to Muhammad over the course of 23 years. Therefore, it is treated with utmost respect by only touching it with clean hands and storing it on the highest shelf with nothing on top of it. The Qur'an should never touch the floor.

In the UK, processions are held to remember Husayn's martyrdom and create a sense of solidarity between Muslims

Read more about the importance of the Qur'an on page 161.

Knowledge recall

1. Define the following concepts: haram, greater/lesser jihad. (You can find these definitions on page 167.)
2. List five practices performed by Shi'a Muslims during Ashura.
3. State two reasons why Muslims may pray all night on the Night of Power.

Evaluation practice

4. Give one reason why marking Ashura is important and one reason why it should not be celebrated.
5. Which do you think this is the most persuasive argument? Why?

Skills practice

On these exam practice pages you will see example answers for each of the exam questions types: **a**, **b**, **c** and **d**. You can find out more about these on pages 5–9.

Question *(a)*

*Question **(a)** tests your knowledge and understanding. You will always be asked to **define a key concept** in this question. You can find a list of the concepts at the beginning of the chapter.*

> *(a)* What do Muslims mean by 'haram'? [2]

Student response

> Haram means eating things that are against Islam. Like pork or meat that was stunned before killing.

Improved student response

> Haram means forbidden in Islam. This can refer to foods that you are not allowed to eat, or actions that you are not allowed to perform, e.g. adultery.

🕐 **Over to You!** Have a try at answering this question:

> *(a)* What do Muslims mean by 'halal'? [2]

Helpful hints

To help you answer this question effectively, you could use the check list below to make sure you include the most important things:

- **Synonym** – Include a synonym for the word 'halal'.
- **Example** – Give an example of an act or thing which is halal.

Now give yourself **two minutes** to answer this question by yourself:

> *(a)* What do Muslims mean by 'ummah'? [2]

what went well

The candidate has given two examples of things that are haram.

How to improve

You must use a synonym for the word 'haram' that shows its wider meaning.

You should learn the exam board's definition of the word at the start of this chapter.

You could give examples from any area of the specification (there is no requirement to only use food laws).

Tip

This candidate uses two examples. There is no need for this. The most important part of this answer is the understanding that haram means 'forbidden' in Islam.

Question (b)

*Question (b) tests your knowledge and understanding. It will always ask you to **describe** a belief, a teaching, a practice or an event that is included on the specification.*

> (b) Describe how Muslims may spend zakat money.   [5]

Student response

> Zakah is alms payments. It is the duty of all Muslims to pay alms to people who are in need. It is 2.5% of a person's income after the nisab and has to be paid every year. It can be a tax in some Muslim countries, but it is usually up to the individual to pay it themselves. Some Muslims could give it directly to the poor, but most will give it to a charity who spends it on their behalf.

Improved student response

> Zakah is alms payments. It is the duty of all Muslims to pay alms to people who are in need. It is 2.5% of a person's income and it goes to the poor, widows, orphans, the homeless or those who have reverted to Islam. It is often given to a Muslim charity or the mosque, who may use it to respond to emergencies or disasters or to fund long-term projects to help people. Sometimes it is used to run soup kitchens, food banks, health care programmes or education programmes. It can also be used to help travellers in need or to pay those who collect and distribute it.

🕐 **Over to You!** Have a try at answering this question:

> (b) Describe how Shi'a Muslims celebrate Ashura.   [5]

Helpful hints

Use the check list below to make sure you include the most important things:

- **How/Why** – Set out one of the actions that will be performed during Ashura (e.g. pilgrimage to Husayn's shrine or grave).
- **Example** – Describe what happens (e.g. ensuring clothing is clean, performing wudu and salah).
- **Repeat** – Then repeat the above process for other features of the festival (e.g. rawdah-khani, processions, self-flagellation, shabih).

Now give yourself **five minutes** to answer this question by yourself:

> (b) Describe how Muslims perform Hajj.   [5]

What went well

The candidate knows what zakat is. They mention that it goes to people who are in need and that it can be given to people who are poor.

How to improve

You must concentrate on the 'how' part of the question. This wants you to give a set of examples of the ways that zakat is used or spent.

You should include specific examples of the people that zakat is used to help.

You could mention how the organisations that collect zakat distribute it.

Tip

The focus of this question is the way that the money is used so aim to include as many examples as possible.

Question (c)

*Question **(c)** tests your knowledge and understanding. You need to give detailed evidence and reasoning to support your explanation of the topic. You may need to show how belief influences religious practice. This is not an evaluation question so you don't need to evaluate different viewpoints.*

> (c) Explain the practices that take place during the pilgrimage to Makkah. [8]

Student response

> Muslims on Hajj perform ghusl and wear white clothing. They perform salah at the Masjid al-Haram and also tawaf by walking around the Ka'ba seven times in an anticlockwise direction. Then they perform sa'i by running and walking between the two hills of Safa and Marwa. They walk to Arafat to confess their sins and they walk to Mina to throw stones at the three walls. At Mina they perform a qurbani sacrifice for Id-ul-Adha. They drink from the zamzam well and shave their heads.

Improved student response

> Muslims prepare for Hajj by performing ghusl, a ritual wash, and wearing white seamless clothing. This shows the equality of all Muslims before Allah. In Makkah, Muslims perform salah and tawaf at the Masjid al-Haram by walking together round the Ka'ba seven times in an anticlockwise direction. This reminds them of their connection with the rest of the ummah and of their connection with the prophets, as they walk where the prophets walked. Muslims perform sa'i, where they walk and run between the two hills of Safa and Marwa in the Great Mosque, re-enacting Hagar's search for water for Ishma'il.
> Pilgrims walk to Arafat and stand on the plain to confess their sins to Allah. This reminds them of how they will stand before Allah on the Day of Judgement. They collect small stones and take them to Mina to stone the walls in remembrance of Ibrahim stoning Shaytan to chase him away. At the end of Hajj, Muslims celebrate Id-ul-Adha and offer a qurbani sacrifice to Allah. They give a third to the poor. This reminds them of Ibrahim's willingness to offer his son as a sacrifice and of Allah's protection for Ishma'il.

🕐 **Over to You!** Have a try at answering this question:

> (c) Explain what the **two** types of jihad mean for Muslims. [8]

Helpful hints

Use the check list below to make sure you include the most important things:

- Include **more than one statement** about the meaning of jihad for Muslims. Note the question refers to *two* types of jihad.
- For each type give an **example** of what actions this form of jihad requires (e.g. observing the pillars or obligatory acts).
- Explain **why** Muslims might consider these actions important (e.g. they are influenced by teaching from the Qur'an, the hadiths or Shariah Law).
- Suggest **how** the two jihads might affect a Muslim (e.g. what their lives may be like as a result or what they hope to achieve).

What went well
This response includes accurate, relevant information about practices that take place during Hajj. It gives several good examples.

How to improve
You must recognise that the word 'explain' requires some detail of the practices rather than just a list.

You should show understanding of specialist vocabulary by defining it or using it in a way that clearly demonstrates what it means.

You could give reasons for why the practices are significant.

Tip
For this question, there is a huge amount of relevant information that could gain you marks and it would be very difficult to cover everything in the space and time provided. Pick just a few central practices and give details about them if you are short of time.

Now give yourself **eight minutes** to answer this question:

> (c) Explain the importance of zakah to Muslims. [8]

Question (d)

*Question **(d)** tests your ability to **evaluate**. This means you need to show you have considered more than one point of view and that you have referred to religion and belief. You will need to be able to make judgements that are supported by detailed reasoning and argument.*

> (d) 'All Muslims must go on pilgrimage.'
> Discuss this statement showing that you have considered more than one point of view. (You must refer to religion and belief in your answer.) [15]

Student response

All Muslims must go on a pilgrimage because it is a duty. Pilgrimage is Hajj. It is one of the five pillars of Sunni Islam and one of the ten obligatory acts for Shi'a Muslims. This point is good because millions of Muslims go on Hajj every year and they all go to Makkah at the same time.

There are other types of pilgrimage, not just Hajj. These types of pilgrimage could be the ziyarah for Shi'a Muslims. But Sunni Muslims often think this is shirk so they won't go on it. Or Umra is a lesser pilgrimage to Makkah that is desirable but not obligatory. This is one that all Muslims do not have to go on.

There are lots of reasons why a Muslim might not go on a Hajj pilgrimage. One reason is because they are ill. If they have a life-limiting illness or a terminal illness it might be too difficult to go on Hajj because it is a very physically demanding event. Other people might be too poor to go. It is very expensive to arrange travel and take a lot of time off work and then to stay there for so long. Or they might be able to afford it, but since they live with their family who depend on them maybe the family would suffer too much if they went away. In these cases, Allah forgives people who do not complete Hajj. They could go on a smaller pilgrimage that is less expensive though.

Improved student response

Pilgrimage is one of the five pillars of Sunni Islam and one of the Ten Obligatory Acts for Shi'a Muslims. It is a duty for all Muslims to perform Hajj at least once in their lifetime and so all Muslims must perform pilgrimage as the Qur'an commands. However, many devoted Muslims are excused from Hajj due to personal circumstances and Allah will not punish them for it. If someone is ill, or not wealthy enough to go, then they do not have to. This does not mean that they are not true Muslims. Yet just because there are exceptions for those in difficult circumstances, this does not mean that the statement is not generally true. All Muslims have a duty to perform Hajj, but Allah is merciful and forgives those who cannot.

Pilgrimage is not performed by all Muslims for many reasons. The number of people who can travel to perform Hajj each year is restricted so that the area of Makkah is not completely overwhelmed with pilgrims. Hajj is dangerous, even though it is safer than it used to be. Those who have people who depend on them may not go in case something goes wrong. However, Hajj is a duty of devotion to Allah. A duty is something that a person is obliged to do, it is not just a desirable act or an optional extra. While there

What went well
There is plenty of relevant material in the response that talks about why a Muslim might not go on Hajj or when it is not a duty to perform pilgrimage.

How to improve
You must remember this is an analysis and evaluation question. Look back at the suggestions in previous chapters about how to structure and develop your reasoning in these kinds of answers.

You should give some more reasons why Hajj might be regarded as important for all Muslims.

You could come to a conclusion about the question.

There are regular references to the question throughout this answer.

The response includes balance and counter-arguments that are backed up with reasoning.

The use of ethical language such as 'duty', 'obliged' and 'desirable acts' adds to the debate.

are other optional pilgrimages, such as ziyarah or umra, Hajj is a duty to be performed by all Muslims. But real life is complicated, and a merciful God would not punish someone who chooses not to go due to difficult circumstances.

In the modern world, a Muslim can participate in a great deal of the practices of Hajj, and therefore show devotion to Allah, without leaving home. Muslims can make sacrifices that will support others to go on Hajj even if they cannot do it themselves. The internet and television allow people to see the sights and participate in the rakahs and du'a at home. It is more important that Muslims show their devotion to Allah than they make the physical trip to Makkah. Those who do go may bring back photos or memorabilia for their loved ones so that they can share in the blessings. There is no need for all Muslims to go on pilgrimage.

This mini-conclusion acknowledges that maybe both arguments are strong, and there is more to be said.

Specialist vocabulary has been used effectively and accurately throughout.

The final decision is brought clearly back to the question and is relevant and well supported.

🕐 **Over to You!** Have a try at answering this question:

(d) 'In Britain, it is difficult for Muslims to fast during Ramadan.'
Discuss this statement showing that you have considered more than one point of view. (You must refer to religion and belief in your answer.) [15]

Helpful hints

Consider what is important about this question:

- **Britain** – What is different about Britain to a Muslim country? (Think about the weather, society, school and work commitments, Western calendars, national holidays, etc.)
- **Fasting** – What is required of a Muslim during the fasting period? (Think of what must be given up, how this affects sleeping patterns, how this could affect jobs that are very physical, etc.)
- **Ramadan** – How long must all this continue for? (Think about the effect fasting might have on activities that usually take place over the course of a month: exams, seasonal events, work and social commitments, etc.)

Study Challenge:

The exam board will only ever ask a question **(d)** that gives you a statement to discuss based on the content of the specification and then asks you to discuss it from different viewpoints, referring to religion and belief.

- Look back at the specification focus boxes at the top of each page in this chapter.
- Choose one area from the list that has not yet appeared in the questions above.
- Create a statement that you can debate.
- Write your own **(d)** question on this area that begins with this controversial statement and asks you to discuss it, using the wording from the questions you can see above.
- Now give yourself **fifteen minutes** to answer this question by yourself!

Tip
This question should show off all the skills you have developed so far. You should be well organised in your response, interpret the question carefully to include the right detail, and make use of evidence and examples. Include key terminology and give reasoning to support your analysis.

Tip
By now, you have learned many skills that you can put to good use when you are answering exam questions. Practise all these skills regularly, just as you would do if you were learning a sport, a musical instrument or a clever trick. The more you practise, the easier it will become.

Tip
Remember, if you decide to repeat this challenge for any of the material on life after death, this is the only question that requires you to include non-religious beliefs as well as religious ones.

Glossary

Terms with a **yellow background** are key concepts which you will need to make sure you remember.

abbess and prioress – superior roles governing nuns in an Abbey or Priory

abortion – when a pregnancy is ended so that it does not result in the birth of a child

abrogates – cancels or revokes

absolute morality – the belief that moral rules are the same for everyone regardless of the situation they are in or the consequence of following them

absolute poverty – an acute state of deprivation, whereby a person cannot access the most basic of their human needs

absolution – forgiveness for sin

Adalat – belief in Allah's justice; one of the Five Roots of Usul ad-Din in Shi'a Islam

adultery – voluntary sexual intercourse between a married person and a person who is not their spouse

afterlife – life after death; the belief that existence continues after physical death

agape – a Greek word that translates as 'unconditional love' or 'charity'

Ahl al-Bayt – the family of Muhammad. For Shi'a Muslims this consists of the twelve Imams and Fatima, his daughter. Sunni Muslims include Muhammad's wider family

akhirah – life after death

Al-Ma'ad – (resurrection) restoring a dead person back to earthly life

alms – money or goods, given to the poor

altar – a table at the front and centre of the church from which the Eucharist is celebrated

Al-Qadr – predestination; one of the Six Articles of Faith in Sunni Islam

annulment – a legal process in which a marriage is declared invalid or void

anthropomorphised – given human characteristics, such as walking or speaking

apostasy – abandoning or turning away from Islam

atonement – the belief that Jesus' death on the cross healed the rift between humans and God

barzakh – a state of waiting for the soul

Believer's Baptism – Baptism as an adult

Big Bang – the idea that the universe began at a single point that quickly expanded

Bismillah – the words that preface all but one of the chapters of the Qur'an: 'In the name of Allah, the beneficient, the merciful.' Used in prayer and as a blessing

blended family – when a divorced person forms a new relationship, the family may contain a mixture of step-parents and step-children

burqa – a one-piece veil that covers the face and body with a mesh screen to see through

Caliph – the deputy or successor of Muhammad in Sunni Islam

capital punishment – the death penalty; execution as punishment for a criminal offence

celibate – remaining unmarried and not having sexual intercourse. Monks and nuns take a vow to be celibate

censorship – the practice of suppressing and limiting access to material considered obscene, offensive or a threat to security. People may also be restricted in their speech by censorship laws

chalice – a large cup or goblet used for carrying and sharing the wine during the Eucharist

charismatic – lively, informal worship that emphasises the Holy Spirit

chaste – refraining from sexual intercourse

church planting – starting a completely new church where one did not exist before

cohabitation – to live together in a sexual relationship without being married or in a civil partnership

commitment – a sense of dedication and obligation to someone or something

commune – a group of people living and working together who share all possessions

conception – the point at which an egg is fertilised by a sperm

confession – admitting wrongdoing and saying sorry to God. For Catholics this may be done through a priest

consecrated – made sacred

conscience – the ability of the mind to think about and make moral decisions

consummate – to complete a marriage by having sex after the ceremony has taken place

contraception – methods used to prevent a woman from becoming pregnant during or following sexual intercourse

convert – to change to a new religion or belief

corporal punishment – physical punishment intended to cause pain

corporate – shared by a whole group, not just an individual

covenant – an agreement or promise between human beings and God

Creationist – someone who believes everything exists as a direct result of the work of a divine being. Some Creationists take creation stories literally and reject scientific accounts

cumulative selection – favourable changes in an organism that are retained and built on

deacon – an ordained role, often reserved for men, who take some responsibilities assisting a priest

deaconess – a non-ordained role, mainly concerned with helping the priest to minister to other women and girls

democracy – a system of government, elected or run by the people

denominations – organised groups of Christians with their own leaders and traditions

discrimination – acts of treating groups of people, or individuals differently, based on prejudice

divorce – to legally end a marriage

diyah – a financial compensation to a victim or their family in cases of murder or harm

DNR – 'do not resuscitate'; an order to not try to resuscitate someone if their heart stops beating

doctrine – a set of teachings accepted by the Christian Church

dominion – having control or sovereignty over someone or something

double effect – when an action has two outcomes, one intended and one unintended

doxology – an expression of praise

ecumenical – encouraging the different Christian churches to unite

ensoulment – the point at which Allah gives the foetus a soul

environmental sustainability – ensuring that the demands placed on natural resources can be met without reducing capacity to allow all people and other species of animals, as well as plant life, to live well, now and in the future

epistemic distance – a distance from full knowledge of God

eschatological – concerned with the end times or 'last things' in the history of the world

eternal – with no beginning and no end

Eucharist – the celebration of the Lord's Supper with bread and wine during a church service

euthanasia – from Greek, *eu* 'good' and *thanatos* 'death'. Sometimes referred to as 'mercy killing'. The act of killing or permitting the death of a person who is suffering from a serious illness

evangelism – preaching the gospel to others with the intention of converting them to the Christian faith

evil – that which is considered extremely immoral, wicked and wrong

evolution – the process by which different living creatures are believed to have developed from earlier, less complex forms during the history of the earth

excommunication – to exclude or expel people from membership within the church

ex nihilo – out of nothing

extended family – a family that includes near relatives such as grandparents, aunts and uncles in the same household as parents and children

extremism – believing in and supporting ideas that are very far from what most people consider correct or reasonable

Fairtrade – products that are produced by workers in the developing world who are ensured a fair wage and decent working conditions

fitra – natural disposition or in-built nature

Five Primary Precepts – five absolute rules that guide moral action

Five Roots of Usul ad-Din – the fundamental beliefs accepted by all Shi'a Muslims

fixity of species – species remain unchanged from their initial, created state

font – a large container for baptismal water, often made of stone

forgiveness – to grant pardon for a wrongdoing; to give up resentment and the desire to seek revenge against a wrongdoer

Free will – the ability to make choices voluntarily and independently. The belief that nothing is pre-determined

fundamentalists – Muslims who wish for Islam to be brought back to traditional roots

Furu ad-Din – branches or ancillaries of faith; also called the Ten Obligatory Acts. The rules and laws that organise life for a Shi'a Muslim

gender equality – people of all genders enjoying the same rights and opportunities in all aspects of their lives

gender stereotypes – generalisations made about male and female behaviour based on their biological sex

General Synod of the Church of England – the national assembly of the Church of England that considers, debates and approves laws affecting the whole of the Church

Gentiles – non-Jewish people

ghusl – a ritual wash of the whole body

global citizen – a person who understands their role and responsibilities as part of the worldwide community

glossolalia – speaking in 'tongues' (languages unknown to the speaker)

Godhead – another name for the one God in three persons of the Trinity

good – that which is considered morally right, beneficial and to our advantage

Greater/Lesser jihad – the word jihad means 'to strive' and there are two forms of jihad:
- Greater jihad is the daily struggle and inner spiritual striving to live as a Muslim
- Lesser jihad is a physical struggle or 'holy war' in defence of Islam

hadiths – Islamic scriptures, a record of the words of Muhammad

Hajj – the fifth pillar of Islam; pilgrimage to the city of Makkah

halal – actions or things which are permitted within Islam, such as eating permitted foods

halal slaughter – 'permitted' slaughter that requires the recitation of the Shahadah, with rules over how the animal is to be killed and the meat managed afterwards

hanif – a true monotheist who is not Christian, Jewish nor an idol worshipper

haram – any actions or things which are forbidden within Islam, such as eating forbidden foods

harmonise – fit together, expanding or completing the story

heresy – a teaching that is against accepted doctrine

hijab – a scarf that covers the head and neck but not the face

Hijrah – migration; Muhammad's journey to Medina that marks the beginning of the Muslim calendar

hospice – a place of health care that attends to the physical and emotional needs of a dying person

hudud – punishments that are fixed by Allah

human rights – the basic entitlements of all human beings, afforded to them simply because they are human

hypostatic union – the one personality of Christ in which his human and divine nature are united

hypothesis – an explanation that has been proposed but not yet tested out

Iblis – (Shaytan) the devil/Satan

Id Mubarak – 'Blessed festival'; a greeting used by Muslims during Id-ul-Adha and Id-ul-Fitr

iftar – breaking fast with a meal at sunset

ihram – clothing of seamless white cloth for men, or plain, modest veil for the head and body, with uncovered face and hands for women

imago Dei – a Latin term that means 'in the image of God'

Imam – for Sunni Muslims: a Muslim prayer leader. For Shi'a Muslims: one of the twelve infallible successors to Muhammad chosen by Allah to guide humans towards Him

Imamate – the religious and political leadership of the Shi'a Muslim community, consisting of twelve Imams

Immanuel – 'God with us'

impotent – powerless or weak

incarnate – made flesh

incarnation – God becoming human in the form of Jesus

inconsistent triad – three ideas are possible but only two of them can be true at the same time

indulgences – pardon for sin, granted by a senior priest through good works or, in medieval times, through payment

inerrant – cannot be wrong

infallible – incapable of being wrong

intercession – to ask on behalf of another person

ISIS – a terrorist military group that has been condemned for its harsh interpretation of Shariah Law and violent attacks

Jahannam – hell

Jannah – paradise

jihad – to struggle or strive for Allah. The lesser jihad is the outward struggle to remove evil from the world and has been used to justify some military or even terrorist activity

jinn – a spirit made from smokeless fire (e.g. a demon)

justice – fairness; where everyone has equal provisions and opportunity

Ka'ba – a cube-shaped shrine at the centre of the Great Mosque in Makkah

kalam – the word of Allah in scripture

khalifah – a deputy, steward or Viceregent. Allah's representative on earth

khums – annual tax for Shi'a Muslims of 20% of their wealth. Half is given to religious leaders to fund education and half to the poor

kiswa – black cloth with gold Arabic writing that covers the Ka'ba

liturgy – the prescribed set of words and rituals that take place during a church service

living will – when a person writes down their wishes for their care and whether they wish to refuse certain treatments before they lose the ability to communicate

logical problem of evil – the attempt to show that it is logically impossible for God and evil to exist at the same time

madrasah – an Islamic school, often attached to the mosque, for learning about the faith

mahr – (dowry) the money or goods given to the wife to fall back on in the instance of divorce

mahram – a member of one's family with whom marriage or sexual intercourse would be considered haram. Women may not be alone with men who are not their mahram

malaikah – the Arabic word used for angels

malevolent – wishing others harm

martyred – being killed for refusing to reject one's religious faith

Masjid al-Haram – the Great Mosque of Makkah

Matthean exemption – the exception to Jesus' rule forbidding divorce, allowing it if one partner has been unfaithful

Messiah – another word for 'Christ'; a saviour or liberator

ministry – a period of service or work

miracle – a wonder or marvel that occurs in the physical world, as a direct work of God

Missale Romanum – Roman Missal. Contains the exact wording and pattern for Catholic worship

mission – spreading the message of Christianity, often overseas, and offering practical help to those in need

modernisers – Muslims who wish for Islam to be reformed for the modern world

monastic – monks or nuns who live simply under a vow of chastity with few possessions so they can dedicate themselves to worship

monogamous – having only one sexual partner

monogenes – an Ancient Greek word translated as 'begotten', meaning 'one of its kind'

morality – principles and standards determining which actions are right or wrong

mortal sin – a deliberate, serious sin against God's law

Mosque – ('Masjid' in Arabic) a 'place of prostration' for Muslims; it is a communal place of worship for a Muslim community

MP – Members of Parliament; elected politicians who represent people from a fixed area when the government make laws

muezzin – the person appointed to recite and lead the call to prayer at a mosque

myth – a fictional story that contains truths expressed as symbols to explain the world view of that religion

natural selection – the organisms that are best adapted to their surroundings are the ones that survive and reproduce

Nicene Creed – a formal statement of the main Christian beliefs, initially adopted by the first Council of Nicaea

nikah – Muslim wedding ceremony

niqab – a veil for the face that leaves the eyes clear and is paired with a full head and body covering

nisab – the threshold of wealth that a person can have before they must pay zakah

niyyah – the right intention

non-violent direct action – using civil disobedience that causes no harm to people or property to bring about political change, e.g. sit-ins, strikes and blockades rather than petitions or negotiation

nuclear family – two parents – one male, one female – and their children

occultation – the belief that the twelfth Imam did not die but will be hidden by Allah until the Day of Judgement is close

omnibenevolent – the state of being all-loving and infinitely good – a characteristic often attributed to God

omnipotent – all-powerful or almighty

omniscient – all-knowing

ordained – to be given priestly authority in a holy ceremony

Original Sin – a tendency to sin that is human nature as a result of the actions of Adam and Eve in the Garden of Eden

Paraclete – Holy Spirit

Parousia – the second coming of Christ on the Day of Judgement

Paschal – relating to Easter or Passover

pastoral care – help with personal problems

Patriarch – the highest-ranking authority in the Orthodox and Catholic Churches (the Pope is the Patriarch of Rome)

patriarchal – a system controlled by men

penance – demonstration of remorse for sin through the performance of prayer, good works or sacrifice

penitence – confession and repentance for sin, resulting in forgiveness

persistent vegetative state – a continuing state of having no apparent consciousness but having a beating heart and appearance of being awake but not alert (usually with life support)

personal conviction – something a person strongly feels or believes in

pluralist – distinct cultural, ethnic and religious groups existing together in the same society

polygamy – the practice of a man marrying more than one wife at a time

polytheists – those who believe in or worship more than one god

predestination – the belief that all actions are willed by Allah in advance and that he has already chosen some for Jannah and some for Jahannam

prejudice – pre-judging; judging people to be inferior or superior without cause

priory – a building where monks or nuns live, work and pray

promiscuity – having several sexual partners on a casual basis

prophethood – ('risalah' in Arabic) is the term used to describe the messengers of Allah, beginning with Adam and ending with the Prophet Muhammad

protected characteristics – a quality of a person that the law keeps safe from harm

pseudoscience – practice that claims to be science but is not properly following the scientific method

punishment – a penalty given to someone for a crime or wrong they have done

purgatory – the purification of souls still tainted by less serious sins

qibla – the direction of the Ka'ba building in Makkah

qisas – a law that allows retribution for certain crimes to ensure justice. For instance, a life for a life

quality of life – the extent to which life is meaningful and pleasurable

Qur'an – Islamic scripture, a record of the words of Allah to Muhammad

qurbani – (slaughter) the sacrifice of an animal to Allah during the festival of Id-ul-Adha

rakah – the procedure for salah. A unit or cycle of prayer movements that is repeated

Ramadan – the ninth month of the Muslim year in which fasting is performed during daylight hours

reconciliation – bringing people back into a good relationship with God

relative morality – the belief that what is right or wrong may change depending on culture, upbringing or circumstances

relative poverty – a standard of poverty measured in relation to the standards of a society in which a person lives, for example living on less than X% of average UK income

religious sister – a woman who takes some vows as a nun would but helps in the world instead of living separately in a convent

repent – to be sorry for or to regret a past action

responsibilities – actions/duties you are expected to carry out

resurrection – the belief that Jesus rose from the dead on Easter Sunday, conquering death

revelation – God's direct communication to humanity

revert – when a non-Muslim becomes a Muslim; they 'revert' because they return to the state that Allah created them in

riba – the term used for usury in Islamic banking

risalah – divine message or prophethood

rite – religious ceremony or practice

roles – position, status or function of a person in society, as well as the characteristics and social behaviour expected of them

ruh – soul

sacraments – an outward sign of an invisible and inward blessing by God. For example, Baptism, the Eucharist

sacred – holy, devoted to God for a religious purpose

sadaqah – voluntary charitable giving

sa'i – the act of walking seven times between the hills of Safa and Marwah

salah – ritual prayers

salvation – being rescued or saved from the punishment for human sin

sanctity of life – the belief that life is precious, or sacred. For many religious believers, only human life holds this special status

Sanhedrin – an ancient Jewish council of judges or elders

scapegoat – one that is made to bear the blame of others

schism – division or separation

scientific theories – a hypothesis that is tested extensively and repeatedly to see if it is true or false. Theories may be altered or changed if new evidence is found

scripture – a sacred writing or book (for Christians this is the Bible)

scourged – whipped/flogged

secular – non-religious; having no relationship to religion

segregation – laws enforcing white and black people to be separated, e.g. on buses or at school

self-flagellation – a disciplinary practice of punishing oneself as an expression of faith

Shahadah – the declaration of faith: 'There is no God but Allah, and Muhammad is the messenger of Allah'

Shariah (straight path) – a way of life; Muslims believe Allah has set out a clear path for how Muslims should live. Shariah Law Is the set of moral and religious rules that put the principles set out by the Qur'an and the hadiths into practice

Shariah Council – an organisation that rules on Islamic laws derived from the Qur'an and hadiths

Shariah Law – the set of moral and religious rules that put the principles set out by the Qur'an and hadiths into practice

Shaytan – (Iblis) the devil/Satan

Shi'a – a branch of Islam that regards Ali as the successor of Muhammad

shirk – an unforgiveable sin of associating other beings with Allah (idolatry or polytheism)

sin – deliberate or immoral action, breaking a religious or moral law

single parent family – one parent raising a child or children alone

Six Articles of Faith – the fundamental beliefs accepted by all Sunni Muslims

social justice – promoting a fair society by challenging injustice and valuing diversity. Ensuring that everyone has equal access to provisions, equal opportunities and rights

soma pneumatikon – a spiritual body

soul – the spiritual aspect of a being; that which connects someone to God. The soul is often regarded as non-physical and as living on after physical death, in an afterlife

speciesism – the belief in, and practice of, treating humans as more important than animals

steward – someone who manages the world on behalf of God

suffering – pain or distress caused by injury, illness or loss. Suffering can be physical, emotional/psychological or spiritual

suhur – a pre-dawn meal consumed before fasting

Sunnah – example, practices and teaching of Muhammad

Sunni – a branch of Islam that accepts the first four caliphs as successors of Muhammad

survival of the fittest – the process of natural selection

sustainable – causing little or no damage to the environment so that life may continue for a long period of time

tafsir – commenting about the meaning

tahrif – the change or corruption of an original text

tallaqtuki – in Arabic: 'I divorce you'

Taliban – a political and military fundamentalist movement that has been condemned for its harsh interpretation of Shariah Law

tawaf – walking around the Ka'ba seven times in an anticlockwise direction

tawassul – intercession or intervening on behalf of someone else

tawhid – 'oneness' in reference to God and is the basic Muslim belief in the oneness of Allah

ta'zir – punishment that has not been fixed by the Qur'an

testimony – the story of someone's personal journey into the Christian faith

theistic evolution – science is correct, but God is the power behind the events that science describes

theodicies – attempts to justify the existence and qualities of God in the face of evil

Torah – the Jewish books of Law; the first five books of the Old Testament in the Bible

transubstantiation – where there is a complete change in the substance of the bread and wine to become the body and blood of Christ

Trinity – the three persons of God; God the Father, Son and Holy Spirit

Triune – three in one

turbah – a small piece of moulded clay on which Shi'a Muslims place their forehead during salah

Twelver – the largest sect of Shi'a Islam that recognises twelve Imams

ummah – means 'community' and refers to the worldwide community of Muslims who share a common religious identity

usury – earning or charging high rates of interest on money that is borrowed

Vatican – term used to describe the chief residence of the Pope and his authority and government

virtue – a positive personal quality or characteristic, often called moral excellence of character

wali – guardian or father

World Council of Churches – an organisation that coordinates hundreds of Christian churches so they can work together

wudu – ablution; ritual cleaning performed to purify a worshipper before salah

Yawm ad-Din – the Day of Judgement

zakah – compulsory annual donation for all Muslims of 2.5% of their wealth for the relief of poverty

zina – unlawful sexual intercourse, e.g. sex before marriage or adultery

ziyarah – visiting places connected with Muhammad or other important figures

zulm – depriving someone of their rights or failing to fulfil a duty towards someone

Index

Headings in **bold** refer to key concepts.